GORGEOUS
TRAGEDY

R.E. LEE'S FINAL MONTHS

JOHN ELLSWORTH WINTER

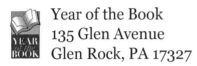
Year of the Book
135 Glen Avenue
Glen Rock, PA 17327

Print ISBN: 978-1-949150-48-3
E-book ISBN: 978-1-949150-49-0

This narrative is historical fiction. Both facts and fact-based information are used in nearly equal proportion. Only a few names, events, or incidents are products of the author's imagination, yet even those are based upon authentic milieux and records.

THE THREAD

Sometime

let gorgeous Tragedy

come sweeping by

.   .   .

Where more is meant than meets the ear.

Il Penseroso
John Milton

DISCLOSURE

In regard to authors who say, "my book," "my commentary," or "my history," French mathematician Blaise Pascal wrote in his classic *Pensées*: *"They would do better to say: 'Our' book, our commentary, our history, etc., because there is in them generally more of other people's* [ideas] *than their own."*

So I present a narrative, "our book" about R. E. Lee's last months of life. I do so with unfeigned thanks to many people uncited but with vibrant clarifying ideas.

One indication that R. E. Lee is different from popular, and scholarly, attention is how he specifically named himself. He signed his name "R. E. Lee" in correspondence, even love letters to his wife, to his children, and in military communiques—not the romanticized "Robert E. Lee" of entertainment mentality, nor even "Robert Edward Lee" of formal history presentation. His most famous biographer, Douglas Southal Freeman, entitled his *magnum opus* properly: *R. E. Lee, a Biography*. He was R. E. Lee, period.

At most, a narrative is a snippet of what occurred, extracted from a whole to represent that whole. Much like a book of 500 pages, a film of two hours, or a lifetime of study, a narrative can carry the warp and woof of the reality of its subject. R. E. Lee's actual "vacation" trip to improve his deteriorating health the last months of his life is a snippet that portrays the tragic hero he became, far surpassing other American military leaders. He is the iconic American general.

The largest library in the world, the U.S. Library of Congress, notes most publications in it concerning any American are about Abraham Lincoln; the second-most publications concerning any American are about R. E. Lee. No other American of any stripe comes close to those two. As well, only Lincoln has surpassed Lee as a tragic hero. They lived at the same time on opposing sides of national unity versus separation: tragic heroes *contra* one another. Finally Lincoln's patriotism preserved the Union. Lee's acceptance of and desire for "a more perfect Union" after his defeat in the Rebellion approached Lincoln's love for the United States.

Secretive, as he had been in warfare, the loser Lee did affirm most everything "American" in order to reunite America. Strange to say he was something like another American—Benedict Arnold, who deserted America in the War for Independence and became a general in the British Army, then lived in England for eighteen years afterward. Arnold died wanting to be buried in his Continental Army uniform: "the only uniform I have ever worn with honor and would be buried in it." Then "14 June 1801 Gen. Arnold expired... He lay across the bed, half dressed... in buff breeches... an old blue coat... [that] had been his American uniform."

Both Generals Arnold and Lee wanted to be American again. Lee succeeded.

DEDICATION

To the brave ones of my family, unknown to the world, who serve(d) to free the world from slaveries in modern times and now form a "bright squadron of angels who for us fight." (Edmund Spenser)

Among the living: older brother, Jack, U.S. Army sergeant in World War II and Good Samaritan; three bright nephews, brothers Terry and Jeffrey Toomey and Eric Winter in World War II; son-in-law, John Blazy Navratil, Agent Orange survivor in Viet Nam; grandson, Max Ellsworth Winter, presently aboard the U.S. Navy aircraft carrier *Harry S Truman*, CVN-75.

Among the dead: fraternal grandfather, Emanuel Winter, U.S. Army "mule doctor" in the Spanish-American War; uncle, Mann Winter, U.S. Army gassed in WW I; uncle, Earl Corrigan, U.S. Army wounded in WW I; older brother, Russell, U.S. Army artillery radioman in World War II Battle of the Bulge and a gentleman; older brother, Jean, U.S. Air Force in World War II and creative artist; younger brother, Glenn, U.S. Army paratrooper in World War II, author, and inspirer of this narrative; brother-in-law, Richard Toomey, Senior U.S. Army in World War II; brother in-law, Ronald Williams, U.S. Navy in World War II; as well as brother-in-law, U.S. Army Lt. Charles Hoffman, World War II valiant volunteer, *still in France* in the American Military Cemetery at Epinal, near the eastern city of Nancy.

RATIONALE

This novel is true. Facts and fiction based on facts in nearly equal proportion, it's R. E. Lee's story: an American hero who became anti-hero then hero again.

Only Abraham Lincoln soars higher than Lee. Lincoln was a hero of sorts for the whole nation, then hero of a half-nation—thereby anti-hero to the South. Assassination brought iconic status.

R. E. Lee almost became the embodiment of Lincoln's citizen of the Second Presidential Inaugural Address: "with malice towards none, with charity for all... to bind up the nation's wounds... to do all which may achieve and cherish a just peace among ourselves." An embodiment, *almost,* for Lee remained uncharitable about black people and "lesser breeds."

His last seven months were marked with ill health and poor medical care. Academic colleagues prevailed upon him in Spring Semester 1870 to take a vacation trip to the warmer South. Begun amidst terrible rains, the trip southward turned negative. Afflicted, he wanted to go home most every day for two months and four days.

At first warm Florida was mysterious, then inspired Lee immensely. Later, the homeward trip by another route was filled with delights and highlights.

Back at Washington College, Autumn 1870 rains fell in biblical proportion. One evening after leadership duty as Senior Warden of Grace Episcopal Church, in Lexington, chilled to the bone, Lee walked home in the rain; no umbrella. Immediately in bad health he waned swiftly, yet spoke "a word a day." Even so, no one engaged him. His empty casket floated away in a flood; he was buried shoeless.

CHAPTER 1

"Sigh, therefore man; with bitterness, sigh"

R. E. Lee's passage was bracketed by blustery March weather from the first day of his long-needed post-war vacation until the very end of his life months later in October of 1870. It ranged from the small rain to a Great Flood articulated in his treasured Bible, mostly the latter kind. He came to abhor seemingly divine-sent deluges.

Stormy blasts immersed his hometown of Lexington, Virginia, that very first day. His poor health was short of what could be found in the warmer, more southern states. Book-ended by squalls and lashes of rain, it replicated the tumults of his disrupted childhood: deserted by a father who had abandoned his mother after squandering her estate. Stormy from childhood to old age, R. E. Lee was submerged in a dramatic and haunting human Niagara.

His departure from Washington College had been preceded by a freakish downpour that persisted unrelentingly into the late morning. Gusty cloudbursts laid down torrents of rushing water. The trip showed signs of being traumatic before it had even begun. He shivered in bed during the frigid March mountain air and did not want to rise after a shattered night's sleep. He groped for stability but there was only the staccato beat of rain against his bedroom windows.

Lee decided a healthful breakfast would break the miserable spell, but learned that water had dampened and extinguished the cook-stove fire overnight. Instead he ate but one slice of buttered oat bread. He was discomfited to say the least and infuriated

1

actually; he had to submerge his emotional state. He dared not disconcert his severely physically compromised wife; R. E. Lee did not want to leave grief in his home when he was departing it for several months.

Lee and daughter Eleanor Agnes huddled on a riverside wharf under a single bumpershoot, the old-style umbrella of Pennsylvania Dutch origin he had "procured" during the drizzly days after the Battle of Gettysburg seven years before. Wrapped in wool blankets, they looked more like ne'er-do-wells than father and daughter, college president and beauty.

The rain-sodden wharf along the North River at Lexington creaked under the weight of well-wishers. Because it was overly filled, many who felt for his well-being stood on soggy hillside soil, not adding anything to their own safety in the mud. Others slipped and sloshed on the bank trying to find solidity on stone or fallen log. Under poor conditions all sought to bid "Farewell, Sir" to the father and "Godspeed" to the daughter. There was a dearth of joy expressed in that "mudville" on the North River's banks Thursday morning, 24 March 1870.

"All those people around us are getting soaked," Lee observed. "It's Job's 'great rain,' and won't stop for hours and hours. They need not have come today." Though unspoken, he would have preferred to wait until the morrow to travel. That he couldn't, or wouldn't, express such peevishness bespoke his Southern gentrification.

"But Father, they're here to bid you farewell," responded Agnes. "They're interested in your welfare. They want you to take a vacation for your health." Unsettled by his adverse attitude, she pluckily declared, "They love you."

The old man just peered at her. Mulish, stubborn, and old, Lee did not shrug a shoulder, did not blink an eye; whether or not he paid attention to his daughter could have been debated easily—in better weather.

"What will I do if it rains all night? Did we bring all my medicines, Agnes?" Already, the former general—who often slept on the ground like his troops, or on a cot in a tent in bad weather—could feel the dampness, the power of rain to control human existence.

Agnes, nicknamed Wig or Wiggie, replied softly, "Yes, we did," though it was she, not "we" who had gathered his medicines for the trip.

Some Washington College students, and all of his faculty, formed a semicircle around the family present. Mary—Lee's severely arthritic wife—had remained at home, and rightly so, for all on that slippery wharf were distressed, and were distressing one another.

A larger company surrounded the semicircle from literally next door to Washington College... the Virginia Military Institute where his brilliant son Custis taught. Cadets in uniform sought to send off the former military commander with some degree of seemliness, some propriety. With pomp and circumstance, in fact.

Rain hindered their actions. Bugles and drums had to be covered and flags furled fast lest the dyes run. Cadets sloshed about with wet feet, numbed hands, and saddened hearts. Faces dripped disappointment. One could not possibly tell by the weather that the trip was to become "the last and most beautiful chapter of his life," as Douglas Southal Freeman, newspaper editor and historian, would later note.

When the packet-boat departed the landing, Lee stated with a sham smile, "At least I didn't have to speak. Maybe the rain was a blessing."

Wiggie wasn't placated by the slight look of glee on his face. Yet she hoped he might not be downcast for long.

The canal boat left quickly. From days of exposure to the near constant downpours, rain had seeped through the freighter's roof in several places. Water stood in puddles here, there, and everywhere.

"Winter weather clothing would still have been appropriate, Father," Agnes said.

"True. But we must endure through the mountains of western Virginia. We're going to the Deep South. We must endure."

True Lee: *endure*. And endure. Always endure.

Lexington along the river was a minor stop for packet-boats—freighters, primarily, but with restricted room for passengers. The vessel would travel southeasterly through the night to Lynchburg about fifty miles away. The freighter had space for social events if passengers so desired, providing simply a bar, kitchen, and toilets. As a hauler it carried pig-iron from small, local Rockbridge County mines to Richmond's industries, as well as agricultural produce from area farmers to markets. The vessel was laden to the top of the gunwales yet still seemed adequate, a decent riverboat... not a yacht but acceptable nonetheless.

The storm reached epic proportions. High winds vexed even the small crew. The few passengers were frightened, huddling together for some comfort or strength, neither of which arrived. For R. E. Lee it was another sleepless night. He tied himself in emotional knots wishing to be back in the shielding sanctuary of the commodious President's House at Washington College. Then the old man thought of Herman Melville's Ishmael in *Moby Dick* riding out a cruel storm, as Melville, the sailor, had done on several occasions.

As well Lee recalled another storm, centuries and centuries before Melville, wherein the prisoner Paul of Tarsus encountered the tempestuous Mediterranean Sea storm called the Euroclydon. Roman legionnaires had prepared to jettison a hundred-plus prisoners to lighten their ship for safety's sake. The weary college president pondered, *How did Paul survive? How could he ever endure being cast into the stormy brine?*

Such frenzied thoughts, however, didn't assuage his irritation. Not much kept wind and rain away from a body. Miserable co-travelers, both Lee and Agnes, became heart-sick but did not tell the other.

Journeying down the North River and Kanawha Canal to the James River, about fifty miles away, father and daughter's feelings and composures deteriorated faster than the boat could move.

At Lynchburg the next day they transferred to a train to Richmond. Both still were blighted by low spirits, by shivering in wet garments, by leave-taking from family, friends, students, comrades. For two days the duo was disgusted and bedeviled. Discomfort turned into annoyance—for the trip, possibly even for one another. Though at least the train was dry, rain still drowns even the best of human beings.

Melville had written that "meditation and water are wedded forever," but not for R. E. Lee, who remembered the retreat from Gettysburg and how he had almost lost his army in a storm rivaling the Euroclydon. Water is a cruel conqueror. A conflagration can be fought but a flood covers everything, nature's one-act drama.

And what comes after a flood? Ruination! young Wiggie thought. The only thing worse than "rain" was perhaps "train." *Things had better get better, or we may return home quicker than lightning.*

She never mentioned her thoughts to her father, but saw them mirrored in his facial expressions. Her chief concern became his ability to survive the next months.

CHAPTER 2

Richmond was different

Richmond was fresh, mostly because of the southern Spring. Flowers, trees, bushes, and bees predominated. The sky was not foreboding as the previous day. High, stringy clouds wafted rapidly above, while on the horizon southward, assorted puffy clouds with gleaming pure white tops floated along.

But those conditions touched only the physical senses of father and daughter. Neither captured the total atmosphere of Virginia's capital five years after the end of the war.

A person walking along Richmond streets or a horseman riding slowly by could discern a low hum coming from some houses or cottage shops, likewise a number of small factories, possibly cottage industries. "How different from Lexington," noted Lee.

"It helps revive my spirits," said Agnes, "that we will prosper again as a people, all over the country." She intensely wanted to forget the Rebellion. Richmond's discernibly civil public atmosphere corroborated her innermost yearnings for national unity.

As they walked through town, Lee couldn't help but be mindful of small groups of people milling about, some at street corners, often draymen and hucksters plying their wares, or visitors to official government buildings each dressed properly to do business of one sort or another. Once in a while, larger gatherings formed near shells of houses not yet torn down nor rehabilitated—buildings which fleeing Confederate troops five years previous had burned to prevent use by Federal troops.

Daughter and father noted a true Southern, not revolutionary, spirit had returned. A *dolce vita*—a sweet life—seemingly waited just around the corner.

"Better ambience than in Rockbridge County's hill country of western Virginia along the North River," mumbled Agnes.

Her father instantaneously stopped walking. He internally knew she was right. He did not reply, though; the emotional weight of her statement was leaden.

The day was invitingly warm, not dazzling sunshiny, but warm enough to heighten human spirits. Still tired and somewhat frazzled, Lee became no longer downcast, not grouchy but fascinated.

Easily father and daughter slipped into favorable small talk. Both were considering in differing degrees the spring chills of mountainous western Virginia. No question they were happy, glad, on the first away-from-home day of their vacation. Wisely they set aside yesterday's wicked weather, and their crabby counteractions.

Daughter and father always performed the same ritual when entering the public sphere. First she would brush her hair thoroughly then gently massage her cheeks while he would rub his hands together several times and bump them together to get the blood circulating. Individually prepared, Lee then would take Agnes' left arm and tuck it under his right elbow. Declaring themselves thereby a couple, they made ready to stroll the streets.

Richmond was different to both sets of eyes. They recognized few people at the train station or outside their hotel. There was no talk of defeat or secession. And unlike the hill country where people often dwelt in the past, the "Rebel Yell" was not heard in the city. Though previously devastated by its own Confederate garrison, the attitude in the Virginia capital was "that was then; this is now."

Nonetheless, as soon as the Virginia State Senate learned Lee was in town, it wanted to capitalize on his fame. It unanimously extended him the privileges of the floor and would have accorded him a formal reception. Lee declined the honor, knowing the Senate wanted fame and credit rather than his own well-being.

Of course there was talk. It's only human to do so. Not war talk; that was passé. Not of defeat; that was still bitter emotionally. Instead, it was talk of "reconstruction." The two visitors noted that subject several times. Father remained quiet; Wiggie talked in. And on. She had opinions, strong ones mostly but not malignant; she believed a new time deserved a new attitude.

Favorite topics encompassed reconstruction of structures public and private—homes and schools, churches and hospitals. Factories, too. Then talk of another kind of reconstruction emerged: the political kind. Reconstruction that Northern Radical Republican Congressmen applied to the South shortly after the war, was as much punishment as restoration.

That legislation's unspoken value was that intelligent people saw a way that formerly opposed citizens with their own values might still converse but not shoot one another, analyzing not attacking one another, to re-Unionize the nation. But talk is never cheap; it has costly ramifications, exorbitant tolls and taxes on human relationships. The good point about talking is it doesn't murderously blot out human life.

The Lees discovered Richmond had a wealth of talkers about political Reconstruction *pro* and *contra*. Father and daughter were cautious in their remarks but listened perceptively, nodding their heads in different directions at different times to indicate attention without further commitment.

Marvelously once in a while there was some talk about reconciliation. Reconciliation with the North!

Reconciliation with the North? True, there were more nay-sayers than yay-sayers but those fault-finders were not able to daunt nor deter those who wanted to be good citizens of the *United* States of America. Lee had already encouraged reconciliation, chiefly to his Washington College students and faculty, quite regularly so.

Somehow Richmond seemed to them a befitting place beyond *academe* for acknowledging reconciliation with the re-united nation as a whole. R. E. Lee needed such a setting, but his present lot in life was the challenge of living in the Valley. After the vacation-for-health trip, he would serve as Washington

College president one more academic year then look for ways to enhance reconciliation of the American people with one another.

The old man thought big because America was big from Richmond to Washington, Boston to New Orleans, Atlanta to Chicago, Florida to Maine, Minnesota to Texas, Atlantic to Pacific, the Gulf of Mexico to the Great Lakes and all the other grand lands within.

CHAPTER 3

After astonishment, marginal medical review

As planned, Lee consulted three physicians in Richmond for more evaluations. The big-city experts were to verify his small-town physicians' assessments.

Wiggie assumed the role as auxiliary to the medical team, to ride herd on her father, so he would make time available amidst an ever-burgeoning social schedule. Necessarily setting up appointments with four parties—the three physicians and one patient—was difficult enough for a single event but became onerous when multiple appointments became necessary.

The old president didn't take notes, scrawled or mental, nor did he heed Agnes when she broached the subject. "What are we doing," she curtly asked several times, "if you aren't going to help yourself—and me—to see the doctors?"

"I presume the 'three wise men' will this time perform their magic by having *me* give *them* the gold, frankincense, and myrrh." Chuckling, R. E. Lee seemed pleased with his attempt at humor.

Agnes fought back a hearty laugh. "May you be forgiven for such an interpretation."

Like a petulant child, Lee was not only fretful but touchy and ill-humored. "I'll pay attention to you, Wiggie, strict attention. Then we can be on our way to even warmer Georgia and Florida, even nicer than here."

Their social life in Richmond consisted of visitors to their hotel lodgings. Most were just to pay respects, which Agnes attempted to keep to brief dialogues about the South's future in the restored Union. Others thanked Lee for changes he had made in their lives or in the lives of family members. Agnes was thrilled to hear such stories about her father. But neither did she take notes.

R. E. Lee was grateful, yet as a sweet-tempered person he sought to turn those visits in other directions. Sometimes he asked about the weather, other times the visitors' post-war circumstances. Compellingly, however, he enjoined visitors to consider the welfare of the re-united nation. They were Americans after all, not just Southerners.

He told Agnes he hoped he was not an overly optimistic Pollyanna. "What we've seen and heard in Richmond gives evidence I'm not concocting confidence in our people."

And then he snapped into a popular folk song: "Old MacDonald had a farm," and pronounced the vowels in a long drawl, "E-eee, I-iii, E-eee, I-iii, O O O."

Wiggie stomped her feet, twirling around to her father's tune. Feeling like a girl again, she joined the chorus, inviting her father to dance. He demurred; in its place he sang louder, and shambled his feet, sort of dragging them around.

Meanwhile the Richmond physicians' assessments were as close to guesswork as they were to the systematic structure and behavior of the physical and natural world. Merely five years removed from the war's inadequate medical conditions, that poor methodology was barely improved in anesthetics, sterility, or sanitation.

Nonetheless Agnes relished the fact those medical reviews were not detrimental to their further vacation plans. President Lee agreed, whether in mere acquiescence or in actual belief. It didn't matter; he needed to be away. The call of the "open road" permeated his waking hours. Vacations are usually better for the soul than the body.

Then... an astonishment. They heard a piece of news. If their spirits had recently subsided a measure or two, most certainly they were revived, energized, in fact. Upbeat more than usual, the city appeared to manifest a spirit not unlike the day before Christmas.

"The Gray Ghost is in Richmond!"

CHAPTER 4

The Gray Ghost

Wherever he went there was some obscurity about this Gray Ghost, a fountainhead of mystique one might say, from birth onward into old age. John Singleton Mosby, a Confederate cavalry commander during the Rebellion, was *sui generis*: "of its own kind" and there weren't doubts about it.

Something "shadowy" was the kindest term Northern troops used about him during the war. They knew him to be insubstantial, more murky, dark, and dirty than any other Confederate officer. Federals at all levels from Abraham Lincoln to the lowliest Yankee private did not know where... or when... or how... the Gray Ghost would strike in northern Virginia. But they did know why: they were enemies. And they feared him—rightly so.

After the war the Gray Ghost changed his political affiliation from Democrat to Republican as had former Southern General James Longstreet. The "Ghost" became a fast friend of General "Unconditional Surrender" Grant, Victor of Vicksburg, Vanquisher of Lee. The Gray Ghost had actively boosted Grant for the Presidency of the *re-United* States of America—and was amply rewarded, while the South remained staunchly Democrat for another century.

Factually, nearly nothing is known of his birth or childhood, prefiguring a lifetime of puzzlement couched in ambiguity. In his University of Virginia years he had studied ancient Greek and Roman histories, literatures, and languages plus mathematics, seeking to become an American Renaissance man. But then he shot a fellow student, killing him outright, for which he was jailed.

In prison a learned jailer befriended Mosby. That friendship opened for him the study of the law, and he followed that profession after receiving a pardon. For an unknown reason, never discerned, the governor of the Commonwealth released him from incarceration. Virginians were flabbergasted. The governor was grateful he was not personally lynched, or at least not tarred and feathered for such a collapse of impartiality.

Mosby married a soul mate, Pauline Clarke, daughter of a former U.S. Representative from Franklin, Kentucky. The couple spent gobs of time reading ancient classical literature aloud to one another. That endeavor provided a double impact: the author's viewpoint and the reader's exegesis, elucidation. It was a practice R. E. Lee also engaged in with his wife Mary every evening during his presidency at Washington College. Reading to one another made up for some of the years they had to live apart during his military careers in the Federal then Confederate armies.

Both couples, though not social friends, had energetic mouths and unstopped ears. Reading aloud to one another engendered an additional dimension to each marriage, not merely communication (as valuable as that act is) but a *raison d'être*, a new, expanded reason for living life with another human being. Reading to one another engages a triple-sided *tête-à-tête*, not just two but three entities. The third is not simply the married partners talking confidentially, but *"from the central deep"* something new arises in creation. It is a spontaneous creativity that goes beyond morals and laws to—possibly—create life again. The Mosby and Lee couples lived a fine truth, not together, but each with a soul mate, and each couple different from the other.

After the infamous 1859 raid by John Brown on the Federal Armory at Harpers Ferry, Virginia, the future Gray Ghost patriotically joined a local Virginia militia unit, but was quite passionless about such service. To be kind, the word "passionless" is a gift because he was not only without passion but had a couldn't-care-less attitude and skipped over the drilling and discipline of military life. Bad motivation plus poor preparation for a future soldier.

Like Lee, John Mosby had opposed secession—before the Confederacy was formed—as the route Virginia should take after Fort Sumter was bombarded, solidifying South Carolina's effort to withdraw from the Union. Hotspurs started the conflagration; South Carolinian pols felt they could only follow the example of impetuous foolhardiness, bad and inexpert though it was, even with militarist P. G. T. Beauregard at its head.

Human emotions might be good ways of ending wars, but they are horribly inadequate ways to begin them.

Emotions most often are imaginary states of mind; non-rational, they are conspicuously fictitious—consequently befuddling, even dangerous. Emotional states are too easily aroused, but then are held tenaciously—and often fail in the end. That failure devastates losers. Furthermore, it disillusions winners who do not get what they thought they earned. Emotions often twist out the "juices" of thoughtful, planned humanity, leaving a mangled, crumpled residue that has to justify its tactless flippancy.

Virginia became one of the last states to join that unconstitutional action, secession. There were people in Virginia—for example, the large population of Quakers of northern Virginia, but not exclusively such pacifists—who opposed secession. R. E. Lee, himself, when approaching the Virginia convention hall for the final legislative vote for the Commonwealth to secede or not, stated in opposition, *"Now we shall be done with that talk."* But the Virginia hotspurs out-shouted and out-voted peace lovers, and seceded.

Various groups of Virginians honestly were concerned about the rightness of secession as they sought to discern what kind of respect such an extreme action would be to the memory and political values of Virginia's Founding Fathers of the Constitutional Convention in 1787: George Washington and James Madison. Both helped formulate the Constitution at Article 1, Section 10.1: *No State shall enter into any treaty, alliance, or confederation.* No confederation. No confederation yet they formed a confederacy! It was evident Virginia lived a

"South Carolina skimble-skamble" at the beginning of the war until questioners were shouted down. The Gray Ghost lived with that inconsistency, too, at first as one opposed to secession, then, as an impetuous believer—a hodge-podge intellectuality accepting an unconstitutional confederation.

Mosby had signed onto actual military service as a private in the 1st Virginia Cavalry led by Jeb Stuart, a favorite of R. E. Lee when Superintendent of the U.S. Military Academy at West Point and then in the War of the Rebellion. In the private's first engagement with the Northern army, excitement of chasing and capturing Federal troops changed him. He was so bestirred as to become a sudden convert to military life, just as religious fundamentalists do, without further analysis. Galvanized for action, in off-duty time he put his scholarly abilities to use, no longer studying Greco-Roman classic literature, but reading books on military strategy and tactics. He wanted to become more proficient at the war game, in fact, to excel at it.

No wonder then that he quickly was appointed 1st Lieutenant under his military expert Captain Jones, later General Wm. "Grumble" Jones. Upon doing scouting work for Jeb Stuart, who was mightily impressed, Mosby was made a member of his staff. Therein he concocted plans to raid Union General McClellan's army surreptitiously from behind. Following that successful operation with only nine troopers, Stuart gave him fifteen men for further "independent" actions. These guerilla raiders rode into battle after which they would "disappear" one by one into civilian homes in northern Virginia to meet again at prearranged times and places for further actions. Such "disappearances" not only irked Federal army officers but spooked their men, as neither officers nor troops knew when or where they would be accosted. Mosby's Rangers were phantoms of fear, wrathful warriors as well as wraithlike, chimerical. They hid, then lunged upon unsuspecting quarry anytime, anywhere. Not only irritants, they were feared way beyond their numbers and actions.

Interestingly, the Rangers were allowed to divide their spoils of war, making their military tasks all the more inviting. In short order Mosby's unit was incorporated as the 43rd Virginia

Battalion of Cavalry comprised of eight companies of Rangers. He, himself, would ride into battle shouting the military *Psalms* of the Bible, scaring the hell out of Federal troops who knew their Bible, too. He appeared a madman, using his religion to kill others, then dissolving, so to speak, into the woods.

In April 1865 Mosby disbanded his command but did not surrender to any Northern unit. He instead headed southward to join General Joseph Johnston's army in the Carolinas, still in the field after R. E. Lee's surrender at Appomattox. On the way he learned of the final surrender of Confederate armies, so he returned to his father's home in Virginia. Thus ended his shadowy, even spectral or weird, military career.

Post-war he became friendly with U.S. Army General Grant, soon to be President of the United States, supporting his elections and administrations. Little wonder then that he warranted censure and lambasting by many Southerners for turning from Democrat to Republican. He called Southern opposition to him a "fiery ordeal in Virginia." It was par for the course—a final ambivalence he neither tried to moderate nor suspend, thereby remaining displeasing but always illusory. People normally don't understand such actions; shadowiness, renegade, mirages, specters, ghosts are too nebulous, unclear—and scary. Rather effective, though, in guerilla military actions particularly. A ghost indeed, gray and uncertain and indistinct and unclear: the Gray Ghost.

In Richmond!

CHAPTER 5

"Wiser not to keep open the sores of war"

The Gray Ghost, J. S. Mosby, and the Gray Fox, *nom de guerre* by which R. E. Lee was ever-so-often styled, were in the capital of Virginia at the same time five years post-war. Was it a fluke they met in the formerly rebellious Richmond just seven months prior to Lee's death?

Most would contend it was simply a bit of luck, or fortuitous serendipity. Most would thereby rule out—even eradicate—the possibility of an invisible or divine predestination. It is so easy to dismiss anything that does not come through the seven orifices of the human head as valid truth.

Who would want to have missed it had they known such masterminds would meet years after the historical event that defined them both? Expressly because each man had changed his military views, drastically, a 180-degree turnaround.

Could such radical coincidence or accidental encounter have brought them together as ephemeral ghost and fox? If so, then it was neither coincidence nor chance... but something paranormal, something cryptic, something unfathomable.

In the former colonel's *Memoirs,* Mosby would write: *"In March 1870, I was walking across the bridge connecting the Ballard and Exchange hotels, in Richmond, and to my surprise I met General Lee and his daughter."*

Neither giant of the vanquished Confederate Army of Northern Virginia knew the other was there. Conceivable; yet mystifying, as well.

When the two former military giants met, they did not talk about war—at least not the *War of the Rebellion*. Their conversation was instead a revision, a re-vision or re-envisioning of the American dream for the whole nation—South, North, West.

Neither Ghost nor Fox sought to be stoned into granite of a mountainside in Georgia or cast in bronze on a battlefield pedestal in Pennsylvania, nor painted in oils on canvases in state houses across the South depicting their ventures. Theirs was a riveting image. Attractive because unusual. Two great former warriors *not* talking about their war.

The Gray Ghost had that image fastened, fixed tightly in his memory, and wrote:

> *The general was pale and haggard, and did not look like the Apollo I had known in the army. After a while I went to his room; our conversation was on current topics. I felt oppressed by the great memories that his presence revived, and while both of us were thinking about the war, neither of us referred to it.*

A rather generally accepted fact affirms that ordinary minds talk about people. More average minds will discuss events, though what has happened can't be changed. But great minds will discuss ideas, blueprints for the future. Gray Ghost and Gray Fox were idea men who realized the South had been consumed by the inanity of the times. Gobbling down defeat after defeat, the South had been squeezed to death from the Atlantic Ocean, around Florida to the Gulf of Mexico, then up the Mississippi River by General Winfield Scott's all-encircling "Anaconda Plan."

Mosby knew Lee knew that fact; R.E. Lee knew Mosby knew it, too. Instinctively, paranormally, both knew the South would be throttled. Such acute and potent thought routinely leads to verbalization of some sort. We human beings seldom think intensely about a topic without words slipping o'er our tongues.

Gray Ghost and Gray Fox discussed the then Franco-Prussian (Franco-German) War in Europe of 1870. Lee had discussed that stupidity with others, particularly in a letter to his wife, and now shared it with John Mosby:

I have watched with much anxiety the progress of the War between France and Germany and without going into the merits or question at issue or understanding the necessity of the recourse to arms, I have regretted that they did not submit their differences to arbitration of the other Powers as provided in the articles of the Treaty of Paris of 1856. It would have been a grand moral victory over the passions of men, and would have so elevated the contestants in the eyes of the present and future generations as to have produced a beneficial effect. It might have been expecting, however, too much from the present standard of civilization, and I fear we are destined to kill and slaughter each other for ages to come.

It is well known that R. E. Lee did not cross any of the fields of battle where he had been victor or victim, skirting around them to avoid the desecration that war wreaks upon everything around it. It's deleterious to victor and victim alike to go where other men were killed, or mutilated by cannon fire, crippled for the remainder of their lives, or struck senseless by the horror of it all.

Socially, war damages human institutions and natural resources, seriously jeopardizing political entities by replacing ingenuity with makeshift arrangements to meet emergency after emergency before, during, and after battle. Individually, war reduces combatants to naked struggle for the barest survival, a seriously sad decline from and rebuff of the usual need and desire for human relationships.

The same desecration extends to the dead. Thousands upon thousands, losses numbering millions—even billions over the eons of time—of loved ones who have had to suffer depredation and plunder of their normal lives while living long, long after the wars ceased and loved ones buried.

Losses in all ages that human beings have been on this planet from wars and warfare surely are more than the present worth of all human assets, capital, and resources worldwide. The tally of war is beyond calculation, its toll beyond comprehension. The complete horror may be discernible only by God.

On the deeply rooted level—that is the intimately human level—as a major leader in that 1861-1865 debacle, R. E. Lee in the summer of 1869 replied to a request from a Gettysburg attorney David McConaughy, president of the Gettysburg Battlefield Memorial Association, to join in a meeting of participants who fought in the battle at Gettysburg. The lawyer's purpose was to memorialize those people and events.

The former general would have none of such elevation, enshrinement, or glorification of death, destruction, or veneration of warfare in marble or bronze markers or statuary. None. None whatsoever.

Lee adamantly opposed making war acceptable, opposed remembering its clashes, opposed commemorating its victors or its victims. Too many men had been ushered unwillingly into death, or missing-in-action, or life-long misery and pain by war's destructions. War is as grave a human taboo as incest or murder, both engraved in human law codes and exceedingly deep in human hearts.

Lee would not attend the event nor indulge in civil war reminiscence and commemoration. When pressed in David McConaughy's usual gentle style, R. E. Lee responded:

Lexington Va: 5 Aug 1869

Dear Sir:

Absence from Lexington has prevented my receiving until today your letter of the 26th: enclosing an invitation from the Gettysburg Battlefield Memorial Association to attend a meeting of the officers engaged in that battle at Gettysburg, for the purpose of marking upon the ground by enduring memorials of granite the position & movements of the Armies on the field.

My engagements will not permit me to be present, & I believe if there I could not add anything material to the information existing on the subject. I think it wiser moreover not to keep open the sores of war, but to follow the examples of those nations who endeavored to obliterate the marks of civil strife & to commit to oblivion the feelings it engendered.

Very respy your obt Sevt [signed] R.E. Lee

"Wiser not to keep open the sores!" and its corollary, *"Obliterate the marks of civil strife and commit to oblivion the feelings it engendered,"* are words one hundred percent pacifistic. Spoken by a former general who turned against war, and an iconic American general at that! Lee had come to realize that war was a passion play performed by idiots who chose not to understand its long-term terrors.

Strange at least, bizarre at most, in light of Lee's disapproval there stands today on that Gettysburg battlefield in a lofty position his statue on his magnificent steed, "surveying" the indefensible open fields, the blood-soaked losing fields of Pickett's Charge. While, in fact, during that losing struggle which he ordered, Lee sat on a log. On a log, the stump of a tree. And then he had risen only to mount and ride out to the retreating, decimated troops, telling them, "It's all my fault." It was.

Pathetic at least, unacceptable at most, stands the statue of the victor of that battle afar by a mile from Lee's, located back from the roadway without a drive-around, void of specifically evident directions or markers. General George Gordon Meade, who was on his horse the whole time Pickett charged, actively directed the defense of the Republic from usurpers.

Even in commemorations and memorials there is the baffling destructive power of war: infelicitous attribution and ill-advised appreciation. Often said, God is the first casualty in war because both sides claim, "God is with us." The second great casualty of war is that facts and figures are misconstrued to make "our side" the victor under any circumstance. Truth suffers, dies in war. At least God lives on. Truth has textbooks, seldom opened.

Ghost and Fox now together, talked not about that War of the Rebellion, nor seeking to be stoned into granite or cast in bronze or painted in oils. A riveting image those two formerly gray-clad leaders, *not* talking about their war, silent because of shame, because of errors of purpose; wordless because there is no excuse for man's inhumanity to humankind.

CHAPTER 6

A Sword of Damocles

John Mosby and R. E. Lee straightforwardly talked about what they knew. They discussed newspaper headlines, featured stories, even gossip columns. Typical in rumor-filled, hearsay-saturated taverns, it was everywhere. On street corners, around dinner tables, at church and synagogue, during casual meetings, while traveling, at school, when shopping, and at workplaces the subject was omnipresent.

Apparently neither boring nor outdated, that current topic dangled over the South much like the Sword of Damocles. The semi-historical legend was much appreciated for its closeness to fact not only in the ancient world but through all centuries of Western civilization. In Mosby's scholarly study of ancient Greek legends he encountered Damocles who was an excessively flattering courtier in the palace of Dionysius II, the tyrant in Syracuse, Italy, what is now named Sicily, during the 4th century B.C.

Damocles' praises of the king were intemperate, over the top, and bootlicking constant, exclaiming how wonderful it must be to be wealthy, with so much power. The ruler Dionysius offered to switch places with him so Damocles could experience what it was like to have such might. Of course, envious Damocles jumped at the chance to experience the magnificence he imagined. During a grandiloquent banquet, he reveled being mollycoddled like a king, upon finishing eating and before the entertainment began.

During a noonday feast Damocles happened to view the ceiling there to behold a sight of something not of this earth. He blurted out, "A razor-edged sword." An illusion induced by wine? A nightmare at noon. The makeshift king wasn't sure what it was but it was dangling directly overhead, boding what evil he couldn't tell. Swaying on a single strand of horsehair! A doomsday scenario if ever there was one. Petrified Damocles was discomfited thoroughly. Notwithstanding, he begged King Dionysius if he might abandon food, frivolity, and foolishness. Then hightailed it home.

This allusion indicates when one is powerful one is also under some kind of peril. Power implies peril, always. Generally alluding to a hazardous situation or situations stacked full with impending danger, particularly if a situation could be bungled, blown up by a single misstep.

Apparently neither boring nor outdated, the current topic dangling over the South much like the Sword of Damocles was an allusion to the imminent and ever-present perils faced by Southerners from those in power, and to Dixielanders that meant Northern Radical Republicans. Reconstruction was the hottest topic for conversation and the two Grays talked about it much of the afternoon. The war as a topic was becoming passé.

Reconstruction laws were passed post-war in the U.S. Congress and had been instituted by the Northern Radical Republican faction. The goal was strongly anti-Southern: suppress and punish the former rebels for that 1861-1865 catastrophe. *"Make them lose again!"* Adding insult to injury, Northern Radical Republicans wanted deadly hurt and utter humiliation for the South.

President Lincoln, a regular Republican, had wanted Southerners treated as brothers returning to the fold, "to let them up slowly." Explicitly he had stated in his Second Inaugural Address prior to assassination, "Let us judge not, that we be not judged." He emphatically and graciously announced, "with malice toward none, with charity for all."

Identically, post-war-elected President Ulysses Grant—the North's great general—also wanted reconciliation rather than retribution. True, he lent some support to Northern Radical

Republicans in a few states, with the usual political rationale: to keep his Party's position, regular Republicanism, ascendant in certain selective states.

Almost desperately, Northern Radical Republicans were hell-bent on destruction of rebelism.

The chief clash was to mete out *lex talon*—the law of the claw—that is, reprisal on former Confederate officers and officials who previously had taken oaths to serve the United States of America. No longer *lex talionis*—the law of retaliation, "an eye for an eye"—*lex talon* meant to kill, ravage, and despoil, just as Methuselah's son Lamech of ancient Hebrew religion. *"I have slain a man for wounding, a young man for striking me; if Cain is avenged sevenfold, [then] truly Lamech seven and seventyfold."* In other words, rip, tear, destroy, kill the enemy for what was done; if that doesn't work then over-kill, kill, kill, kill seventy-seven times more.

What those hyper-politicized Northerners really wanted was *lex talon*, and they got it. The savage claw: revenge, vengeance of the most heinous sort. Severity was their dictum, to the point of death.

Plainly, Abraham Lincoln was assassinated two times: first in Ford's Theatre in Washington, D.C., by a lone assassin; second in Congressional chambers by multiple cruel Northerners of Radical Republican persuasion for continual castigation of the South.

Northern Radical Republicans made Reconstruction their national policy. At best however, it was an effort to rebuild the nation as a whole, particularly the South after the War of the Rebellion tore it asunder: a noble selling point to the American public. Factually, Reconstruction was "a massive experiment in interracial democracy without precedent in the history of this or any country that abolished slavery in the 19th century." It was effective salesmanship regardless of its ulterior motive; Northern Radical Republican perturbation accomplished its aim; anxiety and uneasiness flooded the South. However, as a law based on horrific hatred, it was bound to reap evil, rotten fruit. Reconstruction was a fancy cover for destruction.

That said, Reconstruction actually had a few good elements. It established the first public schools in the South. For whites! Inadvertently, it undergirded future political actions that resulted in the 13th, 14th, and 15th Amendments to the American Constitution. Reconstruction laws thereby achieved voters' rights for black persons as American citizens. And therein hangs a wondrous tale: the most powerful implication was black people were human beings after all—*not property*. A singular victory, yet necessarily fought for over and over ever since.

The Radical wing of Republicans ruled that political party in Congress making for the first and foremost bad element of Reconstruction. That powerful political lobby set out with un-American, un-Christian intentions to destroy the South of pre-war and rebellion years.

The lobby reveled in perturbation, causing mental uneasiness about standard human codes of conduct which are benchmarks, codes of model conduct and decency in a democratic society. Such codes made for normal functioning among citizens, municipalities, States, and the rule of Law itself. The lobby knew what they were doing: stir, agitate, whip up animosity against the South for its longtime practice of slavery and the rebellion to continue it. They knew perturbation would succeed one way or another as long as hatred lasts. And if hatred doesn't last, lie about it—that is, make the South the post-war source of all unrest in the country. Northern Radical Republicans knew that a lie is a handle which fits all kinds of evil.

Moreover, Reconstruction was a hell for black people, former slaves especially. Countless untold and purposely unnumbered blacks were lynched, hung to death all over Dixie. American "justice" had been denied *in extremis* to thousands of blacks after emancipation and constitutional freedom had been earned by blood. America's "original sin" had been slavery; in Reconstruction the sin became sanctioned murder especially of black men, which persisted into the next century.

Talking about the turmoil surrounding Reconstruction, the two former military officers, Lee and Mosby, could not help but discuss the tragic nature of war. "War has dire effects on present populations and governments," Lee said. "It disarranges everything during its duration and thereafter. From social customs to politics to productivity, finances to Faith, education to employment, war throws things into confusion. Uncertainty reigns. Everything is distorted. Restlessness and turmoil reign during war—on the battlefield and home front."

"Afterwards, too," in muted tone added the Gray Ghost as if it were a piece of incidental information. Then he paused. In a stronger voice Mosby appended, "Usually without bullets and bombs. Instead with laws to stifle and bull rope to hang."

R. E. Lee was caught unaware. *How kindred are we?* In the silent hiatus, the former general decided to keep the initiative. Confidently he repeated a statement he had made public at Washington College: *"The great mistake of my life was taking a military education."* In the present instant he thought, *Had I not been a Military Academy graduate I may not have rebelled— because secession was revolution.*

Hence he added a thought from King David's *Psalms*, to the distinct pleasure of Bible quoting Mosby:

Too long have I had my dwelling
Among those who hate peace.
I am for peace;
But when I speak
They are for war.

Silently repeating that psalm several more times to himself, each word came slower, weightier than in the previous recitation. R. E. Lee chained himself unawares. He clamped mental handcuffs on his reasoning. He caged himself in an emotional prison.

Mosby was left unsettled, weakened. Downright hollowed out.

At that point Lee wobbled in a self-induced vertigo. He perceived his former military prowess—Gray Foxness, he named it to himself—transmogrified into whiteness, blandness much like white bread, tasteless and gummy. Floundering amidst unproductive emotions and lacking logic, he felt naked before the blast of a dreadfully thick, inky warning worse than his compromised physical health. Something hung him up. Something of long, long standing: a fixation, a mental block at least or a phobia at worst from the war operative in his post-war life *a fortiori.*

A weapon hovering above him on the slimmest of strings.

CHAPTER 7

Provisional pacifism

"My opposition to war is a provisional pacifism," R. E. Lee told the Gray Ghost. "The provision is war in self-defense. When— and only when—attacked in their homelands may human beings go to war."

John Mosby responded eagerly, "That makes sense to me as an American and a human being. Where and how we live is a sacred fidelity we owe to one another. To protect our own is stamped in nature; creatures protect their own, down to even insects. True—some insects raid others but they are met with resistance protecting their place. There is something precious in each species and the species tries to save it from invasion."

"Yes," replied the former commander, "though many contend self-defense includes more than homeland and what is within our boundaries."

"But where does that lead us?" Mosby asked sharply. "What limits are placed on other conditions or circumstances or entities considered national interests? Financial investments? Cultural objectives? Historical reputation? Religious preference? Uncontrolled population growth by an assaulting country?"

Lee answered in a fragile voice, "Yes, and sometimes just for hurt feelings on the part of troubled leaders." His answer had sounded hollow, not because inept or wrong, but because it was only too true. "Wars are easily started—peace so difficult to gain. Even George Washington, two years after leading the rag-tag Army during the Revolutionary War and two years before the Constitutional Convention resulted in his terms as President of the United States of America, determined war to be the ultimate bane, blight on human existence. From Mount Vernon on 25 July 1785, he wrote: 'My first wish is to see this Plague to Mankind banished from the Earth; and sons and daughters of the World employed in more pleasing and innocent amusements than preparing implements and exercising them for the destruction of the human race.' Such was the reason his mother and I named our first born, George Washington Custis Lee."

R. E. Lee's 1861 decision to withdraw his U.S. military commission had been gut-wrenching. He had made his fateful choice alone in his office, without fanfare. Before breakfast on April 20, he quietly entrusted his resignation letter to a slave, for delivery at the War Department. Had he been too anxiety-ridden to face his former mentor and chief, General Winfield Scott? Was the use of a slave a slap in the face of Scott? The Union? He had written to a kinsman only minutes after penning his resignation: *"I have been unable to make up my mind to raise my hand against my native state, my relations, my children and my home."*

Of course he had been totally opposed to secession, but that fact didn't matter. *"Secession is nothing but revolution,"* he had written to his son Custis while in the U.S. Army from his frontier post in Texas. Then again on 23 January 1861, three months before the war started, he had declared to Custis, *"I can anticipate no greater calamity for the country than the dissolution of the Union. It would be an accumulation of all the evils we complain of, and I am willing to sacrifice everything but honor for its preservation."* Again on the day in April 1861 when the delegates to the Virginia secession convention were to vote whether or not to leave the Union, and R. E. Lee was in the Capitol rotunda at Richmond, he said to a companion, *"I hope we have seen the last of secession."*

It had been a critical moment in his life, precisely because he did not use his considerable influence to dissuade secessionists. His acquiescence possibly led those sitting on the fence to go along with secession. That choice was regrettable for them. Another burden Lee would have to bear.

Violating the American Constitution's Article I, Section 10: "No state shall enter into any Treaty, Alliance, or *Confederation*," Virginia, as some other states, had joined a Confederation. When resigning his commission in the United States Army Lee had told Francis Blair, Sr., "I would sacrifice all for the Union, but how can I draw my sword upon Virginia?" Previously to General Winfield Scott, General-in-Chief of the Army, he had voiced the same quandary.

Robert Edward Lee was a son of Virginia, a true son. That fact had changed his history, from honor to facsimile thereof.

But he did it. First, because he had felt a deep gratitude to his home state since, as was the custom in those days, the individual states paid the expenses of having a student in the Military Academy at West Point. Though Cadet Lee had excelled at the Point, Virginia had captured his heart. Old loves last and last. To the end.

Virginia's colonial-style culture still emulated that of the Founders of the Republic: Washington, Jefferson, Madison, Monroe. Over and above the Originators' culture, Lee had lived in it, had been surrounded by it, totally immersed in it at Arlington House. Additionally, his marriage to Mary Anna Custis—the only surviving child of George Washington Parke Custis, George Washington's step-grandson, then adopted son, and founder of Arlington House. R. E. Lee had lived amongst George and Martha Washington's copious memorabilia grounding him in adulthood firmly as a lover of tradition. To the end.

One usually discovers that personal feelings are inadequate ways to make sea changes in one's life. Early in the war, R. E. Lee had tried his pacifism on President Jefferson Davis of the Confederate States of America. On 8 September 1862, before the Battle of Antietam/Sharpsburg he had *proposed peace*. In a letter to President Davis he wrote:

The present position of affairs, in my opinion, places it in the power of the government of the Confederate States to propose with propriety that of the United States to the recognition of our independence. For more than a year both sections of the country have been devastated by hostilities which have brought sorrow and suffering upon thousands of homes, without advancing the objects which our enemies proposed to themselves in beginning the contest. Such a proposition, coming from us at this time, could in no way be regarded as suing for peace; but, being made when it is in our power to inflict injury upon our adversary, would show conclusively to the world that our sole object is the establishment of our independence and the attainment of an honorable peace. The rejection of this offer would prove to the country that the responsibility of the continuance of the war does not rest upon us, but that the party in power in the United States elect to prosecute it for purposes of their own. The proposal of peace would enable the people of the United States to determine at their coming elections whether they will support those who favor a prolongation of the war, or those who wish to bring it to a termination, which can but be productive of good to both parties without affecting the honor of either.

It was courageous of a field commander to have contacted his commander-in-chief to plea for a peaceful change in war policy. The single-minded Davis had vetoed the request, squashing a peace proposal the second year of the war.

Thereafter, intensity in battles increased. In the bloodiest single day of the war at Sharpsburg, Maryland, along the Antietam Creek, the battle had become a draw but had started a Southern withdrawal from the North, then had moved onto the horrendous slugfest of Fredericksburg, Virginia, ending in a Southern victory. The South's battle-deaths increased exponentially.

As casualties rose, an increase in desertions nettled Lee's warrior-spirit. So after the great victory at Chancellorsville, Virginia, he again wrote to Davis: *"There are many things about which I would like to discuss with your Excellency,"* inviting him to view the battlefield at the same time. President Davis had begged off since he was seriously ill and requested—not commanded—Lee to visit him in Richmond instead.

It is no wonder after those two victories Lee had wanted to use them as stepping stones to something special up North. It would have to have been much more than another military victory even on enemy soil. His two major victories had not worked for the South, and Vicksburg to the west was under ever tighter siege and readily could have become a great victory for the North. Something special was planned in the east by R. E. Lee.

Such a Northern victory along the Mississippi River would have split the South asunder, east and west. Louisiana and Mississippi east of the river already had been crippled. Texas and Arkansas on the west side would have been immobilized drastically if Vicksburg fell to the North.

Thus, a so-called and hoped for, end-of-the-war military victory by the Army of Northern Virginia would surely have been counter-balanced by defeat in the West along the "Father of Waters," as Native Americans named the river, which divided the Confederacy. The South, therefore, would not have gained headway at all if it had lost along the Mississippi and won a single battle up North.

Continuously surrounded by General Scott's highly successful "Anaconda Plan" on sea and land, the South had been blockaded from the St. Lawrence River spilling into the Atlantic Ocean, down the East Coast and around Key West, Florida, then up to Pensacola and, finally, over to the Mississippi River spilling into the Gulf of Mexico near New Orleans, then up the Mississippi to Vicksburg. And the fever pitch of Northern opposition had been elevated by generals who didn't just sit in their britches: "War is Hell" Tecumseh Sherman and "Unconditional Surrender" Grant had been wreaking havoc in the South, seemingly unstitching one state after another from the Confederacy.

It had been a critical decision in Confederate history. Lee had wanted it to be the final one. His strategy had been aimed at something great: peace, *not combat*. So he readily accepted the President's return-invitation to Richmond. Now he had his work cut out for him: serious work, unconventional work, groundbreaking work for a field commander—not combat but parleying peace.

Consequently, from 14 to 17 May 1863, in the Confederate War Office at Richmond prolonged meetings, some into the night, the President's Cabinet; the President; the Adjutant General of the Confederate States; Samuel Cooper, the Confederacy's senior general; Secretary of War Seddon, all had debated the field commander's plan as Lee had presented it. Some kind of approval to do something about peace was agreed upon. Some kind of peace because the records of the Confederate War Office are missing! Destroyed as Confederates had burned Richmond when they deserted it near the end of the war? Or willfully missing?

We'll never know because—mysteriously, arguably, controversially, and implausibly—President Davis' accounts of the meetings for those days are also missing from his copious records. Blank. Excised? Contrary to other minor correspondence recorded in the official Davis Papers nothing has been found. What had they actually discussed those four days in May 1863?

Lee had the power to amplify his position and use it advantageously to gain shaky approval from the 1863 Confederate official meetings. That power did not last long back in '63 and wouldn't work at all now in 1870. However, Lee's satisfaction was of some value though he did not hear of the President's Cabinet's doubts and suspicions about his irregular plan until after the war. Too late again.

He had moved the Army of Northern Virginia northward for Pennsylvania. Purely accidentally, six weeks later they fought a battle at what one of his generals called a "place of no importance." They lost that accidental battle, making Gettysburg so important in American history.

There does exist one piece of evidence, from an in-house observer—Confederate War Office clerk, John B. Jones. Shortly after the end of the war in early 1866 he had published his diary in which is written, only one day before the fatal Battle of Gettysburg:

JUNE 30 5 O'clock PM

The city [Richmond] is now in good humor, but not wild exultation. We have what seems pretty authentic intelligence of the taking of HARRISBURG the capital of Pennsylvania, the City of YORK, etc. etc. This comes from the flag of truce boat, and is derived from the enemy themselves. Lee will not descend to the retaliation instigated by petty malice: but proclaim to the inhabitants that all we desire is PEACE not conquest.

All that information plus Lee's statement in his official report of the Northern Campaign that "it has not been intended to fight a general battle at such a distance from our base, unless attacked by the enemy," is historical tonnage that badly needs valuation, review, and re-evaluation.

"Not been intended to fight a general battle—unless attacked," is the operative tag. No wonder, then, that Lee had given distinct orders *not* to shoot first, *not* to bring on a battle. It was an order disobeyed—among others at Gettysburg—as a North Carolina unit had started the firing first slightly west of Gettysburg town at Willoughby Run and a soldier had written to his North Carolina governor bragging about starting the conflagration.

Positively contrary to the views of most history buffs, chroniclers, a few of his officers, and hosts of people with but casual interest in the truth, R. E. Lee had not been going to fight a major battle *unless* his army was attacked. Such people commemorate primarily the fighting; they make battle a kind of sacrament emphasizing clashing sounds, mass movements, smoke and plentiful fire, sound and fury, killing and destruction—a spectacle of fierceness. To enjoy? Why not a horror to avoid?

The truth Lee knew about his greatest defeat shadowed him. Many a time.

R. E. Lee had told John Mosby of that hurt, for both had been steeped in the current travails of Virginia: Northern Radical Republicans in the American Congress forcing Reconstruction on the South. As president of private, small, destitute Washington College six months after the end of the war, Lee and it both had suffered severely difficult times.

"War is the enemy of the human race, instigated and aided chiefly by pride," Lee shared. "The great mistake of my life was taking a military education."

CHAPTER 8

A wasted life

For an uncomfortable stretch nothing happened.

Belatedly Lee shook his head. Still and all, he didn't comment nor make a sound.

Mosby wondered, but did not wander from waiting for more from his old commander. Not knowing what to do, he was tight-lipped. Finally he asked, "Can I do anything for you?" *What would I do if he's having a heart attack?*

Laden with torment, Lee dragged out a "Nooooo."

His heartache became evident to Mosby, who promptly asked, "Should I leave?" Though appearing sensitive, Mosby considered departure would be a boon.

"No!" was the razor-edged reply. A frightening pause followed, then a slow whisper, "No... no," as if to apologize.

Again actionless, wordless they faced one another. At some point Lee coughed. The older man didn't feel urgency. Thinking again of a lost cause... Lee knew war's ephemeral content. That diminutive bit of knowing started an impetus to continue human contact with Mosby—or he'd be a deadbeat as a friend. As a result assuring himself at any rate he was humane, caring, Lee felt he was again in the land of the living; somewhat more than tolerant, he became warm about sharing ideas.

His next cough was clearly artificial, desperate to open a truth nagging his conscience.

It worked. The staged rasp caused him to twitch shoulders up and down, then to straighten his posture against the chair. He raised his eyebrows, looked wide-eyed at Mosby, and angled his head considerably to the left, then slowly returned his head to the upright position. Following those painless actions he exhaled heavily.

Mosby looked at him sympathetically.

Lee's emotional baggage was hefty and dense, making him consider that he might understate—or overstate—his position.

Then he made a peep. R. E. Lee made a superficial peep. The naïve noise nearly made him laugh at himself.

It was ludicrous at worst but farcical overall, justifying Mosby's response—a burp-like toot that made him bury his mouth in the crook of his left elbow.

Lee couldn't help but smile broader, not knowing which sound, peep or burp, was the more hilarious.

"I..." This time Lee's singular sound was followed by a lull both tired and stagnant. Even he needed silence as he sifted through alternative ideas to explain his present condition, which was tightening, worsening because of emotional exertion. The lone syllable was hollow as from within an empty barrel.

Mosby felt poignancy weighing a ton on his heart as for a smitten warrior. Sorrow took on a relentless omnipresence as if the hotel room were a mortuary.

Then Lee delivered a hard blow, like a flying-squirrel slamming unexpectedly into the side of a house in the midnight hours. "I am thinking of my own subterfuge. Concealing my own inadequacy."

For the first time silence was a necessary response in every respect. By both men.

What to Mosby was an exploding shock, Lee perceived as brightening relief. "A subterfuge to avoid admission of guilt; subterfuge to steer clear of battling over what couldn't be changed—the past."

John Mosby, now wide-eyed, ears attuned, leaned closer to Lee. He didn't want to miss anything, specifically if it was a negative self-assessment. And then he felt shabby because he had wanted to hear Lee say bad news about himself.

"I told my staff at Washington College, '*The great mistake of my life was taking a military education.*' But I did not tell our students. Nor the public."

Without delay, Mosby sounded his own fake cough. "But I had heard stories to that extent after the war, so some of the public knew your position."

"That may be so, but do you understand there is a high degree of subterfuge in not declaring my great mistake to our young men at Washington College?" Then Lee went on, "They deserve to know what I think as their president about the war since I lead them in moral reasoning as well as intellectual pursuits, even spiritual searching. I have promised their parents our college espouses a position that we will nurture their sons as Christian gentlemen. It is a policy of the institution to tell the whole truth possible. I should not avoid discussion on the tragic nature of war with our young men. I did nothing about admitting culpability. And still am silent. I live a subterfuge."

The Gray Ghost stated, "It is part of the same rationale I've tried to live by. I've endorsed our former enemy general... now President of the United States, U. S. Grant."

Insisting, Lee declared, "War pulverizes everything. Uncertainty overwhelms human reason. Distorts, deforms rationality. Turmoil reigns—on the battlefield then crippling home-life. It makes things ugly as well, as often as not pre-war memories are dimmed or forgotten because of the gruesome events on every battlefield."

"Either way," said Mosby, "the end result is the Grim Reaper swings its scythe, mowing down countless numbers... dark-skinned people with kinky hair, or pink-tinted ones with fuddy-duddy hair of no special advantage, or yellow-shaded people who have nothing but pig-tails to identify them." The former cavalryman knew war firsthand to be a full-time no hokum hater of humankind. "It's a ditch dug out to throw in human flesh we suppose to be of no importance, no value to themselves or us."

Again R. E. Lee was caught unaware. *Does he mean it?* Then he nipped such thoughts in the bud, and resumed questioning his reluctance to share his "great mistake" with his students.

In Lee's late teens, military school had been the only possible way he could get a college education. His mother, Anna Hill Carter Lee, could not afford anything else. Her husband had deserted the family, and she already had one son, Charles, at Harvard College, costing her dearly.

Nonetheless, the Military Academy at West Point, on the west bank of the Hudson River in New York State, was not young Robert's desire. He had been a stellar student from the time he was quite young even though he and his mother's house slave, Nat, had the heavy burden of caring for his seriously sick mother. His personal choice would have been Harvard College to study mathematics, the subject in which he excelled. Academic tutelage in area private schools for his elementary education culminated in a minor miracle: a newly opened school right next door to his home in Alexandria, Virginia, by the eminent Quaker educator, Benjamin Hallowell.

Lee's family had been deserted by Henry "Light-horse Harry" Lee. With a "heavy horse" so to speak, he ran riot through his wife's inherited wealth with ill-advised real estate transactions, mostly failing in the western hills of Virginia, some near the famous Natural Bridge geological formation. As well, money lent—or given—to Robert Morris, financier of the American Revolutionary War, was never repaid to Lee's father.

In military life "Light-horse" had been the famous... because effective... cavalry commander for George Washington in the War of the Revolution in the 1770s. In victory, he served three one-year terms as Governor of Virginia. Later he was chosen by President George Washington to be commander of 12,950 troops in 1794 to put down the "Whiskey Rebellion" in Pennsylvania. Those "dumb Dutchmen" were citizens who wanted to distill, imbibe, and sell—but not pay taxes on—their homemade brew. They had a perverted sense of their usefulness, their value. One of their common prayers exalted themselves above others, illustrating how much they needed correction:

Liewer Gott in Himmel drin,
Loss uns Deitsche was mir Sinn,
Unerhalt uns alle Zeit,
Unser Deitsche freelich Keit.

Beloved God in heaven above
Sanction us Dutch (Pennsylvania Germans) to be just as we
* are,*
Guide and preserve us throughout our days
In our contented Dutch (Pennsylvania German Christian)
* ways.*

Then "Light-horse" was elected a Representative in the U.S. Congress. To his credit he presented Congress' eulogy on 28 December 1799 upon President Washington's death earlier in the month. That plaudit for Washington became instantly famous: *"First in war—first in peace—first in the hearts of his countrymen,"* waxing dear to the hearts of millions of American school children through the years. Shortly thereafter dollar signs filled Henry Lee's head; he made those sub-standard financial investments in frontier properties, and lending money to friends had triggered him to trip the light fantastic out of the country and onto Caribbean islands away from America and family responsibilities.

Robert had been only six years of age, close to seven. Unmistakably the whole family suffered, but a boy with a runaway father easily becomes a butt for awful humor. "Light-horse Harry" had left horse puckies for others to clean up, causing some to question his famous cavalry exploits during the Revolutionary War and his decisions in Virginia politics. No way was he first in the hearts of Virginians... except for his purloined, ripped-off wife Anna. She never allowed her children to speak ill of their father, vanished though he was.

With a vivid memory of things gone wrong and a heavy heart about his original educational misstep, R. E. Lee softly repeated once more, "The great mistake of my life was taking a military education."

Clearly moved, Mosby used a kerchief to wipe his eyes. The ex-guerilla cavalryman, the Gray Ghost shook. War and its consequences do that to strong men, especially those who have "seen the elephant" ...actual battle and barbarity, blood and guts, screams and pleas, savagery and obscenity, and blasphemy followed by prayers, then prayers upon prayers—to the same God—agony without ecstasy.

Each weary moment in front of Lee's twisted and strained facial expressions bespoke emotional instability. The strain was blatant enough that he grew concerned about his own well-being. Then, thoroughly out of character, R. E. Lee began talking about himself. Rambling about various events in his life, some not difficult to grasp, others blue-ribbon and honorable, still others pessimistic. Few were connected in an obvious manner, but were revelatory of his inner self nonetheless.

The discomfort between Lee and Mosby extended to the point of embarrassment. Neither ex-soldier could look steadily at the other's face. War left heavy freight with nowhere to go some five years after the warring. No wonder former warriors are quiet *post bellum*.

Not old age, not military defeat, not even obscurity in the hinterlands of western Virginia had ever misshaped R. E. Lee to the point of such blunt misery as had his candid but emphatic remarks about war. Now, framed prominently by his beard, the muscles around his eyes tightened in anguish; he squinted as if taking aim with a rifle. His lips twitched irregularly then plastered shut against one another, forming an ugly kink to his mouth. Collectively, constrictions warped his whole face, to say nothing of his personality, speech especially. No longer did he appear patrician, not the blue-blooded aristocrat, not the Southern grandee.

Lee was desolate. Dismal in front of a comrade. Pathetic within.

A few throes in several muscles of his arms and legs slowly rippled through the older man's body, never intensifying, however. Never ceasing, either. Lee tried to subdue them by getting up, then sitting down again on another chair saying, "Ouch!" a few times. Seemingly without purpose he grunted like an injured animal. Pathos showed.

Any words groaned aloud he repeated silently, also persistently. He seemed to have considered rehashing would make it easier to understand, but followed that thought with one about activity. *Maybe standing, maybe walking will relieve the pressure.* So he arose; walked to and fro attempting to soothe pain. It struck him that revisiting an inadequate experience is an attempt to vindicate oneself, as if self-justification were a cure for pain.

Rethinking, *"Great mistake... military education,"* didn't soothe either. Like a blacksmith's hammer, it struck red hot iron over and over, hot as hellfire, searing exposed flesh.

President Lee needed a cooling poultice, a soft refreshing treatment of some sort from daughter Agnes, but she had long before dismissed herself and left the hotel room for a walk in a nearby park in downtown Richmond.

Something had to happen to relieve the torture. The intellectual and emotional agonizing over the decisions which caused the deaths of thousands of his brave men didn't melt away at a wish. Nightly prayer relieved the pressure; nonetheless in daylight the old misery returned.

"The populace and the government both had misjudged everything necessary for a successful war—except the Southern Postal Service!" Both knew the importance of the wartime Postal Service. *But what had successful mail deliveries to do with defense of the Confederacy?* It had been a *non sequitur,* an illogical bragging point for the Confederate States of America. Buying stamps does not win a Rebellion.

Lee inwardly indicted the South... people, government, officials. *I could have used that fact as part of a plea for all branches of government to put aside bickering while my troops were lacking food, shoes, even ammunition.* The thought nagged him again as often in the past.

Then, attempting clarification he spoke aloud, "Without a full measure of material resources, without full acceptance by a unified population, the South needed *total* civilian dedication, increasing manpower to continue warring. Additionally, a political situation that would not re-splinter as the seceding states had splintered off the Union."

Mosby appeared to be taken aback by the litany of secession mistakes. Perhaps during the conflict he had not realized the public lack of caring because he had success in military ventures with public help in his own clandestine operations and subsequent "vanishing" in northern Virginia.

At that nib of time Lee added, "Limited resources disappeared PDQ. And fragments beget fragments all the time. It was a disaster." Becoming tight-lipped, he knew what he had done, conscious all the more of what he had implied. It was the next to last time he would make a confession to a former fellow officer.

Thoroughly exhausted, R. E. Lee had to sit. He slanted downward into a chair, tilting it hazardously.

Mosby jumped to his aid by steadying both chair and man from tumbling to the floor.

Lee looked at him curiously, wondering what was so wrong.

For his part, Mosby was also static, unmoving. After a few moments he took steps toward the door, as if to flee. Quickly he halted, realizing he would be in bad odor if he stranded President Lee of Washington College.

Time passed. And again passed. Waiting was now necessary for each man.

In an instant, Lee bobbed up, functioning. Out of character again, he bounced upward on his toes, stretching arms forward and back, looking around but not at anything in particular.

Mosby stayed dormant.

With a faraway look, Lee stood erect, starchy stiff. No feet shuffled. Lapels were not brushed off unconsciously. The only action was a swiveling, rolling his hands together as if keen for participation in something, much like Socrates of old at the battle of Athens against Potidæa, standing silent for hours.

Known for springing victory from defeat, R. E. Lee finally spoke. With nary a quiver of uncertainty he repeated, *"Great mistake on my part."* A clear pronouncement without bathos, without movement from the magnificent to the trivial or ridiculous. No regrets. No pathos either, to evoke sadness or pity. Just a personal avowal. Lee's restatement cleared the air... for him... as the knell of a church bell.

For John Singleton Mosby the knell was as a funereal chime.

Still in a compromised physical state Lee was overcome with a spate of dizzy spells, minutes apart. He was fearful of physically crumbling. *The floor appears moving up to me then retreats, gets bigger and then withdraws coaxing me to fall.* By sheer determination he blocked the feeling, thinking boldly, *I have to get hold of myself.* Instead he took hold of the back of a nearby chair, gripping with both sweating hands.

He stopped short, not falling. Slightly bent over at the waist he didn't see anything clearly even when gazing at John Mosby. No activity or signal; he was hooked by something that wasn't in the room. In such a state he didn't think how his companion reacted; he took no cognizance what or where or who or why he was present. Strange to say and more weird to experience, Lee was not in his own little world. Nor did he seem to himself to be in any world at all.

Am I having a stroke? A heart attack? What? His questions shook him up enough again to stop questioning.

After some fairly long minutes, Lee whispered, "I'm not the man people know. They see me only on a horse."

It may have helped Lee understand, but Mosby—who had stopped leaning on a door jamb and now began circling the room—clearly did not comprehend what was going on. If Lee's *"great mistake"* was of interest and importance, this second statement had cut deeper. It pierced the Gray Ghost's self-image as a soldier.

As former cavalry Ranger, a guerrilla fighter to the Nth degree, Mosby had literally run rings around the Federal army units for two years in northern Virginia. Federal troops were sent often to ferret out the Gray Ghost personally; none were successful.

Mosby—an above average student of Greek and Latin—knew his Bible well. In fact he had ridden into battle citing martial psalms of King David, such as:

Plead my cause, O Lord, with them that strive with me:
Fight against them that fight against me.
Take hold of shield and buckler and stand up for mine help.
Draw out the spear and stop the way against them that
*   persecute me:*
Say unto my soul, I am thy salvation.

*Let them be confounded and put to shame that seek after
     my soul;*
*Let them be turned back and brought to confusion that
     devise my hurt*
Let them be as chaff before the wind:
Let the angel of the Lord chase them.
Let their way be dark and slippery
And let the angel of the Lord persecute them.

To the detriment of Union troops, it was a deadly game but
Mosby succeeded. A Northern sergeant had written home saying
he could not shoot a man quoting Holy Scripture.

In a final strained whisper, R. E. Lee's next declaration was
not subtle. It lunged upon Mosby as he had done to Yankees.
"The greatest mistake I ever made was becoming a soldier."

Mosby lost it; composure fled. Stiffened. Frozen. Immobile.
No Bible verse sprang to his lips.

R. E. Lee's ethical dilemma coursed through himself. He had
sent so many men into battle who never returned alive. Many
more were seriously wounded and then pathetically served by
"medical" personnel. The horror of it all lacerated his Christian
conscience.

Mosby had heard rumors after the war years of Lee's
changed orientation and intentions, but never from the mouth
and heart of the man himself. Now he wrestled with the words,
the actual concepts, a condition notably severe because he
himself as a lucid thinker and straight talker was now blocked.
Self-blocked at that. He failed to speak to his former commander.
The one-time cavalry phantom was veritably washed-out, gray,
blood draining from his face. Like the ghost others proclaimed
him to be.

R. E. Lee paused to select his words carefully. If he were to
flesh out his views in what would amount to a personal lecture to
a former comrade, he perceived it would be like a barroom
argument of feuding opinions. He wanted rather to construct an
argument systematically using reason in support of an idea.

A kind of numbness set in collaterally. Lee examined himself
then analyzed Mosby's body language. Ruminating quickly, he

hit upon something other than logic to present his case. A practical example. It was the reply he had made in a letter to his former corps commander Richard Ewell earlier in the year. Of course it was impossible for Mosby to have known about Lee's postal correspondence with Ewell. Thus Lee would have to tell the Gray Ghost one more statement of his pacifism, piling it on, stacking the deck.

"For my part I much enjoy the charms of civil life. I find too late I have wasted the best years of my existence."

"Wasted!" Mosby responded, patently stupefied. "WASTED!" he barked.

Without quibbling, Lee answered, "Yes, wasted." Military life had wasted his best years. There had to be a better, more humane, way to live.

It was a *coup de grâce* to end all coups for John Mosby. The Gray Ghost staggered and sat down beside Lee on the comfortable settee.

And then nothing at all happened for a long time. Nothing except breathing.

CHAPTER 9

Memories bless and *burn*

R. E. Lee was much like a detective as he noted John Mosby's prevailing silence, yet seeming consternation. The Gray Ghost was unavoidably tense. Mosby had good reason to remain tongue-tied. Of course Mosby's pronounced constraint could have been based on something else entirely.

Conceivably the Gray Ghost could understand Lee's transformation best by an appeal to the former Ranger's efforts as a cavalry guerilla fighter. In well-nigh countless skirmishes and battles his men were brazen in efficiency, bewildering in trickeries, and not far off from incredulous in escapes. His war efforts had tied up Federal forces more than ten times his total command. His Rangers' efforts had culminated with brutal effect on Federal forces for two-plus years throughout northern Virginia—near enough to Washington, D.C., to keep the northern population vexed and fearful, perplexed, pestered, and finally scared spitless that their capital would be captured.

At the end of the war, Mosby never surrendered. *Might the war still be huge in his present life?* surmised R. E. Lee. *Even self-repatriated?* Each question struck with the force of a sledgehammer.

In a deep and somber voice, Lee said, "It is well... that war is... so terrible," then coughed to clear his vocal cords. "Or we would grow too fond of it."

A simple statement but filled with dread about the horrors of warfare: clear and concise, clout filled and guilt laden. The same instant, there was icy churning regret, remembering the butchery of masses on the battlefield.

Yet, in an instant Lee forged a schism between his past and the present, paralyzing himself from an objective evaluation. *What am I doing?* In stiletto-sharp, detached gushes that dulled him, he repeated, "We would grow... too fond... too fond." A pause of unaccounted length ensued, during which Lee reached out to Mosby for physical support.

Support was given lovingly by the guerilla fighter who had himself begun the process of turning from violence after the fratricidal war to do his share in restoring the Republic he had fought against so successfully. Changed man and a changing man supported one another.

The former commander of the Army of Northern Virginia was battered. Tempest-like he tormented his conscience: "O memories that bless and burn; O barren gain and bitter loss. Will I ever forget?" he stated haphazardly.

In darkly shaded memory, R. E. Lee realized that if human beings cannot have a world without war then they are condemned to war upon one another forever. Endless wars. Until war becomes the normal condition of the species.

As late afternoon's shadows lengthened, R. E. Lee's demeanor slipped into total passivity. He did not repeat the words; nor did he intend to do so later.

Stillness unrolled between them again like a gaseous mist in a swamp. Each man sat transfixed in quietness, for minutes, and more. To Lee's relief and Mosby's thankfulness.

Then something beyond social rules of convention but close to the infinite silences of space stirred the hearts of the former warriors. A deeper stillness, not mere muteness. It was a seedbed of discovery: insight. A remarkable perception of solidarity. They looked steadily at one another and said not a word, or two or a hundred. They saw something similar in the other.

The turmoils of belief and unbelief that had marked any previously incompatible words concerning war and war's effects were wiped away in the silence.

Then, at last... a sound. A whisper. As if in a lover's private connection there came one word, "Yes," from one of them.

In tenderness the sound was spoken, breathed by one whose drooped chin was hard against his chest as he eyeballed the carpet beneath his feet for any pattern that might help him end their time together.

The other traced shadows in the room that might suggest closure as well as daylight's descending sun.

"Yes," as in a lover's dialogue, the alternate one responded mere seconds later.

In peace. Generous affirmatives had solidified their friendship. Handshakes were strong; handshakes were long. Warming to their hearts they shared the Lion's Grip of Judah: eye to eye, chest to chest, right hands to right forearms, left hands to left upper arms, torso to torso, knee to knee, foot to foot they stood riveted.

Gray became their royal purple for the remainder of their lives.

CHAPTER 10

"Found again in the heart of a friend"

After several consultations with Richmond physicians concerning his health, Lee's mind was set at ease, though the doctors may not have been thorough enough as practicing scientists, deferring to the college president's self-evaluation.

During their stay in Richmond, Agnes and R.E. Lee met several friends informally and briefly; none caused over-exertion on his part except J. S. Mosby's visit. Lee then encountered a lesser-known friend, and thereon hangs a number of tales.

As life often has it, a snag occurred in their vacation effort: traveling companion daughter Agnes fell ill with her ongoing thorn in the flesh. Beginning from the rain-saturated wharf at Lexington on through Lynchburg where it caught up to her, as often is the case, people worsen and Agnes more so. Some days she was bedridden, empty and unresponsive, yearning to recuperate to aid her old father who complexified her condition.

"Wiggie" was her father's all-around travel agency. Train travel and routes, companionship, hotel accommodations, caregiving nursing, eating arrangements with special dietary needs, correspondence, and socialization with others all continued her concerns, demonstrably weighing on top of her illness.

The grand old man was unable to help his daughter most of the time with any of those demands. They were a hampered duo. Turning back for home was not much of an option either. Yet Florida appeared thousands of miles away. Southern balmy breezes were mere conversation points, and not physically soothing nor heartwarming intellectually.

Then... from out of the blue... a remedy! A rejoinder to life's twists and turns a friend appeared. One James L. Corley materialized.

No way could Corley have been thought of as a resource waiting to assist father and daughter. No way was the friend even remembered in the midst of incessant rain, then pleasant Richmond weather, followed by a skull session with J. S. Mosby. No previous correspondence or meeting had happened after the war. But there Corley was, smack dab in Richmond in front of Lee and daughter "Wig."

Corley had been the Chief Quartermaster of the Army of Northern Virginia. Lee had dealt with him almost daily and befriended him as an efficient officer in a most difficult position. The Confederacy had a terrible time keeping its field armies supplied. Everything from food to equipment to ammunition to horseshoes for its livestock, cash to pay suppliers as well as troops on which the A.N.V. relied for movement to meet the enemy—*everything* was in short supply most every day, including battle days.

Also a West Point graduate, Corley had served in the U.S. Army in the West before the war, but later resigned to join the C.S.A. He was widely known as a skilled and orderly manager of tremendous needs and short supplies for a whole army of sixty or seventy thousand men on the move.

R. E. Lee was startled but thankful, ever so filled with gratitude to see James Corley. A gift. Lee thought Providence was on his side. For the trip, presently, at least.

More often than not, the A.N.V. had been undersupplied by the Confederate government. Lee was thought by Richmond officialdom to be so famous, so powerful a military personage as strategist and tactician, that he could nearly always get supplies from the Virginia countryside, that the populace would respond to his needs if officialdom hadn't. The Army of Northern Virginia needed food, staples, food, uniforms, more food, *et cetera*—it never had enough shoes, never enough for men—horses and mules either—*never enough*. Young men and some old ones, too, marched bare-footed while animals for wagons and riders went unshod.

In that old army, James Corley had made good things happen in poor situations. It would be the same on this trip. Even daughter Agnes felt better, relieved to meet Corley after her father explained the man's history and ability.

The demands upon Corley in the war were perpetual in victory, or defeat. He managed or concocted minor wonders by hook and by crook, by buck and by luck to keep the A.N.V. supplied. Usually minimally supplied, never maximally supplied, was a reason back in the Summer of 1863 that R. E. Lee ventured into enemy territory. Corley savored the thought of copious pickings, there where everything existed, not in Federal government storehouses but on countless productive farms and in numerous successful businesses in Pennsylvania.

Lee's Northern Campaign entered the Quaker State's lush fields, ripe orchards, bountifully stocked barns... cattle, horses, pigs, sheep, chickens, turkeys, guinea fowl galore... and its rolling wheat fields, barley fields, oat fields ready to be "harvested," so to speak, by friend or foe in late June or early July of '63. To Southern farm boys and men it was a bit of the Garden of Eden to feed upon, to "collect" for the Army of Northern Virginia. Those magnificent barns, crisp fields of hay and grain, the orderly accoutrements of fences, sheds, haystacks, trim spring houses, and well cared for farming equipment made for an artist's canvas, pigments and brushes as well.

In preparation for the excursion into Pennsyltucky, as the state was familiarly known, the army "bought" supplies with Confederate currency or scrip paper I.O.U.s, not Federal greenbacks. All together some 60,000 head of cattle, horses, mules, pigs, sheep, sometimes chickens and turkeys were stockaded then herded south to Staunton, Virginia, the A.N.V. base of operations, from the southern tier counties of Fulton, Franklin, Adams, and York all *before* the Battle of Gettysburg.

The soft underbelly of the North was ripe for the picking. And Colonel Corley, Chief Quartermaster, was champion picker-upper for the Confederacy. Especially, he rejoiced there would be shoes! Work shoes, dress shoes, clodhoppers, Sunday-go-to-meeting shoes, dance shoes, boots, galoshes, even sandals. Any kind of leather, any color, almost any condition as long as they had soles. Shoes for men, shoes for horses and mules—all were plentiful.

Soldiers loved it, the plenitude. They may have been tired but they loved the abundance of what they desired: leather shoes from cottage industries, iron horseshoes from the local iron furnaces, and food from the many small merchants who dotted the farming area. Shoemakers, blacksmiths, and vegetable farmers turned delivery hucksters going from man to man selling food and other stores, scores upon scores of times, populating the verdant landscape where Lee's men bought such items cheap and sold them for profit to fellow soldiers in gray and butternut extract dyed uniforms.

Corley had planned his own lavish jaunt in line with General Lee's interesting plan to go to the banks of the Susquehanna River on a very special assignment. It was a secret to troops and officers alike yet apparently known to only one of his corps commanders, Richard Stoddert Ewell, "Old Baldy" his troopers named him. He had been wounded in the left leg, which was then amputated below the knee at the Battle of Second Manassas. Later at Gettysburg he was wounded in the chest by a spent bullet and shot in the wooden leg that had replaced the amputated one. Two men other than Lee—Ewell and Corley—knew the plan for sure; others in the A.N.V. may have known also but never spoke of it.

"It's so uplifting to see you again," Lee said eagerly.

"It's comforting to see you again, Sir," replied Corley the businessman.

Lee thought they could discuss his own limited condition for the trip, and Agnes' condition as well. He thought that Corley, having stated he was in the insurance profession in the Carolinas and visiting Richmond on a business trip, might know a possible traveling companion who would aid the two on their trip to Florida.

Obviously Lee was needy. With Wiggie fighting off a serious cold, her helpfulness was nearly nil if not totally absent. Corley was so moved to see his old leader alive he immediately volunteered to help, without thinking all such an offer would entail. By all shakes, Corley stood ready to serve his old commander without reservation, a true comrade in war... or peace.

He offered to make all the arrangements for their travel to relieve them of such complicated matters. It was he who made the many preparations for various trains, hotels, personal abodes where they might stay and visit. Even eating accommodations— the whole shebang. But, of necessity, he noted, he first would travel to his home in Charlotte, North Carolina, to set his own affairs in order. Then when the Lees arrived at Charlotte he would accompany them on the remainder of their way to Georgia to make further plans as necessary and to be certain as possible their plans would be accomplished. To make sure, as well, both travelers would be in good enough shape to travel from Savannah, Georgia, to close-by Florida, then back northward to Lexington after visiting family in eastern Virginia.

Out of the blue, gratis. A military veteran. A comrade-in-arms still.

"You are a Southern gentleman," Wiggie noted. Corley blushed, actually blushed. All three smiled.

Lee added, "Agnes, he's a Good Samaritan."

Corley's face turned pink again.

No one smiled, but old man Lee shook his own head in solid affirmation. "Thanks be to God," he intoned.

Corley punctuated, "Amen."

Wig smiled. Ever thankful to be relieved of what she had to do, but for which she was not prepared.

Corley was much moved. A blubber reached his lips but its faint cry was instantly caught with a handkerchief. "Thank you, Sir," came forth readily.

"Thank you," spoke the Lees with joy.

Life is spontaneous with small miracles that keep happening when we least expect.

CHAPTER 11

"Seek peace—and pursue it"

James Corley quickly discerned the exhausted condition of R. E. Lee. He promptly recommended the father and daughter detrain late afternoons or early evenings at some—any—station, village or town, along the route rather than endure night-time train travel. He consulted the conductor of the train and station personnel about shelter farther down the line. When necessary he interviewed fellow passengers to discover possible arrangements for overnight accommodations.

Given that the average speed of trains, passenger or freight, was only ten miles per hour on good tracks and a mere five on worn-out rails, it was necessary for Corley to plan carefully for night-time accommodations for their party of three. Most passengers were like Eleanor Agnes, unknowing of the appalling condition of trackage in post-war Dixie. They didn't realize that very few good tracks had T-shaped rails made of steel. The old iron ones rusted dangerously while the steel tracks were susceptible to being pilfered by railroad companies for their own important routes. It wasn't dog-does-not-eat-dog in southern post-war railroads; contrariwise, it was dog-eat-dog with a vengeance.

Railroads frequently substituted cheaper, less efficient, and much shorter-lasting rail type "strap rails," for the purposely purloined—considered "borrowed"—steel T-shaped rails. Strap rail consisted of blocks of wood about five inches high and ten feet long, overlaid with straps of iron about an inch high and several feet long, then nailed to crossties for stability. Made of iron, the straps rusted quickly, flaked off regularly, and easily splintered the wood base from the heavy pounding by locomotives and freight cars. Delays on some stretches were recurrent and numerous, making a mockery of train schedules.

Another substitute rail was U-shaped *turned upside down*, forming a hollow iron rail susceptible to caving in. The weight of the trains caused countless indentations, making for bumpy riding at the least or broken rails which stopped traffic completely. In 1862, the line from Nashville to Chattanooga had 1,200 broken rails and had hardly been repaired eight years later.

The majority of the South's 9,500 miles of railroads were owned by cotton farmers and storage businesses which stood in contrast with the North's 22,000 miles of railroads owned by corporations; the latter had standardized rail gauges and shared railyards. High expenses kept those privately owned, small railroads in the South from keeping their tracks in shape. Southern railroad owners were scavengers and thieves.

Adding to the inadequate rails and speed limitations were the usual halts because of differing track gauges between two railroads, usually across town from one another, as competing cotton growers had not organized common railyards. Southern railroads were chimerical—delusory like the fire-breathing monster of Greek mythology with lion's head, goat's body, and serpent's tail—almost totally unrealistic and unbelievable. During the war it had taken General James Longstreet's corps of 12,000 soldiers twelve days to travel 800 miles by trains to northern Georgia for the Battle of Chickamauga after fourteen different rail changes.

No wonder in 1870 the elder Lee's temperament became shorter than the rail lines. His usual quick temper flared each and every stop. Daughter Agnes and friend Corley sought to mollify him, usually with minimal success. Both became exasperated, as much with him as with the repeated stops, transfers, and forfeited time.

As his company's traveling representative, Corley knew the unpredictable rail situations but thought he could plan around such limitations. All three travelers realized it was Lee's discomfort that served as major mover for Corley's spontaneity in rejecting further night-time rail travel whenever possible.

Subsequent to Corley's leave-taking for home, the Lees' first travel experience upon leaving Richmond had been a generally untroubling ride that ended with an overnight stay at the home of the John White family in Warrenton, North Carolina. Lee's daughter Anne, who was ever "Annie," had died during the war and was buried there. R. E. Lee had never visited her grave because of wartime duties then college responsibilities.

Women of the Warrenton area had raised money for a cemetery plot and a monument for Annie Lee, caring for them thereafter with deference and respect. So before entraining the next day, father and daughter visited her grave site. It had been decorated with fresh flowers for their arrival. R. E. Lee was fully appreciative for their love and care rendered the years before his visit to Annie's grave and told one and all.

He realized an important truth at that monument: human beings are the only species that buries its dead. And the Warrenton women were noteworthily human. A good day all around and if not invigorated, Lee was peaceful: Annie was in God's guardianship.

However, the agreeable night and day in Warrenton, near the border with Virginia, did not foretell the remainder of the train trip southward.

Continuing southward travel was interrupted various times and extended into eventide, often darkness. The train moved slower than the five mile per hour average. It navigated through the countryside as if lost, almost hopelessly seeking its way. The engine headlamp seemed to search for the tracks. Sleeper cars, seldom available in the post-war South, were prohibitively expensive; one was attached to the two passenger cars, making for a length of five vehicles counting locomotive and wood-fuel car. Agnes later wrote her mother that she and her father spent the night in a "sleeping car," but couldn't sleep at all for the unfamiliarity of the experience. And the noise. Noise. Noise. Endless noise.

On the other hand, as on most overnight trips, a few passengers tried to sleep sitting upright in the passenger cars.

Others unashamedly leaned their heads on the shoulders or laps of co-travelers, known or unknown. No method worked for more than a few minutes. They, as well, couldn't sleep for the unconventionality of the situation. But it cost them less to sit than it did to pay the extra sleeping car fee to lie down.

The mileage that first night of travel was minimal; mostly unnecessary. Possibly the train covered 20, maybe 25, 26 miles, supposedly to make up time lost during the previous daylight hours. The few stops along the way didn't help either. And because stops were without explanation, passengers became markedly irritated. Lee among them; loudly so: one time Wiggie was much embarrassed and said so to a total stranger.

"But age has its privileges," noted the other woman in the darkness.

That first overnight episode compromised R. E. Lee's well-being further than he thought. His will to travel lessened. How much longer could he endure was a question for both him and Wiggie. Options ran through his mind. *Stay overnight two or three days at some hotel along the way? Return home?* Ambivalence added dreariness to Lee's already disappearing whiter than white affability, becoming more and more a demanding condition on himself... and for people around him.

Gentle-hearted Eleanor Agnes began to suffer pangs of conscience overtly along with her pains of body. She, who did no wrong, commenced to feel shame.

The train noises—wheels thumping over gaps where rails met other rails, the whistle, then the fuel-stops to take on timber for the engine's firebox—were nothing compared to the terrible inconvenience of arbitrarily placed sanitary facilities along the tracks. They were the pits. Figuratively; often literally with only slight holes in the earth.

Coal was still in tight supply, but though timber was accessible, it burned rapidly and had to be replenished often. Conductors and engineers worked to load the fuel, sometimes helped by black people, women as well as men, who stayed up late to earn a nickel or two. Sometimes pennies only. One time no wood was in the supply box and the train crew—engineer, fireman, even the conductor—had to enter nearby woods to harvest green timber; no black people were available in that instance.

The bad news was green timber doesn't burn readily. On such occasions the firebox could not forcefully heat the water enough to generate steam to budge the pistons to move the drive-wheels. It took an hour to get up a head of steam to do the job.

The bumping and jolting, as the speed of the train increased abruptly or diminished sharply, pestered and bewildered passengers. Physical composure was virtually impossible; mentally, most passengers were dulled into acceptance of the inevitable. All were assaulted by an irregular series of staccato, jerky jarrings accompanied by stinging whiplashes for the elderly and the very young.

Agnes expressed displeasure. It was like having her head jerked down then back up in a schoolyard when a boy would pull her long locks of hair. Overtiring. Hurtful. On the train she worsened matters, causing her father to feel miserable when she asked, "How can you stand it, Father?"

The first time she had asked the question the old man didn't respond. Many minutes later he replied, placidly, "What else can I do?"

Confounded, Agnes kept quiet afterwards. A soft answer does turn away wrath.

The jarring and thumping made sleeping for the ex-soldier more unendurable than a cot in a tent, or even the bare ground he had slept on while on military campaigns. Numerous times he dozed on the edge of true sleep only to be plucked back into the reality with stomach-churning sounds in the darkness. Once in a while he was aroused and alarmed, "What was that?" One time he demanded to know, "Where am I?" Another time, "Who's in charge?"

Wiggie, awakened, had to reply, "We're on a train after visiting Annie's grave."

The elderly father replied, "I'd be so happy to see her again." No recognition of visiting the grave site, however, passed his lips.

Gradually he lapsed into a soft hum of a hymn synchronized with his breathing. The expression on his face was fixed as he scrutinized the cheerless night passing by outside the window.

"Goodnight, Annie. Goodnight, sweet Annie." And then he wept a father's tears, to sleep in lullaby land with memories of his dear mother Ann as well. His heart was breaking in the middle of the night, in the rickety ramshackled atmosphere of a train.

At dawn, he was as exhausted as if route-marching, foot-slogging, dead-tired on a military campaign. Only months later would he fully realize it was a heart condition. For now he knew it only as tiredness. R. E. Lee was fit to be tied and could not, actually would not, speak to the crowds gathered somehow where they transferred railroads.

The fourth morning south of Richmond, however, turned different. Sometime after 6:00 A.M. the conductor ambled through the cars in an apparent attempt to help passengers start an expeditious morning jaunt. He broke into song in each of the three cars as he strolled by, checking tickets again plus the welfare of his passengers. With a silvery, powerful baritone voice he sang a railroad ditty current in mid-19th century America:

> "Captain, go sidetrack your train."
> Clickety clack, clickety clack, clickety clack;
> "CAPTAIN! GO SIDETRACK YOUR TRAIN!"
> Bump-ah-dee-bump. Bump-ah-dee-bump, bump-ah-dee-
>   bump;
> "CAPTAIN! ... GO SIDETRACK YOUR TRAIN!!"
> Engine Forty-nine.
> Commin' down the line !!!"
> Puff-ah-dee-puff, puff-ah-dee-puff. Puff... Puff... Puff.
> "Captain, go sidetrack your train!"
> Ah-humm, Ah-hhummmm. Ah-hhhummmmmmmmm.

In each car he announced their southbound train would travel about two or so miles farther down the line and then move onto a sidetrack to allow a freight train to run on through. There would be a delay of up to an hour, possibly an hour and a half. Various times another train would go barreling northbound, having the right-of-way. Since the railroad line was one track (two rails), only their train would have to pull off the single track onto a side track—and wait. Waiting meant waiting longer.

Sidetracking was normal and would be encountered other times on the trip through to northeastern Florida. Such stops were time lost, schedules broken. Once in a while they were time-rewarding breaks from the monotony of clickety clack, bump-ah-dee-bump. Stops provided breaks from the painful sitting—really ricocheting from position to position, spot to spot—on hard wooden seats. Bounce. Bump. Bounce. Bump *ad nauseum* from side to side, back and forth, up and down enough to produce aches in muscles and the head. Bowels, too.

Curiously R. E. Lee took simple delight during the daytime in that railroaders' ditty, the playful conductor, as well as other passengers' appreciation likewise.

Once in a while he looked at the scenery, but not often. He noted, however, geniality began to seep through the coach and passengers talking to one another. The tone of the trip had altered enough to make for a friendly "How y'all?" or "How do" or "Hey y'all" or "Good day to you." The Lee party, too, became openly sociable. It was a gentle surprise to the old man. A change-of-pace surprise, yet he couldn't discern why it happened. Once in a while human beings just become decently open when there is nothing to fear. It breaks the boredom. *I can use all that and more*, he told himself.

Then a necessary surprise: the third sidetrack area had both men's and women's outhouses... much appreciated because less waiting time. Sometimes life's little surprises are better than birthday gifts. Surprises in many cases make life as beautiful as Nature. For Nature is filled with wee, elfin artistry and blessings. Outhouses qualify.

Even Corley noted, "At least the day is better than the night had been." The ex-Chief Quartermaster of the Army of Northern Virginia added another dimension, enthusiasm, for his companions' sakes. From time to time even laughter. A familiar face made the bad-travel-medicine go down easier. His phrase became a daily ritual, thus less effective: "Better than last night."

Wiggie thought her father sometimes was mildly humorous, not a comedian performing but a humorist sharing life's risibility with peers. At those times her countenance lightened because she knew her father's humor was never for laughs. It was for smiles. He wasn't an actor, certainly not a vaudevillian. The old man knew that life is made up of "sobs, sniffles, and smiles" with sniffles predominating as an American writer had noted.

For his part, James Corley thought of military bivouacs in the line of march, and of one time on a battlefield when he'd heard the muted humor of the quiet man, R. E. Lee. He realized the general again was hurting underneath. Probably from memories of war because they occupy so much of the human mind. "Memories do bless and burn; memories of barren gain and bitter loss." War comes with dense pangs, inky regrets, trailed by hidden remorse that erupts, explodes unpredictably. Memories change a warrior more than medicine or even religion.

Several times passengers shared portions of sandwiches with others, one shared morsels of cookies. Two hucksters traveling together shared unripe early apples and a few hard pears; they took it upon themselves to rub the fruit clean on their shirts and then sliced them with jackknives. They asked some children in the coach to distribute the slices. A boy and also one girl poached slices as they distributed them.

Not all passengers partook, but many got a taste, a taste of human kindness. Simple words of thanks were more abundant than the nibbles of food. And R. E. Lee noted a positive along with his usual pain in chest and left arm. Turned out it was not an imperfect start to the day, for on balance it was an equilibrium of kindness and infirmity.

Life had a touch of goodness that carried onto the day's first sidetrack. The conductor came by whistling a cheery tune and did a jig, shuffling his feet then pranced into the next coach. To applause. But didn't answer questions about the delay.

An hour passed. An hour and a half. Two hours. It was more time the southbound passenger train sat on the sidetrack than before; two freight trains passed by heading northward nearly an hour or so apart. At five and a quarter hours their locomotive's whistle tooted to alert passengers to reboard the train. Three blasts sounded harsh, but not so harsh as various words by its passengers. Lee's face flushed from his own unvoiced thoughts and uneven activities. "In captivity," he said a few times.

The tone of the day changed, back to negativity. Similar to other passengers, the Lee party couldn't help but feel misery; it was palpable. It would become torturous for each as it bled bitterness into their conversations. Difficult to bear the five-hour delay nonchalantly, every passenger was as antsy as the children in the rail car.

"Well... we've had disappointments before," voiced James Corley in a simple attempt to put the long delay in perspective. In the army he had been continually dismayed that flour and foodstuffs, horseshoes and hay, ammunition and firearms were delayed for days, delayed more likely for weeks—or never delivered. The present sidetrack hiatus was next to nothing for him.

I wonder what my former leader is thinking? Corley mused. *Numerous times we waited for food promised by the War Office. Does he ever think of that?*

Eleanor Agnes was solicitous about other passengers, how they coped with the delay, delay, and more delay. Still recovering from her illness she asked, "Would you children like to play a game? Join me."

Three children, a boy and two girls, went to sit beside her. Wiggie was happy. The children became happy and joined in a game of four people clapping hands with one another in a rhythmic manner while singing a music-hall ditty.

Various thoughts coursed through Lee's mind. *What are five hours' disappointment compared to five years' with the results of the late war?*

Such an idea was an explosive indictment. Remembering now, Lee bowed his head low and wiped away several tears: All those thousands upon thousands of dead boys and men. To no avail. *We could have stopped the War in 1862. Again in 1863. Regrets with blood in them never are forgotten.* R. E. Lee labored alone.

The results of the war were monumental, huge beyond compare with anything else the South suffered: death and destruction in their finances, in their futures, in their daily routines... and in their religion. Life-changing disappointment permeated everything Southern. Five hours' despondency couldn't compare with the last five years' dismay in many Dixieland hearts.

"This train trip is grieving me," Lee groaned.

"What?" Corley asked.

"Why?" Wiggie added.

"The war. The men I led into death. The Northern men I slaughtered. The wrong cause at the wrong time, started by hotspurs who wanted their way, not the whole American way. We couldn't have survived after the war as an independent nation; we would have been ripe pickings for the French who controlled Mexico. There would have been easy pickings of the states and territories west of the Mississippi. The remainder of Southern states, already quarreling throughout the war, would have collapsed into financial and social ruin." Vexed by his own words Lee needed to recover.

"But maybe not," Corley interrupted.

In a somewhat louder voice, Lee said, "No. It would have been a Pyrrhic victory."

"What's that, Father?" Agnes asked.

"It's a victory named after King Pyrrhus of Epirus," Corley answered, "whose army suffered irreplaceable casualties while totally defeating the Romans at the Battle of Heraclea in 280 B.C. and the Battle of Asculum in 279 B.C., during the Pyrrhic War. To an officer who expressed happiness about his victory King Pyrrhus had replied *'Another such victory will utterly undo me.'*"

"A victory inflicting such a devastating toll on himself is tantamount to defeat," said Lee. "Someone who wins a Pyrrhic victory has been victorious in name only."

Then the old man stopped short, slightly panting, remembering his own high battle casualties. His silence and turning his body as if to get away bespoke regret.

"Had the South won the Rebellion, we would have become a poverty-stricken cousin of the remaining Northern states and the Western territories. Always in second place struggling to repair, rebuild, and rebound while the United States would mine the 49ers' California gold and Nevada's silver and become a world power." R. E. Lee seemed to surprise himself with that evaluation, which actually did so noticeably for James Corley.

Gentle Agnes was muddled but concerned for her father. She kept thinking of his physical limitations more than his intellectual positions. The protracted railroad delay could entail considerable self-examination, possibly detrimental to his well-being. Consequently she did not pursue questioning him further.

Her father's profile visibly varied: skin stretched as facial muscles tightened; brow grooves deepened; head jerked sharply upwards once in a while, jaw jutted outward, drawing attention to his whiskers. He seemed to be making a display of himself. So unusual. Agnes became sorrowful, but would not interrupt her father's reverie. And Corley had silenced himself; wisely so.

However, it was because R. E. Lee caught himself off base, thinking about the calamitous consequences that could have happened had the South gained independence but lost territory, unity, and rationale as well. He couldn't help it. Something was happening inside. Happening to an old man who had lost a war, but was seeking to save his soul.

Agnes couldn't help, either, as she continued to mull over what had not been said. Why had Corley used the four-year lost war as an example of waiting? He could have chosen another comparison—perhaps waiting days for a loved one to recover from an illness. Wiggie was disappointed not only with Corley but with herself that she hadn't done something to squeeze in levity, or song, or storytelling amidst the dullness, the vacuity of the five-hour sidetrack delay.

And she noted more. She could tell it in her father's now compressed lips jutting outward, too. His swiftly blinking eyes denoted anxiety. And when he jerked his head back and forth she expected storm number two. It came in a semi-growl, deep and slow.

The former general put his pain into words, mostly one at a time, "If... you... want to know... disappointment, you... should... have known... my... mind... have known my spirit... in September 1862." The old man hesitated breath after breath after breath. Another severe disappointment. He was disillusioned by what hadn't happened eight years before.

President Davis had rejected his call for ending the war. Lee might have ended it. But didn't. *Oh, God!* was not a prayer but a deep disappointment with himself that he hadn't forcefully confronted Davis with the hard facts about losing—or winning—the Rebellion.

Shut down totally it could have been in '62—before thousands and thousands of men, South and North, at the battle of Antietam/Sharpsburg were killed, wounded, diseased. Before the lovely land was desecrated by fire and bombs, destruction and annihilation in state after state, forest after forest, pasture after pasture, home after home. Before human beings destroyed God's creation—and God's image: fellow human beings.

Silence trickled into the stale air of the railroad car. Bleak, it dropped stagnant upon Lee's two companions during his agony. Only he moved, using a handkerchief to wipe away moisture on cheeks, in beard, on both hands. He wanted to say that both sides may have overreacted about things social, and racial, and religious. The outcome of such serious issues could barely be answered in more than Lee's whisper. "Politics builds a world unlike the real world, the everyday world of citizens. Politicians argue about ideas that are beyond politics' capabilities of handling. It may be honest on their parts but that doesn't mean it's a rational attempt, a workable attempt. It is not judicious nor commonsensical nor pragmatic."

"Misunderstandings were bound to occur, grow, multiply," Corley suggested. "And bound to grow gruesome. Political situations would easily become willful misunderstandings. Growing pains were barely addressed for many years—except in caricature. Our newspapers were filled with grotesque cartoons of politicians South and North. They were ridiculed with raucous words and ugly representations of leaders in pictures that did no credit to anyone who drew them, those they satirized, or those who read them."

Lee replied, "Therefore they could not propose a rational understanding, some happy middle ground for settling sectional differences back in the 1840s and 50s. Issues then festered and putrefied into intersectional dissents, even hostile acts of Americans against Americans."

The torture of such words wracked all six ears.

Lee was disappointed in political leaders of all stripes, colors, parties, churches, and states, North or South; he reflected a bit louder again than he usually spoke. Heating to his task he declared, "I am not disappointed with the American Republic's founding and its goals. Never. It was solidly rational and conciliatory, attempting in the Constitution to meet the needs of all thirteen former colonies."

Lee was emotional pain enfleshed. Obviously such pain did not ameliorate his physical pain a smidgen. He continued despairingly, "I am deeply conscious of all the dead. They are my greatest post-war concern. After duties to family and the college—not West Point, but Washington College—my concern and anxiety are all the dead who were set up to die because of political and sectional misunderstandings."

The old man felt mournful about the non-acceptance of his proposal for peace in '62. And again in 1863. He still felt that anguish in 1870. And it made him wretched. Downright heartbroken. Constantly, he thought: *What will release me?*

"Then we justify what we do with simplistic talk such as 'All's fair in love and war' or 'nothing is out of bounds.' And we succumb. I, too, succumbed. I've always resented spying, cloak and dagger, double-dealing, yet I resorted to it prior to the Northern Campaign."

More than James Corley, Wiggie was dumbstruck. Her father seldom talked about his interior life to the family and the upshot devastation war had wrought on him. She couldn't say a word. Neither did Corley say anything to Lee about his morose condition.

"I sent spies into York County before we marched north into Pennsylvania since, as a southern county orientated toward Baltimore in slave state Maryland, there were sympathizers we could use to help us secure York for the peaceful effort we wanted to do there on the 4th of July, 1863.

"When General John B. Gordon passed through York on the way to the huge modern wooden bridge crossing the Susquehanna River between Wrightsville and Columbia a strange thing happened. A lass about thirteen years or so ran out of a crowd at Continental Square and gave him a bouquet of bright red roses. He thanked her; she nodded. He looked carefully at the bouquet and saw a note tucked among the flowers. Gordon pulled other riders around his horse so he could remove the note to read it. Doing so he discovered a message identifying the Union troops and their positions to defend the bridge at Wrightsville, obviously by a spy who had reconnoitered for the benefit of our Confederate army. We were readily able to get to the bridge as the Federals were easily trounced since we knew exactly where they were, uncovered their redoubts entrenched at various places, and routed them all.

"It was distasteful to me that I had to resort to trickery with spies," Lee added.

Corley appeared unnerved that the former commander responded emotionally to spy work. He so stated but Lee took exception to Corley's exception.

Lee was not impeded but rather stated some content of the letter he had written to President Jefferson Davis of the Confederacy requesting a peace proposal in 1862:

> *The proposal of peace would enable the people of the United States to determine at their coming elections whether they would support those who favor a prolongation of the war, or those who wished to bring it to a termination, which can but be productive of good to both parties without affecting the honor of either.*

Davis replied in the negative. Of course. He had been a hotspur in '61. Most of the Rebellion had been a big negative to thousands of Southerners still opposed to separation from the Union. There existed a divided South always lurking as a possible Trojan Horse throughout Dixie that Davis feared.

The battle at Sharpsburg, Maryland, along Antietam Creek occurred nine days later on 17 September 1862. The Army of Northern Virginia had to withdraw. It was bloody; the bloodiest one-day battle in American history. Especially bloody in defeat. Lee suffered the whole way back to Virginia.

It is easier to go to war than to make peace. And, staying at war most often is seen as a righteous decision. God is inserted much like a replacement in a sporting event. God becomes an imprimatur, a stamp of approval used automatically to make things right for the side imploring him. And when the side imploring God loses, he is blamed. God always loses, for both sides implore him. God always is the first casualty in war.

Then the dead in defeat pay two times! It is unreal stupidity to declare the dead in defeat to have paid "the ultimate price" because their cause paid the same price. Double defeat. The dead in defeat can't do anything right.

R. E. Lee had struggled for months after the Gettysburg fiasco whether or not he was in the best frame of mind to command an army. He wanted to resign. The loss at Sharpsburg had shaken him to the core; he realized he was not at his very best along the Antietam. Probably because Jefferson Davis had turned down his peace proposal. Nor would the same man accept Lee's resignation after Gettysburg, thereby compelling him to suffer more until it became too much. At Appomattox in 1865 physical starvation and emotional poverty—plus human debate about whether war settles anything justly—compelled him to seek peace through surrender.

He was tortured by the struggles, the woundings, the deaths of men in the ranks who did what was asked of them—and more than was asked. "Those men we lost in Maryland could have been saved from the bloodiest day of the whole war. We should have tried again the next day if we wanted to win a battle," Lee bemoaned. Multitudinous deaths are ponderous. Impactful. Remembered. Remembered too well.

More importantly, Lee discerned he should have tried harder for peace than just a letter. President Davis should have been shown the terrors of fratricidal war. On the battlefield, not in a report—official or not. There were too many deaths, too many wounded. And way too many desertions after Gettysburg. Unbelievable many. Replacements were terribly difficult to find.

We're foot-slog-slog-slog-sloggin' o'er Merica
Foot-foot-foot-foot-sloggin' o'er America—
(Boots-boots-boots-boots-movin' up and down again!)
"There's no discharge in the war!"

Seven-six-eleven-five-nine-an'-twenty mile to-day—
Four-eleven-seventeen-thirty-two the day before—
(Boots-boots-BOOTS—boots movin' up and down again!)
  "There's no discharge in the war!"

Don't-don't-don't-don't-look at what's in front of you.
(BOOTS-boots—BOOTS—boots movin' up an' down again!)
Men-men-men-men-men go mad with watchin' 'em,
  "And there's no discharge in the war!"

Try-try-try-try-to think o' something different—
Oh-my-God-keep-me from goin' lunatic!
(Boots-BOOTS-boots-BOOTS-movin' up an' down again!)
  "There's no discharge in the war!"

It was serious, stony-faced serious, grave disappointment for Lee the peace-seeker! Disappointment of the severest kind, because he knew he should have tried again and yet again to get through to Jefferson Davis. Lee realized he had blood on his hands. And, as Shakespeare's Macbeth, it could not be washed away. Nor wished away. Not even prayed away.

There was always the image of a bridge, the stone bridge over Antietam Creek, the bridge over the Susquehanna also. All those good men from the North ensnarled in clumps trying to rush across at Antietam and the fewer before Wrightsville. They were wiped out by good men from the South defending a bridge and good men from the North defending another bridge.

Lee especially visualized courageous Southern troops flattened dead on Antietam's Sunken Road—become Bloody Lane—as they, too, were mowed down. Their blood flowing and soaking the earth for hundreds of yards, shot by Northern men doing their duty to defend a piece of ground.

And the image in his head of that white Dunkard Church of "the plain people," a pacific symbol, with gaping holes from cannon balls... blasted by which side no one ever will know... standing in whiteness as much an emblem of peace as any great cathedral.

That good man, R. E. Lee, was accustomed to submitting to authority so had not opposed President Davis. He hadn't tried to reason with him to convince him of the peace-seeking position. It was against his training to disagree privately or publicly with a superior official even when that official made such a wrong decision. West Point had done its job.

Meanwhile the starving, shriveling Confederacy went down in flames, hardly knowing what hit, since it thought it was doing God's will. God, the first casualty.

Lee was the one who loved Davis yet opposed him on the proposal of peace issue. But no one could veto Jefferson Davis' veto. Even Davis could not veto Davis; it is the way of irrational leaders.

A similar situation happened again the next year before the Northern Campaign. Lee wanted a fake army—"an army in effigy," he named it—to be placed between Richmond and Washington, D.C., supposedly to threaten the North's capital and keep the main Federal army from following Lee's army into Pennsylvania.

If an army could be organized under the command of General Beauregard and pushed forward to Culpeper Court House threatening Washington from that direction, it would not only effect diversion most favorable to this A.N.V., but would, he thought, relieve any apprehension of an attack upon Richmond during their absence. The well-known anxiety of the Federal Government for the safety of its capital would induce it to refrain a large force for its defense, and thus sensibly relieve the opposition to the South's advance into the North.

What a brilliant strategy, at such a minimal cost. So good. A workable plan. Just too rational for a hotspur! Since Truth is the second casualty, Davis turned down Lee's proposal. No wonder they sang in the South as in the North, "We will hang Jeff Davis on a sour apple tree."

The regretful Lee could not hold back breathing heavily, nor quiet a thudding heartbeat during the five-hour sidetrack delay. His misery was plain to see.

Agnes wondered, *How does one help another who blames himself for thousands upon thousands of deaths?* R. E. Lee's sighs and intermingled sobs caused her to react in kind. Weeping relieves pressure but does not solve problems.

And brave comrade-in-arms James L. Corley, desperate for relief, had to turn away. He walked to the far end of the railroad coach so as not to be heard. His chest heaved in deep despair for his self-shattering, tormented friend.

All three knew the elder Lee should have done more than write a letter seeking peace in 1862. He should have pursued it. Again in 1863 he should have.

Seeking peace is good.

But not good enough.

One must pursue peace.

Doggedly!

CHAPTER 12

Discovery on a different day

Travel on the southbound train the next day differed only by degrees. Agnes and Corley were not perturbed, except to the extent the older man was perturbed. They tried to keep Lee calm, even unaware of any irritant, to no avail.

R. E. Lee was genuine in his reactions. In hard-bitten post-war Dixie he had to work diligently to keep his temper under control. Post-war he'd use sarcasm or the cold shoulder rather than raise his voice in anger. He worked generally to smother other semblances of rage. Anger was a sin, particularly for a Christian gentleman, so he damped down his indignation to such an extent that few could penetrate what was deemed remoteness and coolness on his part. Old age didn't help, though, because people routinely expect, even accept, an oldster to be a crank or a pain in the buttocks.

Just the same, Lee's suspicious, jerky head swivel persisted at those problematic railroad stops. He apparently never realized it telegraphed his anger.

Disturbing events had happened two times the first day out of Richmond; the next day again. One happened early the third day after leaving Charlotte, in fact every two or three hours. Gatherings outside on station platforms became more intense and larger each time. These out-of-the-ordinary occurrences usually entailed a train stopping at a railroad station or a village for passengers or freight to change to another train. Or regularly stopping to take on water from a water tower, water needed for the locomotive to generate steam to operate the pistons that propelled it along the track.

The old former commander wanted to demand an answer but realized he wasn't head of any man's army anymore. He did think of bribing the engineer to blast the engine whistle to clear up the situation whenever the stopped train was ready to move again so people who had detrained could know when to reenter the cars. He satisfied himself thinking of doing something constructive for others on the trip. A bit smug, he then realized he'd only thought about doing something useful... but actually had not done a thing to help. He couldn't help disturbing himself.

Then he re-thought the matter, immediately knowing a martial tone would have evoked only opposition by the conductor who would have had to relay the message to the engineer, who then might have told the conductor to tell the passenger it was none of his damn business. Lee perceived it would have been unworthy of an old man to tell professionals what to do in their line of work. They were not soldiers to obey dictates nor students to earn approval.

The former problem-solving Chief Quartermaster insisted he would speak to the stationmaster at the very next station where the train paused for refueling or to take on or exit passengers.

At that stop the conductor reluctantly introduced Corley to the station agent. It was in a small town in South Carolina with a re-fueling bin of wood to replenish the locomotive's supply. The conductor then stepped outside to talk to the people gathering around the building along the stopped train. What he was saying gave the impression that it could not be a happy occasion because his voice was getting louder by the minute. The people, however, were in a smooth mood and did not detect the conductor's negativity. They had, so to speak, a "bigger fish to fry." It was a repeat of previous days' events. Passengers were looking for an answer not a confrontation.

Within minutes they broke out in cheers, and called, "General Lee. General Lee, come out. Come out. Come out."

It was a crowd; Lee wanted to hide. His skin itched all over. Here was the problem again, neither lessening nor increasing irritation as happened sundry times already.

At Agnes' prompting and presence, Lee emerged onto the back platform of the last passenger car. He was agitated, then consternated, close to being outraged. His trip was being commandeered, preempted by sightseers. Interfered with, and not to his liking at all; his life was being circumscribed, delimited, at someone else's decree.

His slow burn was easily evident to his daughter. Eleanor Agnes was enjoying the event but could not—again—fathom how the people knew her father was on this train.

R. E. Lee chewed over the same problem. *How do they know we're on this train?*

A youth in the gathered crowd had a Stars and Bars Confederate flag draped over his left shoulder and a sharply-shined bugle in his right hand which he blew irrespective of the correct notes. People cheered the lad nonetheless. The crowd sang "Dixie" in lustily animated tones as might be done at a political rally or church picnic. It was composed in 1859 up North in New York as a "walk-around," ending each minstrel show. Southerners made it into a *faux* anthem, anything to irritate Northerners.

Agnes was all smiles, happily forgetting her bouts with sickness. Youth and adults laughed and shouted for no reason in response. Even Corley was part of the gaiety. Children shouted happily regardless of any other reason than to be loud. Everyone clapped except the old man.

Lee looked on. Said nothing. At any rate, did not smile. He gazed. And wondered, taken aback, puzzled over the calls to speak, yet remained stone-cold silent.

"Speech. Speech. Speech," echoed through the crowd. The people were eager for R. E. Lee to say something to them.

Lee looked on.

More calls of the same nature were shouted louder. Then the crowd started to chant: "Lee, speech. Lee, speech," lasting two or three minutes. Irritating R. E. no end.

Lee looked on. Did not smile. Did not visibly react. Said nothing.

Finally Corley emerged from the railway station, climbed up to stand beside his former commander, nudged him and slyly pointed to his own hat and made a quick dip of his head, just a nod. An awkward moment passed before Lee realized he should acknowledge citizens' cheers, music, requests in some manner. Lee knew he should acquiesce. He didn't know the reason and was about to tell the crowd what to do with its chanting his name when he thought, *They won't know what to do with it.*

Lee tipped his hat ever so slightly, never losing contact with his scalp. In a distinct move with head held high, shoulders back, he turned around, and re-entered the passenger car.

He couldn't understand how people knew he was on the train. Nor could the former military giant understand why they would acknowledge him—a defeated general, a loser. It was a repeat of his emotions the other times the train had stopped southward of Richmond—but had not happened the day before arriving in Richmond.

Lee seemingly was saved by the bell as the engineer pulled the whistle chain for three short blasts indicating firewood had been loaded, the train would move, and people should get the dickens off the tracks. The journey southward continued.

The Lee party returned to their seats with questions and an answer. In fact the answer to the phenomenon that puzzled the traveling trio was simple. James Corley resolved it by telling that the stationmaster had received a telegraph message from the previous stationmaster: "General Lee is on the train!" citing its number and name. Gossip did the rest. Love does something much the same, chattering on and on.

R. E. Lee's response was simpler: anger.

Upon further question Corley had been told that message had started back in Richmond and preceded Lee every station, every day, the whole way. In the bargain, it would continue all the way southward through both Carolinas, Georgia, and into Florida.

R. E. Lee was distressed deeply and replied, "How terrible. Terrible. I don't like it one bit."

Only he knew his history. All the disturbance about the public greeting by unexpected turnouts and crowds and throngs and multitudes went back to the time he had been selected to lead Virginia's militia.

Lee's last two employments had not been applied for, nor requested in any way. The more recent, as president of Washington College, the trustees had elected him without any inquiry or offer. Notwithstanding, he had accepted the challenge. The older employment came before the war began when the Virginia Assembly had selected him to head the Virginia State Militia without asking his interest or willingness to serve. R. E. Lee was drafted two important times in his life, but all he ever wanted was to be a small time farmer.

The Virginia Assembly conscription had shaken him up badly when traveling from Arlington House to the capital in Richmond. On that train trip, unknown to him, the public heard of the Assembly's choice and swarmed along the railroad and collected at railroad stops, refueling points or water replacement towers. Everywhere he went they had shouted, "Lee-Lee-Lee," or "We want Lee-Lee-Lee." Multiple places; multiple times. He had been unclear of meaning, then became muzzy, befogged, overtaken by a freakish physical condition of being scared spitless. Whenever cadence and emphasis, tempo or modulation altered significantly he became apprehensive about what would happen next.

At this railroad stop on his health-vacation trip it began with a series of two beats, "Lee-Lee," slowly altering to, "Lee-Lee-Lee-Lee," which was not foreboding or dangerous. But when the emphasis changed to, "LEE-Lee-Lee-LEE," and persisted, it finally became a boisterous, serious chant, "LEE... LEE... LEE... LEE," from which unexpectedly crept dark memories of the 1865 surrender of the Army of Northern Virginia—the "NO! NO! NO! NO!" shouts of his troops shredding his heart strings.

Flashbacks also of similar cadence and downright emphasis the Comanche Indians played on their war drums on the Indian Reservation in Texas where the 2nd U.S. Cavalry had been stationed before the war rushed to the forefront of his reactions. He remembered such drumming as preparatory to Comanche breakouts, terribly long days chasing them, and longer nights protecting his troops from the usual harassment so keen that men and animals could not rest. Now his level-headedness was jeopardized, subconsciously refashioned, affecting him as at the Rebellion's beginning in 1861 when going to Richmond to take command of Virginia's militia and presently on the health-seeking trip in 1870 again. Lee heard on this so-called-health-trip *"more than was meant for the ear."* His composure was unraveling; he feared his soul would be next.

"I want to go home," he told Wiggie. Trouble in his soul needed assuaging that only "Home Sweet Home" could satisfy with his beloved wife and their remaining six children.

The terror of sounds emanating from people repeating his name so methodically rattled him; he dreaded it. Ordinarily, those sounds would have merely aggravated him but now he enigmatically interiorized them, causing strife with himself. Self-warfare differs only in degree from military warfare; it too is a savage god demanding obeisance.

R. E. Lee was in warfare of a soul with itself, for reclamation. Military training doesn't help spiritual warfare. But then, neither does academic education.

He thought his interior might be the "dark night of the soul" which St. John of the Cross had experienced. Yet his own spiritual journey since becoming a Christian at age forty-six informed him that St. John had understood such a comprehensive, exceptional spiritual event happens *only after* a glorious event and its subsequent total *let down;* nothing measures up to the glory of perceiving the True or the Good or the Beautiful and then living each day's ordinariness.

R. E. Lee realized full well that nothing on the trip thus far was so profound, so glorious, so heart-warming or soul-stirring an event, even the time with John Singleton Mosby and James L. Corley as a travel companion. Nor had anything so momentous happened at Washington College in the past year. That being the case, he could not claim a victory over a "dark night of the soul." He was not spiritually destitute; he was, however, intellectually impoverished, needy of answers why people wanted something of him.

R. E. Lee knew himself well enough that his condition was an amalgam of physical ailment, probably his heart—maybe legs, or back—old age, tiredness, lack of sleep, changed eating habits, forced confinement in a wooden box on steel wheels on rough rails, and countless people poking their heads in the passenger car windows or shouting slogans outside for him to speak. He wasn't a dummy, but he didn't know what they wanted. There were too many marching tunes, ragged uniforms, tattered battle flags, limping veterans, and young thrill seekers to suit him.

"What do they want, Agnes? To tell them what? To lead them? Where? What for? Why me? I'm too old even to lead a small college. Whatever is it they want?"

Silence on Wiggie's part caused more pain for him, conceivably already in the throes of... if not despair then anxiety.

"James, do you know?" More silence, and sorrow for a leader drifting in a sea of noise and confusion.

More is better only sometimes.

CHAPTER 13

"Aware of a presence"

As the train continued southeastward across South Carolina and Georgia to Savannah adjacent to the Atlantic Ocean, inadequate travel accommodations persisted. As did the ever present telegraph message noticeable at stops for water, wood, or transfers of freight and passengers to other railroads along the way. Thankfully—but possibly unthankfully—the trip was not rained upon at most stops, though occasional storms materialized while the train was in motion, or parked overnight.

Interruptions continually disconcerted R. E. Lee. Daughter Agnes appreciated the standstills because she detected something positive at each. James Corley smiled at Lee during each stop, showing respect, always deferring to his former commander by standing at attention and looking fixedly at him rather than the crowds.

Lee was the troubled one. When either daughter or friend noted the crowd's reverence for him, Lee rejected their notion. That emotion particularly offended his deep sense of spirituality since he believed reverence is due God, and God alone... not human beings.

Each place the train stopped was a repeat of the platform appearance before: one, Lee was a happy person, the other displeased; the latter resistant to appearing at all before a gathering. The elder was downright nettled when called upon to speak. He could not bring himself to do so, pointedly shaking his head in the negative. Once in a while he would smile when children or youngsters were immediately thrust in front of him.

When considering an occurrence to have taken time enough—that is four, five minutes—or when he was too distraught or too tired to stand another minute, he'd doff his hat—maybe—to the assemblage and seemed remarkably to vanish into the passenger car. Tilting his hat was normally the only show of recognition: a common courtesy, yet bare as a baby's backside, nothing more.

A number of times he'd nod his head as if to bid farewell; it was always followed by a brisk turn, then the fade-away into the passenger car to a seat and sag down. He did not, would not in fact, verbalize thanks to any crowd because he didn't know what he was supposed to be thankful for. Shouts and whistles and horn blasts were screeches to his ear and he'd wince, make a face, then shiver his head in short quivers as if throwing off a fly or mosquito.

Lee expressed nothing from the platform since he wouldn't lie to make it seem he understood the gathering, the music, the calls, the gaiety. He had no taste for them, so did not reinforce them with thanks, or even smiles. Once in a while he'd shake his head in recognition of something—or the other—both daughter and friend couldn't decipher.

Back in the car ordinarily he'd stand briefly beside his seat, distressed, shaking his head again side to side. Sometimes he locked a grimace on his face, tight as a braided whip with puckered lips and furrowed brow, and stared at the nondescript floor. Just stared. Few times and far between he did express a negative opinion, shaking his head jerkily, grousing, "No. No. Bad! Bad manners." Whether he meant his manners or the crowds' he did not clarify.

Agnes sympathized quietly, although she didn't understand his reluctance to accept admiration. Corley... after one large gathering... joined in the sustained calls for Lee to speak, as a band played, and several lads in uniform blared away with bugle calls, and people sang the minstrel tune "Dixie."

Corley had decided he had to do something to cheer up his former commander and friend. Then, glory be! At two stops on the whole trip the first stanza of "The Star-Spangled Banner" was sung by some people in the crowds. They also clapped for their effort.

It had no impact on the old man.

At Augusta, Georgia, Lee had a strange encounter, an inscrutable experience that Corley observed. It involved a boy of thirteen or fourteen years of age. The lad had worked his way through the crowd until, at length, he stood by the side of Lee who was on the ground because the passenger car did not have a platform. The two stared at one another for a long moment. Neither adult nor lad moved; neither spoke. Crowd noise was a mere hum or hubbub without shouts or clamor. The lad stood relaxed, unruffled, appraising the adult in wondering respect. R. E. Lee did not object. Nor smile.

After the three Lee companions were aboard again and the train was underway, Corley said, "Two things amazed me completely. First, I talked to that scrutinizing youth and discovered his name was Woodrow Wilson; his father is a Presbyterian pastor who believes in visions. Do either of you know anything about them?"

Both father and daughter replied they did not. Father Lee, however, tottered ever so slightly, recalling the boy's face and his intense gaze. He didn't have a vision but he did have an "Aha" moment that the lad would make something of himself in later life. He never made sense of it, yet puzzled over it in relation to his young men at Washington College. There they stood before him or behind him in ceremonies, in his office, in public events. This lad had stood beside him: gazed into his eyes, making a difference that Lee struggled with, especially when recalling what it was like to be a lad so young without a father.

The former Chief Quartermaster of Lee's Army of Northern Virginia then pulled from an inner coat pocket a wrinkled newspaper page and began to read, "Someone in the crowd handed me this page which quotes a book, but the man did not give his name, stating only that what I would read was written by a former 'enemy' of Robert Edward Lee about the surrender of his army to the Federal army under Ulysses Grant in 1865."

I was out and between the two lines when I became aware, possessed of night as in the times of old, times of prophets, aware of a presence—I was not seeing with my mortal eyes.

I turned square around, and there my eyes fell upon a wonderful figure, a man venerable and imposing in form, in bearing, magnificently dressed with an elegant gray uniform, superbly accoutered, magnificent sword with the hilt glittering with diamonds, superbly mounted, with an expression of intense emotion as if he were repressing heartbreaking thoughts. Who else, of course, but Robert E. Lee! Seen, and seen for the first time, between my two lines, he had ridden up the road that came between my two lines, riding from Appomattox. I looked, stood as if transfixed, thoughts came over me of all those years, the man whom we had confronted so long, whom we had often feared and sometimes pitied, the man who was in our thoughts so many times and, I don't know but I might say, in our hearts, when on the retreat we saw what care he took of his men. I am almost willing to say we nearly loved him for that.

Then Corley indicated it was written by a Northern hero of the Battle at Gettysburg, General Joshua Lawrence Chamberlain, marshal of the Federal Army at the surrender formalities at Appomattox, who later had written the tribute in a privately published booklet, *Not a Sound of Trumpet*.

Lee was flabbergasted, totally caught off guard. He had to wrestle with the wonderment a former enemy... the wonderment he, R. E. Lee, engendered in Chamberlain's soul... that he, a defeated general was such a magnificent being.

He countered the positivity with thinking about being a negative, disturbed man on the damp canal boat the first night of the health-seeking trip then disturbed thereafter many times on stopped trains during the trip—and now disturbed again. This time disturbed by joy at Chamberlain's words. Personal emotional disturbances come in many colored hues, shades, tints, with many variegated sounds, noise, harmonies, volumes any numbers of which are pleasing or displeasing. This time R. E. Lee was pleased deeply by Chamberlain's tribute.

Agnes was over-the-moon jubilant. Her joy became a family treasure whenever she recited Chamberlain's words to family or friends later in life.

Tears flowed gently from father and daughter, flowed not trickled. He, understanding as a warrior at peace; she, serenely her father remembered and highly esteemed. Corley felt he had done two deeds worthy of his former leader and daughter. And Corley was correct, still another time as he wiped his eyes, remembering that "words fitly spoken are like apples of gold in a basket of silver."

It came to mind to two members of the three that the noble commemoration might help the older man realize what the crowds along the way were about when they cheered, sang, shouted for him, "Lee. Lee. Speech. Speech." He was a hero. Still a hero, even in defeat. The rarest, strongest, and best kind.

CHAPTER 14

Train troubles

At another one of those railroad stops galling President Lee so much, a north Georgia hamlet soberly irked his two companions. The other twenty-six passengers were unsettled, too, many in foul moods. The waiting train crew bitched with the arriving crew for their extremely late arrival. Charges increased and vulgar language exploded. Heard by all in the train and the gathered crowd, the anger never subsided.

The train was comprised of locomotive, fuel tender/water reservoir, sleeping car, and two passenger cars. Because of differing track sizes, at this stop travelers had to change to another with only one passenger car. Overdue arrival and busy transfer of freight and passengers scratched everyone's consciousness raw because the railyards were two city blocks apart; in addition dray animals and dray drivers were in limited supply: only three dray wagons and two dray drivers. Trouble infested the air. And railroaders from both companies were in no mood to be civil.

Unbelievably, war had not been a prime motivation for the companies to standardize into one gauge as the North had done. After the war there wasn't money. The poverty-stricken railroads were muddled and cluttered exchanges of freight and passengers, delaying everything almost 100 percent of the time. Railroad timetables eventually became pointless. Schedules were disrupted time and time again. If ever kept it was by the narrowest of margins. Coordination was not a prime motivation for the companies to change the practice; it didn't pay to modernize.

Dozens of times local children gathered to stare at the entanglements. They'd giggle at what became a bog of goods, passengers, railroaders, townsfolk, and any passing strangers. At best, exchanges were a good laugh. In tough times, though, it irritated passengers like aggravating mosquitoes, or nosy neighbors.

This particular change of trains was an imbroglio. A darkly tainted sky threatened rainstorm or windstorm. Maybe both. Company policies made no provisions for bad weather. Transfer from one rail company to another meant freight and passengers had to be moved in all kinds of weather, at any and all hours. And wet passengers often complained—without any recorded success.

This day nothing was favorable. R. E. Lee, customarily disappointed by such events, was riled up because there was a waiting gathering shouting or trying to sing a rhythmic tune, "Lee. Lee. Lee. Lee. We Want Lee. Lee. Lee. Lee." Bad music, bad transfer to another railroad, bad attitudes all around, bad language, bad weather—all around bad experience.

Lee bellyached roughly to Corley, "The telegraph has struck again."

Eleanor Agnes cringed; Lee about-faced, scorning Corley's attempt with animal-like huffing as in some kind of confrontation with another animal. The ex-Quartermaster General got the harsh message as Lee swiveled around to accost him. Instantly perceived as animus, a spitefulness, Corley bluntly faced Lee because Lee had bluntly faced him.

There was a sense of testosterone in the offing; it was like seeing and hearing in the wild two bucks butting heads as if for primordial dominance.

Something had to give.

R. E. Lee clomped out to the platform, coat unbuttoned, hat tilted to one side, tying his necktie to look decent. Without looking directly at the gaggle of people waiting waterlogged he bowed slightly, tipped his hat, took it off and slapped it against his right thigh as if shaking off dust. At that point he looked at the small crowd, sharply turned, beat a retreat and went back inside, sat down, and fumed, seething that he had gotten wet. Something really had to give for he was near expressing anger out loud. Possibly hostility, too, to his friend. Agnes backed away quickly and went to another part of the car.

His poorly diagnosed heart condition with vague and changing symptoms was ever on his mind because he was physically constrained from time to time in different parts of his body. All of which flooded over him at this jerk-water stop.

After an hour or more the passengers were transferred, they still had to wait nearly another half-hour until baggage and other haulage were finally loaded. Some trackside spectators had climbed up on boxes and stuck heads inside through windows they had opened from the outside trying to view the old man. *Grotesque, utterly weird,* the college president thought. *Unseemly.*

Lee was beside himself and tried to hide in the single passenger car, covering himself with a blanket, changing seats, and finally walked inside to the locomotive/tender end of the single car to camouflage his annoyance then back to the other end, not realizing he was putting himself on display. Repeating the route several times he stopped pacing, recognizing other passengers were looking at him warily. Everything he did was unsuccessful. People outside still shouted, "Lee. Lee." He thought it good fortune as it faded when the train finally departed "no-where's-ville."

Just about all his fellow passengers similarly had been provoked; R. E. Lee felt responsible for their discomfort. A sense of shame welled up inside; he couldn't put a stop to the provocation he perceived as coming from fellow passengers not himself. He hated intrusions, and now ascribed that fault to the people around him. He was doing a job on himself, foolishly not recognizing it.

Unforeseen, he soon realized what he was doing unnerved him. Besides, he didn't know how to make amends. But he did understand something important: he was the source of his problem, not the other passengers, some of whom were totally unaware of any problem he was having. Lee forgot the wet crowd and dealt with his nearby travelers—and himself.

Corley had exacerbated the situation before the train had departed, having exited the passenger car and walked to the locomotive where the engineer and conductor were talking. They were surprised to see a passenger climb the ladder to the locomotive cabin and to hear, "What's holding up departure?"

At that point, without answering, the engineer pulled the whistle chain and tooted three short blasts indicating departure, clearing the tracks of people. He cursed under his breath then barked at Corley, "Get the hell out of here."

Neither engineer nor conductor answered Corley directly, who could not grasp their lack of verbal response. However, he got what he wanted, jumped down from the ladder and ran back to the passenger car, mounting the steps as the train lurched forward as if to outpace him and leave him behind.

Corley felt satisfied to a fault, much like Little Jack Horner who sat in a corner eating his Christmas pie. But the ex-Quartermaster found Lee still unnerved, though the train was moving. It took only a few more minutes before it moved swiftly, heading southeastward. That result didn't suppress Lee's anger; he was not satisfied with the crowd, nor himself, yet much less with his fellow passengers to whom he ascribed—falsely—a crowd mentality. Whence the old man could not settle down; whence he could not write off a lousy railroad transfer incident; whence he could not be at ease with himself. All his inabilities were negative consequences lumped in a heap of emotional trash.

Corley sat down beside Lee, and at once told what happened about his engagement with the railroad crew. He felt happy with himself, a sense of self-satisfaction, recounting it as if it were a personal victory of some sort. He said so to traveling companion Wiggie. He forgot plums on thumbs only look pleasing to people with sticky fingers; others see them as smeared messes. Good man Corley had misjudged the situation.

The businessman's self-assertion didn't impress Lee a bit, whose quick reaction was triple shakes of his head as he turned away and looked out a window, to avoid a confrontation.

Confused, the former Quartermaster of Lee's army didn't know what to say, if anything were to be said at all. The confusion didn't make for good choices whether in actions or thoughts.

Wiggie, as often the case, detected some bad feeling between the men, and deferred entering the tight situation.

Corley was thus left to his own devices, which were minimally existent in this minor incident, for the train had already been primed to leave the very moment he had entered the locomotive cab. Not even a trifle came to Corley's mind for he had no room for a thought other than he had moved a locomotive! Some people sometimes think they are Atlas holding up the globe.

A somber mood smoldered on, drenching three travelers who truly cared for one another but didn't know how to express appreciation in the middle of disagreement.

Poor Corley: gracious helper, good companion, competent guide but not able to bring his old friend out of the dumps, or himself out of the intellectual jungle he had entered. Silence would have been better: it is the best policy. Much underused, however.

Poor Lee, too. Poorer Lee, in fact. His doldrums were self-inflicted but he kept trying to place the blame elsewhere. James Corley was a target. Yet Lee knew better than to make a minor incident a major stumbling block; he used a familiar operating principle: "When in doubt, don't."

Knowing that "music has charms to soothe the savage breast," Agnes tried to help her father by gently humming a lullaby. But nothing! Her father neither thanked her nor looked at her; nor moved. Nothing changed.

R. E. Lee wrestled with the truth about human beings: "We love our sicknesses well, specifically emotional, psychological sicknesses." In fact we cater to ourselves even in our foulest moods.

Then dear, sensitive Agnes made a mistake. Though she, too, was contending with a physical malady that flared up from time to time, even on the trip, her first concern was intense, to help her father, so she chirped lively, a favorite of her father's:

Oh, I wish I was in the land of cotton,
Old times there are not forgotten.
Look away! Look away! Look away, Dixie Land.

There's buckwheat cakes and Injun batter,
Makes you fat or a little fatter.
Look away! Look away! Look away, Dixie Land.

Then hoe it down and scratch your gravel,
To Dixie's Land I'm bound to travel.
Look away! Look away! Look away, Dixie Land.

Darnation! Another time. Wiggie succeeded only in wounding herself. Her lively music and worthy purpose did not soften the situation. It got more obscure though not thornier, poisonous, or deadlier. Then the young lady thought of praying. *Aloud. Gentle down the atmosphere.* Another thought followed: *Southern young women don't pray aloud. Not in public. Not amidst strangers.* Wiggie gave up, just gave up, closed her eyes, hoping neither companion would notice her. Boxing in her emotions didn't help her slowly deteriorating physical condition either.

Three companions traveled soundlessly with each other for long, long minutes. *I wonder who will break the ice,* thought Corley to himself. *Not I. No way!*

Other passengers paid no attention to any of the vexation as they continued to adjust to their own changed situations from the previous train.

Then something popped into James Corley's mind to compensate for his ostensible part in the unpleasantness. *But will it backfire?* He halfway admonished himself. Only halfway.

As most rational people discover... nine times out ten, but late in life... things that just "pop into their heads" are just as likely to be unhealthy as healthy, undesirable as desirable when expressed out loud. Speaking, which is such a mighty human tool, is not always helpful. It is not always as golden as Silence.

CHAPTER 15

Liar?

"Why do they make you a liar about Gettysburg?" asked former Quartermaster James Corley. It was something to do in the midst of the oppressive atmosphere as the train moved away from another of those excruciating transfer stops.

Lee's instant thought was, *Corley should know better! Much better. I don't talk about Gettysburg.* In his misery he missed the agony in Corley's voice, just as he had missed his daughter's musical sensibility. His own continuing illness was exacerbated by the daily intrusions which he could not understand at all except as discourteous and irritating. He quizzed himself several times over the last few days of railroad travel. *Do they want another rebellion? Why acknowledge a defeated general in a failed cause?*

A few exceptional times R. E. Lee raised a foreboding thought about himself: *Am I a monkey in a zoo? A freak in a sideshow? To be viewed and hooted at?* The ramification of such uneasiness and cynicism about himself at an old age was so nauseating he felt himself tremble under his clothing.

In attacking himself more than Corley's question ever could, Lee was chewing away at himself, devouring himself to bits, obliterating himself. It was autocannibalism!

His condition was urgent beyond serious. It was grim beyond grave. Terrible, therefore terrorizing. It was so acute an emotional illness that he didn't know whether or not he could, whether or not he would, live through a physical malady with additional mental instability at the same time.

James Corley repented of his question, but as with many who repent, they do not tell anyone else. The previous error stays "on the books," so to speak, and is repeated by many who don't know anything except the error.

The question about Gettysburg had plagued Lee's former comrade-in-arms ever since he had read R. E. Lee's Official Report to the Confederate War Office of that battle. For over five years the question had rankled Corley, bothering him like a noxious injury that wouldn't heal or like a neighbor's hurtful, shameful words over one's pet dog that followed Nature's call on the next-door property. All Corley could do literally was say, "I'm sorry, Sir," calmly. He spoke the words then gave an impromptu yet sincere hand salute, without clicking his heels or snapping to attention.

Lee acknowledged the salute with his right hand over his heart but remained silent. *Yes, James should be sorry, for he is a sensitive soul.*

But if Corley's question had merely exasperated Corley, it had increased Robert Edward Lee's anxiety. Unfortunately the apology didn't make the matter disappear for the older man.

Wiggie was frightened more by Corley's question than by his admission of guilt. Her continuing, ill-at-ease condition worsened marginally. She knew her father's longstanding, genuine dislike for talk about that war. *That defeat up North sorrowed him the deepest. He attempted something else up North and the battle interfered.*

The present situation compelled Lee to the point of an old game of mumchance, that is maintaining a rugged silence for time on end. *"Mum's the word"* is often the best expression in a bad situation. Mumchance is often... very often... the way out of a foul-up, a debacle.

Lee stayed silent, emotionally poverty-struck. Scrawny desolation set in amidst his turmoil. *I feel wretched every stop where I see veterans of my defeated army.* At each stop, wretchedness touched him and he felt it overcome him every time he saw a veteran in some semblance of a uniform. *Was it because we were defeated? Or because those men suffered so much for nothing?*

Lee knew how to dissect himself. As the ancient Greeks realized, "A person who has himself as his physician has a fool for a physician." It follows that a person who has himself as his surgeon has a *damned* fool for a surgeon, one bound to kill.

Many a clickety-clack and thumpity-thump sounded repeatedly, repeatedly, repeatedly without concluding any message good, bad, or indifferent. Many a spark flew out the funnel-shaped smokestack of the locomotive, sometimes igniting brush fires along the railroad tracks before Lee and Corley could communicate meaningfully with one another. Seconds became quarter-hours, minutes became half-hours, hours became mornings or afternoons as they rode portions of the day in silence.

Lee could not stop himself from thinking about Corley's question. Each time he mentally framed it, anguish dripped from every syllable. The word "liar" however became a poison, a venom in his head. His thoughts were a far worse state than the harassments of train stoppages or the perceived hassles from waiting crowds. It was a sickness unto death of not just a defeated man, but a spiritually wounded one. He remembered George Washington had been defeated more often in the Revolutionary War than he'd won. It was not enough to settle Lee's disquiet. An immediate illness gripped him. Incessantly gripped.

James Corley had made a soul-shaking mistake, not purposely yet nonetheless damaging of mind and spirit. His own body reacted with a tremble in the upper torso followed by a sour consciousness of soul knowing, all within a moment of having spoken about liars, that the question had impaled his friend.

Wig's soul, too, shook. *I've never heard father called a liar. What is James talking about? Why did he bring it up now? On a health-seeking trip?* And then she began sniffling, trailed by several tears but no outright crying, which she stifled effectively, making her both satisfied and dissatisfied by the same incident.

The young woman knew instantly what would happen to her father. It had.

From years of living with him, she perceived his reaction beneath his silence. It was a soul crumbled, collapsed as if in a grisly accident. Near dying at any instant. *Dear Father in heaven, save my father. He is a good man. He needs Thee. In Jesus' name, Amen.*

Corley's mistake was asking about what seemed simple: what he and R. E. Lee had actually experienced. Yet it was what historians had already misinterpreted in the war. He and Lee both had "seen the elephant," the bone-chilling, alarming phrase soldiers South and North used to tell about hand-to-hand combat. However, in this instance the words implied *defeat* because "Gettysburg" had been mentioned. And that name meant the beginning of the end of the Confederacy.

Defeat also implied a dismaying, harrowing event of being prostrate before the enemy, or running away, retreating. Or maybe deserting. Those notions compounded with the realization that the defeat at Gettysburg never should have happened—never, for several reasons—made a miasma of bleakness and grief and sorrow all over again for Lee.

He had felt similar misery within a month or so after that battle seven years earlier. Out of his mournful condition and into the unfortunate undertone of the three travelers' thoughts about Gettysburg, Lee spoke heatedly to the complete surprise of daughter and friend: "I wrote to Jefferson Davis wanting to resign from my duties as commander of the Army of Northern Virginia. The President would not accept my resignation. I wrote requesting a younger officer take my place." Attempting to say more he stuttered, "But, but again he, he..." then caught words already on his lips. He swallowed them tightly and gulped two distinct times as if in place of each word in his unfinished sentence. "I've said much, too..."

R.E. Lee had suffered the same agony two years after Gettysburg at the surrender at Appomattox where a fierce storm of emotions overcame him. He didn't want to surrender to General U. S. Grant but needed to do so to save his starving "boys." He really wanted to lay down a challenge to Grant but didn't know how to frame it: that is, to propose an armistice rather than a surrender.

"But I had no bargaining power," he burst out in front of Corley and Agnes, again utterly surprising them. He realized, *I was afflicted in that war because conflicted from the very beginning. The Confederacy would be out-numbered, out-produced, and out-maneuvered.* Then he spoke what he thought, satisfying his sense of truth, of history.

Brutal insight about the war followed by honest self-judgment about Gettysburg and Appomattox swamped Lee.

But Lee knew duty, his duty to soldier on. He was duty bound. He knew full well from his mother Ann. *I must go on now, too. James did not ask the question maliciously. That he asked was unexpected. Why he did is baffling.*

His affliction still continued. *On a vacation trip for rest and restoration, at that.* Misery solidifies itself firmly over time, becomes a solid block against reality year after year when death is involved. *Misery breeds woe for a lifetime when thousands upon thousands of dead are involved.* The old man could not shake jeopardizing himself with his thoughts. Truth hurts extra when one has to tell it to oneself.

R. E. Lee was laying bare his soul, by his own admission.

The companions' moods sullied. Neither was able to pose a question aloud since it could easily drip like a curse and, no doubt, start an argument in one or the other of the co-travelers.

R. E. Lee sank into emotional mire, a quicksand of sadness. Fitfully he drummed his left-hand fingers on an armrest, then stopped with a short-tempered grunt. In a delayed move he rubbed his right thigh with his right hand increasingly forcefully until he switched to a fist. Quickly the fist became white-knuckled and ill-suited to the task of soothing discomfort. He hammered his fist—not the fleshy heel of the hand but the bare knuckles—on the hard wooden seat... one time only. It stung like a maddened hornets' attack. *What reason can I give for reacting dangerously in front of Agnes and James?*

Feeling for them, he assaulted himself mentally.

Wordlessness and some foolishness reigned over three of the twenty-nine people in the railroad car that day who heard bits and pieces of the Lee party's talk yet understood hardly a thing. For an extended span, each of the trio faced his or her own embarrassment at that display of fierce emotion and irrational responses. Lee himself perceived that his physical features were tormented, and evident to his two traveling companions as well as several other passengers seated close by. Some of the latter stared open-mouthed at the atypical demonstration of emotion by the well-known former general, recognizable by most every adult Southerner.

R. E. Lee put an end to all movements. Save for sighing. It sounded gravelly and thick, much like a wounded animal seeking cover. The sighing stopped further finger tapping, rubbing; it cut short a fist full of anger.

Passengers couldn't help but hear Lee's sighing; they kindly turned away to avoid eye contact with the old man, lest he would feel belittled, unworthy of the respect they had shown him upon boarding the train.

The thumpity-thump, clickety-clack, thumpity-thump from hot wheels on cooler rails reverberated relentlessly and predominated as a dictatorial sound throughout the coach. The sounds surely did not let Lee's anger-filled statement die. The coarse noises seemed to be his message reiterated over and over: *I don't know why, I don't know why, I don't know why.* He had to break the continuous spell of hot and cold revolving wheels on rigid rails accompanied by hot argumentations turned cold turned hot again. He had to break his own distressed mind about that battle lost seven years before.

Briefly he shed sighing, turning to indignation. A mouth-battle ensued. He flung a series of sour inquiries as if not in control of his emotions: "Where did they ever get such an idea? ...What makes them deny my words? My official report to the Confederate War Office details the exact opposite of their words. Why do they make me out to be a liar? What do they think I was doing? Who are they to question? They weren't there!" The questions rumbled fitfully, some razor-edged, some fading groans.

The emotional atmosphere in the passenger compartment was not unlike atmospheric thunder in the mountains of his western Virginia home. Pressure waves resounded in the minds of his two companions, only not so exciting, not so breath-taking as lightning. But they compelled echoes and re-echoes through their minds, causing them discomfort and sorrow for the older man.

R. E. Lee was uncommonly agitated. Nearly overwrought, in fact. Bit by bit his sighing brought on seething anger. It cramped his gut as the cannonade had done on the third day of the Battle of Gettysburg. That barrage began the Confederacy's downfall, simultaneous with the fall of Vicksburg along the Mississippi River.

The question—though posed by his kind friend and traveling companion—had sought a simple piece of information: how did ordinary soldiers respond to him personally after Pickett's catastrophic charge? The last day of the battle back then was... and persisted to be... a miasma, a vaporous reeking of fear and smelling of blood on a muggy, oppressive July day when everything went awry in a beautiful setting.

All three travelers in the train coach felt something frightfully appalling was happening. And silence reigned amongst them, though broken often by mental pain and a soft guttural sound.

Corley had not asked about faulty strategy nor botched tactics. Had not presumed to question Lee's generalship. Did not mean to humiliate his former general. But because Lee had admitted complicity—on the actual battlefield—for that military collapse of his troops by saying, "It's all my fault. You must help me. It's all my fault!" Corley felt free to seek information; he was not fault-finding. His intent was to correct false history, incomplete storytelling and to know the well-being of ordinary soldiers after the disastrous assault.

The ordinary soldiers Lee had trusted implicitly to repeat the great victories at Chancellorsville and Fredericksburg just months before, then turned to him after Pickett's disastrous charge to garner something helpful, some meaning from their sheer defeat.

So, too, Corley sought enlightenment. *How did he keep defeat from becoming capitulation?* "You must have worked assiduously among the retreating men to keep up their spirits." He wanted to keep Lee from succumbing to ennui, weariness, even depression. "No army succeeds with whiners, grumblers, carping losers. Or deserters."

The question dismayed Agnes because she knew it might deface her father's emotional blueprint for their present trip. In fact, Agnes quickly turned her head aside, not wanting her teary eyes and wet cheeks to be seen by her father, who was gruffly discomforted and awkward after the question had been asked. She pitied him so much it hurt. Her heart trembled; she nearly fainted.

Defeat was affliction enough, she thought. *But being misunderstood all these years after the defeat at Gettysburg is disastrous for Father.* It was disastrous because it affected history, she reflected: *His history. His family's history. His country's history.*

Simple searching had sucked out Lee's original rasping response about Gettysburg. His reaction had been so quick, so spirited that it was somehow rousing, close to electrifying. So powerful to him that he found himself unnerved by his own ardor. It was like a lightning strike a mere stone's kick away. Sudden. Petrifying. Dangerous.

He had to save himself.

He recalled in no time his most-liked ancient hero: Job of the Bible. Job had listened to his wife after suffering the loss of seven sons and three daughters plus all his wealth in herds, packs, folds of sheep, cattle, camels, and goats due to a natural disaster. She had told him to admit his sin, curse God, and die. Job told her he could not do so for he had not sinned, not at all. And he would not lie to save his soul.

Then three friends came and told Job he must have done something wrong to warrant such punishment from God. Friends indeed; who needs enemies when one has "friends" like that? Job replied in similar fashion as he had to his wife: "I am not guilty. If I say, 'I am guilty,' I will be lying—then I actually will offend truth and God."

God then arrived on the scene and spoke of all His grand works in creation. God asked Job where he was and what he was doing when all creation was occurring. Naturally, Job was dumbfounded, tongue-tied; he had missed the big show, the "Big Bang."

God then made an amazing revelation, fairly unbelievable to religious minds with rigid ritualistic demands and artificial theological constructs:

Gird up your loins now like a man!
Deck yourself now with majesty and excellence.
Array yourself with glory and beauty.
Cast abroad the rage of your wrath and
Behold everyone who is proud
And abase them
And tread down the wicked in their place.
Then will I confess unto you
That your own right hand can save you!

Robert Edward Lee knew enough true biblical religion to realize, to make actual his full humanity in all its power and purpose, all its essential substance, all its intellectual acumen followed then by shutting down proud, arrogant, obnoxious, self-important persons so they not lead others astray. How to do both tasks was Lee's lifetime quest. He had to find a way to do them so that his own right hand would save him to fulfill God's "confession" to him—R. E. Lee.

The reaction to his friend's question opened President Lee to indicate statements by writers mistaken about his wartime purposes. He had noted one or another writer who completely had misunderstood his Northern Campaign in '63 as a supposed war-ending victory up North, though there had been documentary evidence to confirm Lee's side of the question that he did not intend a general battle at all unless first attacked.

But he had stopped trying to explain to friends. Friends understood and accepted the facts of his efforts in Pennsylvania in 1863. Ceasing explanation in his day-by-day life after the war now carried over to further inquiry by his traveling companions.

Lee remained on the vacation trip seeming in even more advanced age, weakened condition, and mood. His eyelids drooped, his voice softened, and he spoke seldom. His gaze took in more of the passing countryside than of the interior of the railroad car. He was loaded with thoughts that he was still being misunderstood by those people who recorded some history of his campaign up North. He thought, weightily, *I want to be done totally with misunderstanding: to deal with the facts, the truth in the case.* Emotionally he had been weakening; burnout was close at hand, yet he was sticking to the truth as it happened.

The question of how to rectify the misunderstanding remained. It was a dark question, presenting a quandary because *all* the official records of the Confederate high command planning sessions in the Confederate War Office for the Northern Campaign were missing. Missing by wartime destruction? The War Department of the Confederacy had not been wrecked when Richmond was burned by retreating Confederates in '65. But "intentionally destroyed or illegally concealed" as noted by the legitimate investigating authorities from South and North post-war. *What happened to the records?* Lee and others asked after Appomattox.

Far worse, President Davis' papers had a mammoth gap for the dates 14-17 May 1863 when the invasion of the North had been planned in his office, and its rationale stated. *Why the gap?* thought Lee. *Who did what with the official Confederate records? To what avail?*

Thinking on that situation... and far-fetched truancy, vanishing of official Confederate records... called forth further sighs. His companions could only imagine what he was thinking.

Some of Lee's sighs were sonorous, signifying a sleep-like condition. Then he'd quicken. Some were murmurs similar to a sleeping child, signifying a comfortable rest without troubling talk. Then mumbled after others. Length and volume varied, and seemed to signify something: either a coming to terms with alternate realities, or else a conflict between alternatives. Whichever view was true, each hurt as much as the persistent memory of Gettysburg itself. There was trouble in R. E. Lee's soul as well as his intellect.

When he was fully aware he mentioned to Corley some of the supposed "experts." They were writers who especially disrupted his physique, gnawed at his composure. "Some of my former officers, comrades-in-arms, misunderstood my aim up North. It is true, I told only one of my corps commanders what we were planning to do in the Northern Campaign in '63."

Lee began rubbing his right arm from shoulder to wrist, repeating the procedure erratically. It was a kind of ritual to abrade, scrape away the loss of strength, physical strength of a warrior's sword arm, fighting arm. But the previous time he scratched his skin as in psychological penalty—even punishment—for his part in losing that accidental battle. The knowledgeable ex-warrior realized great errors, much like great truths, take on a life of their own regardless of actual facts. And affect the human condition for long, long periods thereafter.

The trouble in R. E. Lee's soul was huge, possibly unsolvable. His daughter and Corley witnessed within spitting distance a dissolution, a winding down of the dynamic of a leader of men. Neither knew what to do except how to make him physically comfortable if possible on a rocking, swaying, passenger car. Agnes betook herself to ask another woman for a drink to slake her father's thirst. She received with grace the water given in a clay cup with a broken handle. It was like a sacred chalice for her to give to her father.

The noble man swallowed all the water and said, "Tell the dear lady, this was the cup of cold water given in our Lord's name."

When fully aware, he ruminated about the problematic issue of misunderstanding by history writers regarding his mission in late Spring 1863. He had known back then that his purpose was unique, a "surpassing raid," the Confederate War Office named it.

However, he had not realized he would be misread, misconstrued, falsified after the war. He thought scholars would have read the records and realized the exceptional, once-in-a-lifetime nature of his plan for that Campaign. However, important records were missing.

Tired to the core, Lee couldn't keep his mind from sprinting through memories of the official meetings, the plans, the objections, the approvals that took place seven years before. He wasn't helping himself by remembering there were minutes that now were missing from the records. The more he wanted to stop thinking about them, the stronger the questions became.

Agnes, who was anxious about her father's health felt—no, feared for his health—he was still up to a face-off with people who misconstrued his plans. Primed, so to say, to hold forth about something important in his life from his past. *A liar? No way on God's green earth. No way would Father lie!* bolted through her mind. *No way. Not Father!*

She sat on the edge of the seat facing him. The backs of the seats could be moved so passengers could view frontward or backward as the train progressed. Much like Mary of ancient Jerusalem who viewed her son drag a rood up a rocky hill, Agnes could see her own father lugging a mighty burden, one similarly fabricated by poorly informed and deficient critics.

A well-desired silence enveloped the three travelers for a length of time that no one recorded. The "well-desired" dimension of the silence prevailed because all three travelers knew *not* to speak. Chiefly the silence covered a mass of heartbreak: aching by the former general; torment by the ex-companion officer over the same lost battle, coupled with sorrow for his old leader. Daughter Eleanor Agnes desolate, of course, by nature and nurture.

After more miles of thumping wheels Lee's annoyance lessened, absorbed into the background mechanical noise. Quietness continued to surround three travelers.

At what seemed a propitious moment for R. E. Lee, with quieter demeanor, he gave a calm explanation, almost an apology, fleshing out his previous declarations. "I wrote in my Official Report to the War Office: '*We did not intend a general battle... unless attacked.*' I wrote clearly and definitively. The battle at Gettysburg was an accident, not a planned campaign. It was not—decidedly not—a 'Gettysburg Campaign.' Historians have misnamed it, purposely misnamed it: *Why?* Because they don't want to deal with the total purpose across southeastern Pennsylvania as a 'surpassing raid' for a grander reason than combat."

James Corley reiterated Lee's argument for confirmation: "People have missed its meaning. Scholars seem not to want to know why it was a 'surpassing raid' that our Confederate War Office named it rather than an attempt to have a war-finishing battle up North which was never your intention, Sir. One victory in the East could not have saved Vicksburg under siege along the Mississippi River in the West."

R. E. Lee then fleshed out his truth, "We were going to use the 4th of July, Independence Day, our National Holiday North and South, at a special place within our reach, to proclaim peace, not conquest, to a weary nation. Two weary nations, in fact.

"An accident. No one intended to fight at Gettysburg. Nothing was there except dusty cross-roads for traders and merchants. Our Northern Campaign is misconstrued dreadfully. History is distorted. The war was prolonged. I'll regret it to the end of my days."

Pausing, the older man slid forward and backward on his seat in the railroad car. Nodding his head affirmatively R. E. Lee now looked out the window at the passing scene. Pausing again he then focused on his daughter and their companion a longer time. He nodded at them, too. Both views were life-affirming to him. *This peace*, he thought, *is what I wanted as the result of going North.*

He self-validated the purpose of that Confederate campaign. "Even the Confederate War Office clerk, John B. Jones, personal friend of Jefferson Davis, recorded the truth one day before the battle at Gettysburg:

JUNE 30 5 O'clock PM

The city [Richmond] is now in good humor, but not wild exultation. We have what seems pretty authentic intelligence of the taking of HARRISBURG the capital of Pennsylvania, the City of YORK, etc. etc. This comes from the flag of truce boat, and is derived from the enemy themselves. Lee will not descend to the retaliation instigated by petty malice: but proclaim to the inhabitants that all we desire is PEACE not conquest.

He continued, "I was up north in Pennsylvania to declare *peace*, not conquest on the 4ᵗʰ of July 1863, Independence Day, at York, Pennsylvania, where Continental Congress sat as the capital of the United States of America, 1777-1778, while General Washington was at Valley Forge in the Revolutionary War. There Congress promulgated *The Articles of Confederation and Perpetual Union*, forming that first constitution of the thirteen united colonies into the original Confederacy. And the rest, as they say, is history. Distorted as it is."

The shrill locomotive whistle sounded several times. It seemed to compel attention from the now tender-hearted Lee, giving him further permission to speak. In tones contrasting with the whistle he asked in a subdued manner, "How is it that anyone could deny my clear declaration, for Heaven's sake? We were not to engage in a general battle." He waited a while then asked in a whisper, "Why do they contend otherwise? Why *do* they make me out to be a liar about our purposes up North? Why?"

R. E. Lee expelled a sigh, close to a whimper, in anguish.

The former general now college president lived pathos. Yet, as a puzzled face oozing throbbing sounds does not answer questions, so pathos noiselessly spreads the grief of a breaking heart to other portions of the human being to help bear the pain.

"Some former generals would have read that report," he said defending comrades of yore in familial tones of a father explaining away his children's errors. "Or at least heard of it. They would know what I intended, or what I did not intend. I gave orders."

Deliberately the old commander of tens of thousands turned away from his two companions on the opposite bench. In punctuated fashion he probed, "So why would a few—such as Jubal Early—pretend we were on a campaign of devastation and conquest? Where did he get that idea? Not from me. Not from his Corps Commander General Ewell who explicitly told Early what to do."

Lee held his temper totally in check although his analysis was accusatory.

Despite the previous ragged questioning that saddened Lee, both his daughter and former comrade-in-arms noticed a changing dynamic. The authority figure slowly unveiled a lenient attitude.

The friend who had first asked the upsetting question about being a liar then picked up the tempo. "What the hell are they doing it for? What's in it for them?" James L. Corley was taking weeks out of his life to be "tour director," their "Man Friday"...for free, out of devotion to his former general. He was taking weeks from his business to accompany Lee and his daughter, all for love of his former superior. But now he had added something to his kindness, a mission.

In blunt surprise, Corley curtly—almost huffing and puffing—opened up. "Where do they get the authority to question your intent as field commander? Who appointed them as god? Second-guessers. Bastardizers all!"

Corley's heated outburst instantly cooled off R. E. Lee several degrees. "Now, now, Sir. They may be wrong but they're not the Devil. Wrong-headed, that's all. We'll talk of them another day."

That quieting by the general lasted through another whistle stop station at a "jerk-water town" on the way southeastward to Savannah.

Time off the recitation of July 1863 events was time well spent. In fact the interruptions together lasted not quite half an hour totally. They were used for relaxing walks outside the stopped train, mostly searching for outhouses. Lee's companions both gave thought to continued conversation. Lull before a storm?

Back in their seats in the coach after the engineer blew the steam whistle for passengers to reboard, Lee picked up the intellectual cudgels. "There are others—story tellers, writers of so called histories, "professional" protestors, saga-makers, bickerers, occasionally at one another's throats—who weren't present up North yet make extensive errors reading my mind."

It was unlike R. E. Lee to be so definitive in judgment of people. But he had donned an academic persona. As President of Washington College and sometime visitor to Virginia Military Institute next door to W.C. he knew academic types well. "Their modus operandi: 'What I have written I have written' permeates the academic world. Pontius Pilate has his followers today, some in the academic world.

"They also think—write and speak, too—that we went on the Northern Campaign to have a spectacular, win-the-war in a one-move operation, a real theatricalizing of truth. They play too much chess.

"They don't realize that war is more than spectacle, more than smoke and fire, sound and fury, even more than death and heroism to be written about. They know gore attracts readers.

"War is a pivotal point in national policy; it has more to do than deal with what turns out to be brief—for even battles are brief, except sieges. National policy deals with all dimensions of national life. It is a long-life phenomenon. It provides people with purpose, protection, day after day after day. The long haul. Long, long haul in fact. Centuries long sometimes."

Warming to his task as the one who planned and officially reported the battle, President Lee asked pointedly, "Why would such scribblers, talkers, tale-weavers be silent—oh so silent—about my clear statement that we intended *no* general battle, except if attacked in that Northern Campaign into Pennsylvania? Why their silence?"

The traveler-for-his-health's-sake then hushed himself into sustained quietude.

The two companions knew better than to interrupt. He was tired, a dispirited state of being, evidently lost in pain caused jointly by the misunderstanding interpreters of his noble purpose years before and as much as by compromised health and the physical exhaustion of travel. In fact his stomach ached, brow sweated, and chest tightened as if a weight were on it.

Five years after the end of the Rebellion that almost dis-united America, it was evident to the old man that some people continued to be rebels against reality. When he did speak... long moments afterwards... it was nearly as soothing as a dove's cooing. "Some people use only their emotions and pre-conceptions to guide them. They intentionally shut their God-given eyes and God-given rationality to the truth." The lament was his normal style.

Daughter Agnes whispered to companion Corley, "It would not be good for my father to continue talking." She detected further diminishment in the old man's health, heeding his mood changes, slow but observable. She was his goodly protectoress, when he heeded her.

The questioning and responses were morphing a trip intended to improve his health into a taxing tour instead. Mentally and physically heavy; too heavy for R. E. Lee in the present moment.

Part of the heaviness was due to the years of an emotional fire smoldering in the former general. Now in a private setting with Eleanor Agnes and James Corley he'd given free rein to exasperation. "Those people have misread the crucial character of our Northern Campaign. They miss the fact that its failure was a broken pivot in the life of the Confederacy. We died politically before we succumbed militarily."

With its ups and downs... mostly downs... the trip was becoming essential nonetheless for Robert Edward Lee. When he had heeded the medical advice he had named the professor of philosophy as the temporary president to operate the college. He was aware the man was the intellectual center of the college, and, better yet, lacked pride—the deadliest of sins. Particularly for academics. All would be well at Washington College. And when he returned from the trip he knew that professor would do what all true philosophers do: fade into the classroom.

With compassion Lee had turned over the care of his wife Mary to the tender mercies of their daughter Mildred and to his eldest son Custis, who was teaching next door at the Virginia Military Institute. Custis was a source of intellectual and physical strength in the family. All would be well at home. The family would coalesce when he was away.

So much of that positive thinking had not materialized on the trip. His health did not improve, complicated by the many train stops and waiting groups and crowds of citizens and former Johnny Rebs. Agnes' health, too, became compromised. And his interpreters would continue to misinterpret him about a pivotal point in the secession movement. He was a post-war target for misinterpretation of his peaceful purpose and many Northerners despised him for forsaking the Union. R. E. Lee was a sitting target.

As private as he was about his life, he considered it necessary that he explain himself to two people devoted to him and his well-being. Therefore he could not help but deal with the unthought-about, uncared-for elements in the planning and operation of the Northern Campaign of the Army of Northern Virginia circa mid-year 1863. So he put himself under constraint to tell the fuller account.

In actuality he went into an important part of his plan for the invasion of the North. He described to his two companions his wartime General Orders No. 73 issued to his troops back in 1863. "I did not want our troops to ravage the Northern countryside, not to wreck villages, towns, or citizens. As general, I made clear to my comrades-in-arms they were not to offend Pennsylvanians."

Surprise! An invading army was not—in any way—to wreak havoc on the country invaded. "The citizens of the Commonwealth of Pennsylvania, like those of the Commonwealth of Virginia, were to be treated civilly, respectfully, honestly, even kindly. My soldier 'boys' were not bushwhackers, rapists, wreckers, destroyers, violators of good order, or outlaws. This invasion was to be a new kind of warfare. Anyone who violated General Orders No. 73 would be answerable to higher command and to me."

Definitively he asserted to his co-travelers, "Confederates were not to bring on a battle. They were not to fire the first shot. I had bigger fish to fry."

At his mention of the order to *not* savage the North in '63 Lee became almost placid. He was confident his 1863 plan would make eminent sense to them. Therefore he said no more about it.

Unforeseen by his co-travelers, Lee turned the subject to their travel plans through Georgia, then Florida. Speaking quietly of their visit to North Carolina to the grave of his daughter Annie, who had died during the war, he told the companions something more. R. E. Lee noted that he had visited his father's grave one time on Cumberland Island, offshore in Savannah,

Georgia, years before the war when he was a young lieutenant in the Federal Army Corps of Engineers. "I need to visit it another time in my life." The death of a father—a hero figure, no matter what—is a significant point in a child's life, even unto adulthood.

Wiggie agreed wholeheartedly. "Of course, Papa, and then we'll decorate grandfather's grave with flowers that will brighten the day for all to see. Just as I placed her childhood locket on Annie's gravestone to hang forever and the brooch Mother sent engraved with the figure of an angel to be buried above her until we meet again so I have a spur you saved of your father's that I'll place in Grandfather Henry's grave."

Corley averred, "It will be a glorious day to put bunting or an American flag on your father's grave, honoring a Revolutionary War hero and friend of George Washington. I want to commemorate not only his wartime deeds but his political wisdom as he originally pronounced—in the halls of Congress no less—that the Father of our country was 'First in War, First in Peace. First in the Hearts of His Countrymen'."

The college president followed their loving remarks with kind words about his malfeasant father: General "Light-horse Harry" Lee. The same "Light-horse Harry" who had abandoned his family—and the country—years and years before when Robert was a child five, maybe six years old.

But the old man also asked, with bowed head and choking voice, "What do you do about a father who ran away?" Emotional pain just seemed to slog doggedly after Bobby Lee turned Old Man Lee from moment one of his trip to restore good health. "Life is strange; unforgiving in mysterious ways, beneficent in wondrous ways; often on the same day or in the same situation." Nevertheless the oldster was working at establishing his own equilibrium.

Stumbling over words, R. E. Lee spoke in restrained tones sometimes inaudibly, that as a boy he felt terrible. "I was abandoned. Deserted by my father's desertion. It was a disastrous emotional storm for me. Mother, too. Family, as well. And our Homeland." Tears flowed down the wrinkled pathways in his cheeks into his gray beard.

The train drove on making its rough noises, so at odds with his gentility as to make the scene absurd. His beard wet, tunic moistened, he was not ashamed nor upset by the improbable railroad setting of his fragility. R. E. Lee postulated a thoroughly human perspective when dealing with long-ago but persistent pain: "Tears are the final, the great tribute to departed loved ones, noble or mundane flesh and blood. They are one in the grave with all our forebears, as we will be for our progeny. 'The dead have all the glory of this world'."

The evening could have devolved into desperate lamentation and torture for all three. Nonetheless Corley eagerly seized the moment. He was a bulldog, just as fierce as he had fought unsparingly for shoes... horseshoes as well as soldiers' shoes. Now Corley re-embarked on an indictment of people who denied Lee's Northern strategy. "The denial of your purpose, Sir, is a greater loss than the battle."

Lee was much startled. His lower jaw quavered in surprise.

Wig was astounded. She felt compelled to ask, "How can that be? Why?"

"The war has been over five years," stated their friend and guide. "Second guesses are the fare of losers and justifiers. They don't merit anything. They cover up reality. They give an untruthful view of life. A view that can hurt the South in the future. They perpetuate a defunct way of being American. And we are American regardless of who won, who lost. True for all of us in 1870.

"Such views aren't worth even the vinegary vomitus they spew: sour, not even good for pickling prejudice. Those views preserve only ineptitude. Ineptitude that caused the war. Ineptitude that perpetuated the war. Ineptitude that will stigmatize the South with lies... for a long time, of decades surely, possibly longer."

Of the same mind but without Corley's aggressiveness R. E. Lee added a poignant assertion: "Such people become the fog of history."

Agnes bowed her head with affirming motions. She stood beside her father as he stopped sliding around on the hard wooden seat. Bending over, she kissed his forehead. R. E. Lee, still gallant as a Southern gentleman, kissed her hands, holding them before his eyes a long time. Her warmth became his warmth. His grandeur became her grandeur. And his tears fell gently on lily skin.

She thanked him; she thanked a gentleman. He thanked her; a lady in more than name.

Tall Corley, within the frame of a door of the railroad car, arms uplifted, formed an image as if making a speech before the Roman Senate. He stood erect, rigorous and regal. He was exhilarated, triumphant in voice. "They are lies; lies of the misbegotten. Lies perpetrated by sore losers, narrow-minded people who purposely want to reframe truth. May God correct their souls."

The old military master responded intuitively, "They are the fog of history which is settling over reality. They'll mislead the South—again!"

CHAPTER 16

Savannah's charisma never fails

The rail journey thus far was uncomfortable, to say the least. At worst, it could be said the days had been a torment. Misery stormed like clockwork time after time, mile after mile along the railroads' diverse inconveniences and the raggle-taggle groups at jerk-water stops.

There came a day when those nightmarish conditions ceased immediately. A Savannah day.

Savannah's charm was evident as soon as the train stopped and passengers alighted from the coach. The weather was perfect, glowing with sunlight, and warmth for skin, muscles, bones, joints, internal organs, too. Soft summer breezes veneered each person though it was but early April. Billowy clouds, brilliantly white, scudded along making a spectacle of themselves. Spring flower scents still floated over the platform eclipsing the acrid stench of burning wood smoke huffing and puffing from the locomotive's firebox. And—little wonders never cease—the train station was clean, quite the contrast with various others on their trip. It even had clean toilet facilities.

Savannah had not suffered much damage during the late war, as both sides admired its beauty, probably from envy as well as appreciation.

"It's a great day already in Savannah. I can do business here today," entrepreneur Corley observed playfully, yet honestly.

R. E. Lee announced, "Make hay while the sun shines." However he did feel the beauty, smiling broadly to everyone's enjoyment. It was a new day. He felt like a new old man with something to be pleased about.

Wiggie rejoiced. *Father's happy or he wouldn't be so genial after those wretched railroad stops. A new beginning of something different. Possibly.*

Savannah exuded Southern comfort from the start, capturing each visitor, even the trainmen getting off from their duties.

Agnes, having previously visited Savannah, voiced, "I trust this wonderful weather is preamble to what is to come."

Both men sensed all she meant and asserted the same sentiment. Wig's father was the louder of the two, but Corley did so much longer, repeating her words several times as he gazed around the station and at the slowly gathering crowd.

However, it wasn't a customary crowd.

What does that portend? Lee thought, already on the defensive.

He surmised, correctly, a telegrapher back up the railroad line had taken it upon himself as per usual: "Lee is on the train."

The crowd was not raucous, exasperating, nor rude. Yet the females, children and young, as well as adult, wore many-colored raiment bedecked in stripes, splashes of shapes, and patterns galore; the men, of all ages were coated in togs of every sort, pastel to sparkle and glimmer. For Spring 1870 the gathered citizens seemed to give a party appearance: good cheer and salutation for the special guests arriving from Virginia.

Someone on the Savannah Welcoming Committee had asked for such a clothing display. The population was to vie with the beds of flowers in bloom around the station and all that would be displayed along the way downtown.

The five flower beds at the depot were placed aesthetically, so one side bloomed blue while the other side red; fronting the train station were three flower beds with a prominent central bed of all white flowers, the other two were a potpourri of tints, shades, and hues of varieties still pleasingly aromatic.

Savannah had a method in such gentle madness, a motive. Its goal was a delightful gaiety of colors with zesty fragrances which would help prevail over locomotives' smoke. It was an easily detected intention to greet people with delight rather than unpleasantness. Savannah was not dull nor discomforting, so why should a gateway to Savannah be otherwise?

From the crowd a number, possibly four dozen, give or take a handful—no one was counting—assorted people, men and women, youth, graybeards and baldheads, beautifully coiffed women and latest-style braided and curled hair maidens—then three black men, former male slaves, one with a trombone the other a violin, stepped to the fore with their companion who had "bones" held high for all to see.

Such bones are ancient in origin and consisted of dried animal bones. Later in time they were carved from fine wood to be seven to eight inches long and one inch wide, then varnished. One was carved with a slight curve and the other almost straight which was held unmoved between the fingers of one hand while the movable one was clacked against it in a slapping motion causing a richly resonant sound to which listeners often responded by clapping hands or stomping feet. Bones are musical instruments poor people can make to be merry and rhythmic.

The trio was an instant hit.

Before he knew it R. E. Lee was gently stomping his feet while his daughter laughed; Corley was open-mouthed; then hooted. The crowd applauded; several youngsters howled.

Cheering and laughing, numerous crowd members started clapping and dancing. Among the people who formed a musical ensemble, instruments appeared and people played mouth harps, others small drums including a tin drum and skin-head drums of various sizes, even a set of sleigh bells from Christmastide. It was not an orchestra, it was a pick-up band with assorted instruments sounding slightly cacophonous notes once-in-a-while to everyone's enjoyment... even the old bearded traveler they were honoring.

Corley danced a brief jig around Agnes to her embarrassment. She did thank him afterwards, consciously identifying it as syncopation with the marvelous reception they were receiving from Savannah citizenry—and there were no outcries for "Lee. Lee. Lee."

Some people sang along with the homemade band when it played folk songs. Others clapped in rhythm. A number of old men plus a few youngsters all in faded gray jackets or trousers, with military kepi or forage hats... one even had on a tarred Havelock covering on his kepi in case it rained... their feet on the hard brick pavement. Among the loud calls and hoots several of the old men stomping yelped in pain sporadically because their rheumatoid joints reacted badly. Yelping and jowling noises struck most everyone's funny bones, eliciting laughter, giggles, and full throated hollering from some women and most men. Oldsters enjoyed their pains for probably the first time in years, hilariously tittering and twittering right along.

It was a gay old crowd ready for a festival.

When Lee alighted from the train the band stopped its repertoire post haste and snappily began to play for him, moving directly in front of him, sort of capturing him in a semi-circle.

They played a lullaby. Not "Dixie" nor a nostalgic Stephen Foster "Old Kentucky Home," not a ballad nor a barcarolle from Venetian *gondoliera*, not a martial tune nor a Mexican mariachi, not a polka nor a praise song. A lullaby, of all things.

R. E. Lee was put at ease immediately. He smiled, but did not doff his hat until later, having forgotten he had it on since he had so immediately joined the merriment.

Unknown to Lee or his daughter, James L. Corley had asked the railroad telegrapher in his hometown back in Charlotte, North Carolina, if he knew another telegrapher down the line in Savannah where his party was traveling. If so, would that Georgia telegrapher know a musical group to meet the Lee party at their hometown railroad station and play or sing to revive the ex-general's spirit. He explained his request because of Lee's health issues. Corley never heard whether or not the telegrapher succeeded so he, too, was put at ease immediately.

Knowing days before Lee's arrival that the former general was doing poorly, the band leader took the message seriously and planned a surprise welcome. Only two years before in 1868, the German musical perfectionist Johannes Brahms had published his famous "Brahms' Lullaby," based on German folk music.

Lullaby and good night
In the skies stars are bright.
May the moon's silvery beams
Bring you sweet dreams.
Close your eyes now and rest.
May these hours be blessed
'Til the sky's bright with dawn
When you wake with a yawn.
Lullaby and good night.
You are mother's delight.
I'll protect you from harm
And you'll wake in my arms.

It swept the music worlds of Europe, Canada, and the States. The response by ordinary people, fathers and mothers, grandparents was a social marvel. That musical style easily became popular and spread near and far. America's South was an excellent setting for that music with its *bona fide* emphasis on family and, after the bitter defeat in war, it nurtured peacefulness in place of fear.

Shortly afterward the orchestra started playing a locally popular tune from decades past. Scores of people, certainly mothers and women young and old, sang the love song for children.

When R. E. Lee was safely off the train the orchestra re-played the tune. This time he sang along with the crowd, the portions he could remember from singing to his year-old grandson Robert Edward Lee III, son of "Rooney" and his second wife. In the quiet moments after the group sang he said to daughter and friend, "I remember that boy so well. And also Rooney's two other dead children by his first wife deceased early in life. He has suffered greatly."

Tears started, then slid down his cheeks and he looked to Agnes for help. She kissed her father in public; most of the crowd clapped in agreement. Others in the crowd also wept, several children. They asked, "Why? Why are you crying?" One little boy asked, "Why is everyone bawling?" His father picked him up, hugging him tightly, and said, "We'll tell you when we get home."

Agnes heard; she was surprised enormously. *Papa singing; then his tears... so different from the past days. So different.* She couldn't truly fathom her father's depth, nor comprehend his breadth. *So different. Deep. So wide.* And then a prayer of thanks under her breath for her father satisfied her questioning mind.

Corley, too, joined in the echo and re-echo, thinking of his youngsters. "I miss my family, each one. Each day." He just had to say the words aloud, then turned aside to cover his aching.

Lee was happy, quite happy; he felt at peace. That feeling graduated into sleepiness. *I feel at home.*

Neither the crowd nor the travelers wanted to leave. The old man yearned for sleep having slept so poorly, so irregularly on the trains. A sense of home bound him to his family back in Virginia, to his family long gone to where there is "no night there" but Eternal Light. He missed his magnificent mother-in-law, his wonderful sorrowing mother, his brave yet faulty father, his precious Annie, his noble sons, his genteel daughters, his endearing grandchildren and the many, many, multitudinous gallant men who died under his command in war. R. E. Lee did not need rational thought to understand the warmth, the depth, and the longevity of home, in this world and hoped for after this existence.

They were in Savannah; a home. A beautiful, peaceful home.

What a celebration the old college president experienced. Totally unexpected by him and his two companions, although James L. Corley had hoped for something good to greet them when they detrained in the beautiful coastal city. Lee thought he could make up his lost sleep undisturbed. *As in the President's Home back in Lexington,* he reckoned.

From the final braking by the locomotive engineer and the ever present scents and colors of the train station plus the first step off the passenger car by Agnes into another world right up to the lingering lullaby sung by the crowd, R. E. Lee acknowledged Savannah was a prize at the end of a difficult railroad trip.

A prize to last a lifetime, long or short: Savannah, the charmer.

CHAPTER 17

What a difference a place makes

"I think I'm at home in Savannah," the gray headed, salt-and-pepper bearded former general observed.

"Why do you say that, Father? Don't you miss Lexington?" Wiggie asked, instantly disturbed.

"I didn't say I was 'elated', Wig. I feel at ease here."

"But it's not home, Papa."

"Well, Agnes, I have a history here you may not know. Children seldom know much of their parents' life story."

Corley chimed in, "I know a bit about it, Sir. I heard about you around campfires in the Army of Northern Virginia. It wasn't gossip, not bad news; it was men, soldiers, old warriors who went through Hell with you and new recruits about to experience the same. All of us wanted to know who and what our leader was. After all, not just where you learned soldiering and how you would get along with and talk to men who might well die young under your leadership. We wanted to know you, Sir. About anything decent that would help us to know, to trust you."

"We'll talk of that another time, James. Right now I feel safe, home, happy. I calculate I have a home here and one there in the mountains of western Virginia."

"Maybe talk tonight, Sir? You may remember I'll be leaving you and Agnes in two days to return home in North Carolina to tend to my insurance business."

"Right. Tonight. Or tomorrow. Soon."

Agnes was not so much excited as annoyed that she would have to wait to discover something about her father she apparently had not known. *But... discovery would be later tonight, or tomorrow; I'll just have to wait. Father is his own time-keeper—and time goes by and by and by,* she told herself. She had minimal confidence he'd remember to talk about the matter.

However, she recognized something else that made her anxious: *Father hasn't said a negative word today about those rail stop misadventures. I get the impression he's forgotten how disturbed he was. He's non-combative. Altered somehow.*

Wiggie was becoming more than a little concerned about the changes she noted in her father. The good changes, too, simply because they were changes, alterations he was making for undisclosed reasons.

Boldly she asked, "Has Savannah worked its charm on you already? Neutralized you? Papa, an answer would help me care for your needs."

Taken aback, the elder Lee looked her in the eye, resistant to the implication of apathy on his part. The same instant he caught a glimpse of defiance in her demeanor. "I haven't noticed, except I'm not sick, though you think I am," he declared.

And that's that. Take it or leave it! was his daughter's perception. The next one frightened her knowing he'd pronounce: *What I said, I've said.* A Pontius Pilate moment. Her thought not only stung but harrowed Agnes keenly.

The intransigency of such a dictatorial statement was so like, "'What I have written, I've written'—and I'm not about to change it."

That mindset became an order and worked evil on the third day at Gettysburg in July of '63 when Pickett's Charge failed miserably. It was his fault as he openly admitted then. Presently he didn't admit he was ill because he was emotionally vibrant in old Savannah, but that attitude compromised Wiggie's ministrations to help him heal physically.

It was an existential draw, a standoff between father and daughter, old age and young adulthood. All the while sparkling Savannah passed by outside their carriage. Amidst the genteel panorama Agnes stifled a murmur then stuffed down a retort followed by assorted coughs and tears. She didn't want to aggravate his condition—whatever it was—anymore. Old Wild Bill Shakespeare had it right when the harlequin-like Puck said, *"Lord, what fools these mortals be!"*

True. In many instances we put not just life and limb on trial, test run, legalistic plague but our very souls, our integral being, the verily innermost being of our Being on exhibition.

Butt-naked show at that. *"What fools!"* Even the best of us make fools of ourselves. On piddling occasions. We are poor poker players.

Both daughter and father paused, stumbling over one another's misunderstanding and stared at the carriage ceiling, which made Lee senior chuckle and the other Lee then smile widely. They glanced outside the vehicle and started to take in the visual delights. That change from emotional skirmish comfortably moved them beyond their respective mis-apprehensions. The discord that might have developed into a rupture slipped away. Agnes dried her eyes; R. E. Lee looked the other way, smilingly thankful.

Their carriage traversed streets paved with brick, bouncing up and over red chunks of broken bricks, split by dray animals shod with thick iron horseshoes. Yet, passing rational belief, a horseshoe—split inadvertently from a hoof—as a faultily thrown off object magically becomes a good luck symbol for human beings. *Sacré bleu!* Supposedly at that point good news cast-off horseshoes when turned open end up will contain good luck for the finder. Truly, *"What fools these mortals be,"* on an assortment of occasions, as if our lives are without purpose.

Of course a thrown shoe is bad news, for the animal. Quite bad. Horse or mule and driver have to steer clear of more impediments in order to avoid foot injury. An animal without a shoe or shoes would often stumble, having to change its gait at the least. The human driver or rider involved had to change driving habits for fear of injury to the animal.

The carriage driver for the Lee party had consciously sought to avoid potholes in the muddy alley used for a short cut, thinking the dray mule had thrown a shoe. He brought the carriage to a full halt in the middle of a huge puddle of dull red muddy water. During the few minutes pause he studied the slow motion of the animal and steadily urged the mule forward, without a harsh voice or a whip.

Lee was so appreciative that he called up from the cab to the driver, "Thank you for looking to your animal's safety. I constantly tell riders to look to the welfare of their animals."

"That's kind of you, Sir. I'll tell old Balaam when we're back at the stable. See, Balaam's come from one of the two jacks... or one of the two jennies... of Andalusian donkeys given to George Washington by King Charles III of Spain back in 1785."

Each of the three passengers was struck by that tid-bit, and the driver's ease in telling the brief history. James Corley couldn't help but ask the black man driving the cab to reiterate the story about President Washington. His request went unheeded as the driver had his own tale to tell.

"Or... so Balaam tell me... 'cause Balaam's a talking ass just like in the Bible!" With a rough guffaw he bellowed out nasally, "Heehaw... heehaw... heehaw," then snorted through his nose in a lower key, "Ah huh, ah hee," much like old Balaam. He followed that performance with a good-natured chuckle, "Heehee. Hawhaw. Ho, ho."

Corley laughed; Agnes giggled. Lee sort of rumbled, clearing his throat, not knowing whether or not he was being mocked as was Balaam in the biblical account. Lee seemed to have missed the simple humor from an ordinary drayman. As an old man he was on sterilized ground, sort of neutered, neither angry as before nor joyous as in victory. Just relieved that he was kind of at home. He did thank the man, "You drive a fine cab and tell a thought-provoking story."

"Thank you, Masser Lee. I bet you can top 'em by a mile." Both men laughed, not at one another but because the simple statement was tremendously true. Yet old man Lee pondered, *Mine would be bloody red.* Then paused until a worse thought crossed his mind. *They'd hurt a hundred people at a time,* and he became morose. Quickly he perceived himself as crusty, bad tempered. *How quickly gentle humor becomes hurtful,* crossed his mind, so he decided to shut up.

Within minutes they exited the alley; the driver stopped the carriage and discovered with relief that his animal was still fully shod. That is, the driver's relief. No one checked with the mule.

The party moved onto a corduroy avenue of logs ribbed together to make a somewhat smooth ride on a main street to center city. The logs had wheel grooves where countless vehicles had gone before, yet it was difficult to stay in such ruts. Not an especially comfortable ride, Agnes squawked in pain each incident the cab lurched side to side. The two men laughed at her response, and bumped into one another several times.

"Sie sind stumm Esel, beide!" Agnes squealed, knowing her father didn't speak German. Whether or not Corley understood she couldn't have cared less. Her hope was her malediction would touch at least one of the two louts who forgot they were Southern gentlemen. But the mule Balaam drawing the carriage would agree for he was one smart jack, hee-hawing and shaking his head up and down, twisting it around and around. Shortly afterward, her expletive penetrated the males who realized what Agnes intended by her mild imprecation. She said nothing else. The men took her cue and did likewise.

The trio was headed to a downtown hotel. Lee actively peered out the cab window, pointing to an assortment of houses and gardens and taverns and churches and flop houses and government buildings along the brick streets and the corduroy road. His familiarity with the anatomy of the city surprised Agnes deeply. It didn't amaze Corley much because he remembered Lee's personal military acumen and early years spent in Savannah as a newly minted Second Lieutenant in the United States Army Engineering Corps back in the 1830s.

Especially—then thought friend Corley sorrowfully of Lee at another place in the old man's military career—*at the Battle of Gettysburg where he fouled up terribly. Miserably. Seven divisions on the same road at the same time at the very same juncture, scrambling to cross South Mountain to get eastward toward Gettysburg or farther east to York. Serious delay by a prime military engineer before a defeat!*

James Corley needed to stop thinking negatively or he'd ruin the present trip for all three companions. In such ruination he'd destroy Savannah as a haven, a home for R. E. Lee. A deal with the devil, for sure.

CHAPTER 18

"We are what we do repeatedly"

It couldn't be helped. No way could he be in such a major city and be unrecognized. But this recognition was different, singularly different from the previous railroad imbroglios. When the Lee party got to a hotel where they planned to stay—a hotel whose name none of the three could ever recall because they never got to stay there—something good, something old, something true happened.

Friends. Old friends. Military friends. Civilian friends. Friends of friends. Friends galore were waiting. Most everyone recognizable to other people who were present.

Lee was greeted by great news when he inquired about the MacKay family, the family of his great friend from West Point, John "Jack" MacKay who died early in life in 1848. The MacKays had just returned from their retreat in the mountains; Lee was overjoyed that they were again at their familiar Broughton Street home. "Savannah will be a home away from home, Wiggie," but Agnes hadn't known of the family and could remember only the name "Jack" from her early years.

The elder Lee halted his jubilant frame of mind because Wiggie didn't react in a similar way. "Is something wrong? Are you sure you don't remember your mother and I talking about the MacKays?" Then he asked again.

She told him point blank, "I only remembered the name 'Jack' being used in our home, a few times."

The wind went out of his sails. It took him moments to recover, but he began to fault himself for not mentioning the

MacKay family more often. An exceptional sorrow filled much of his being, especially for his younger children. Children do miss important parts of their parents' lives; more importantly parents fail to impart much of their own lives to help their offspring know valuable conditions that contributed to making them who and what they are.

Awhile later Lee turned to greet other old friends and to make new ones, trying to forget his sorrow. It was a lame attempt. *I can't undo the past. I need to remember to include Wig in as many of my friendships as possible.*

The elder Lee was stumped intellectually by facts he noted in Savannah: former Confederate officers in particular but ordinary ex-troopers, too, who looked more prosperous five years after the war than he had noted elsewhere in the South. And definitely more prosperous than veterans in his home state of Virginia.

Almost peculiarly, only a short day later, Lee received disheartening news. Samuel Cooper had been the highest ranking general of the Confederacy, outranking Lee and Joseph Johnston, and P. G. T. Beauregard, also Albert Sidney Johnston, killed early in the war. Cooper was originally from New Jersey and entered West Point at age fifteen, graduating in only two years. He became a personal friend of Jefferson Davis, later marrying a Virginia woman. His sympathies lay with the South. Cooper was also the highest ranking officer from the Federal Army to join the Confederacy. After the war he became an impecunious farmer near Alexandria; farming was not his forte.

R. E. Lee clamped his intellectual eyes on the disparity between prosperous Savannah veterans and the chief Confederate veteran. "I must do something to help Cooper, and do it quickly," he told his two companions. Post haste he contacted three Savannah veterans, two former officers of his acquaintance, and a former enlistee known by one of those officers, about the sad condition of Sam Cooper. Within two days he collected $300 for the Virginia veteran and then added $100 of his own money.

Agnes was happy for her father, and said, "You won that battle in two days, Papa."

Corley made the arrangements to have the money sent, with a note from R. E. Lee telling Cooper of the helpful veterans from Savannah.

The day after that love offering was sent, the travelers' carriage drawn by a mule became a draw, too—a magnet for a Savannah throng. The ordinary driver was thanked as if he were a member of the Lee party. Balaam the jackass was petted, rubbed, even fed, with bush leaves and flowers from the wayside. Corley was cheered, though honestly few knew exactly who he was. Eleanor Agnes was submerged in joy; and more joy. The college president was saluted three times with a single cannon as a former general. Too, adored as friend of Savannah's *crème de la crème* from years and years gone by of his personal history with them in the 1830s.

Savannah was a sophisticated city of 7,000 souls or slightly more. It was Georgia's largest city and chief port. Not having been critically touched during the War of the Rebellion, it still lingered, along with rural areas around it, in animus for the North. Additionally there was bitterness that it had lost sons, brothers, fathers and uncles, cousins and friends in a cause that was questionable at best. Such animus was aimed, albeit amorphously, at former Confederate hotspurs for not having planned adequately for war but just shooting off their mouths as if their sounds would scare off the "woolly bear" up North. A good deal of the South forgot a famous adage: "Proper Preparation Prevents Poor Performance." Savannah's genteel citizenry knew there was more than enough culpability for that bloodiest of fratricidal wars, but did little more than spout blame in the hate-filled 1850s. Silence is routinely rotten when it is not golden.

But that was then, this was now: 1870. Some things were forgiven, some forgotten, more were remembered although not alluded to by the general populace. The present time was beguiling: it was Spring... active, bright, colorful. In Spring things grow, implying five years after the war it was time to grow with a reunited nation.

For Lee, Springtime in Savannah meant reviewing his early life there. Having graduated the Military Academy at West Point back in June 1829 he had been commissioned an officer in the United States Army and formally assigned:

> *Brevet 2nd Lieut. Robert E. Lee will by the middle of*
> *November next report to Major Samuel Babcock of*
> *the corps of Engineers for duty at Cockspur Island,*
> *in the Savannah River, Georgia.*
> *(signed) C. Gratiot Brig. Gen. Commanding*

He had left for home in Virginia, and following his mother's death the very next month, departed by boat down the Potomac River to the Chesapeake Bay onto the Atlantic Ocean to sail to Georgia with an old black man.

A household slave of Mother Lee's family, Nat was a great help when R. E. Lee was still the fatherless boy known as Robbie. Both slave and boy had nursed Ann Lee during her persistent illness. Robbie learned so much about personal care for another human being from the slave. And now that Nat's health was poor and he was a free man, R. E. Lee took Nat along on his first military assignment, recognizing that "he serves best who serves his fellow human beings."

Back in 1829 young Lee was exultant, triumphantly happy in his assignment because Savannah was home to that great friend and West Point classmate, Jack... of the Savannah MacKays, no less. Few families in Savannah outranked the MacKays in virtue, social standing, or wealth... plus beautiful daughters, "interesting at first sight." Personal appreciation of feminine beauty by human males is rather rational, accordingly motivational. Or, so males assure themselves.

And, to crown his assignment, Brevet 2nd Lt. John MacKay was also assigned to Savannah, to an artillery unit a bit north of the city. *Oh happy day,* thought the newly minted second lieutenants back then, owing to their proximate postings.

Telling that information to Wiggie easily caused her to accept her father's contentment expressed when he thought he was "at home" in Savannah. His seeming neutral emotions then ceased to cause her critical concern. The biblical verse he often quoted came readily to mind: *"I have learned the secret of being content in any and every situation whether in plenty or want."*

Contentment is neutral much like a bridge between opposite shores; it is a way of knowing both sides of an issue—when one uses the bridge neither side is "right" nor "wrong." The bridge, so to speak, "does its duty" providing passage for any and all.

The trouble back then after their assignments to the Savannah area was that Jack MacKay crossed another bridge: the final one. At an early age, 43, Jack died.

Lee underwent extreme agony though by that time they had been long separated geographically in military postings. The two soldiers never disconnected psychologically. Almost daily for months after Jack's death Lee would assure himself, "Grief is the evidence we love one another."

And he quoted it again... two times... to Agnes and James. Compellingly his words sounded just as beautiful to his two travel companions who imagined it was being said the very first time, though neither ever knew Jack MacKay.

R. E. Lee could not help himself. He was compelled to think about his dear friend. Then, under compunction he had to think of himself back when he was in his forties.

He'd had his own serious brush with death. Strange to say, it was not on a battlefield but during wartime nonetheless. He had kept it secret as far as he could, with the exception of his wife Mary. Mary understood the necessity and the value of silence when asked by a beloved to keep information from public view or children's ears.

But again that was then, and this was now. R. E. Lee discerned he could tell a daughter and a trusted friend what had threatened his life, before public fame and military advancement came his way.

Agnes, discernibly, was no longer a child but a grown woman of grace and learning. James Corley was ever so caring... and discreet when asked to be so.

They're both mature. They'll honor my request for silence, thought the master of many planned campaigns about which he held information close to his chest. *They'll accept that Death's bright angel also causes dark shadows for many people. They can handle the account I'll tell. And keep it quiet,* Lee guaranteed himself.

The crowd awaiting him had been the largest ever in Savannah up to that time. "Size doesn't matter. When you're tired you're tired; you desire rest," R. E. Lee spoke quietly still longing for peace, quiet. The crowd didn't help, but then neither did it smother him. People seemed to notice his burnout, and treated him gently.

The party was escorted to the home of the former Quartermaster General of the Confederate States Army Lawton. James Corley was pleased immensely for he had known Lawton well as a superior officer. It was a pleasant interlude, shortness helping its *tour de force.*

Then the party was off to the home of a former friend, Andrew Lowe. Upon his leave-taking from the Lawton home for the Lowe home, a reporter from *The Savannah Republican* newspaper revealed about Lee that "...it appeared to us that an inexpressible sadness was visible in his features." Times of friendship and conversation weighed heavily upon the tired, and ill aged man.

Soon the party was pleasantly ensconced in comfortable rooms in the Lowe's home, ready for sleep. To sleep among friends is a blessing, subtlely reinforcing the sandman's duty.

The elder Lee, however, desired to talk not sleep, to get something out of his heart and head. He introduced his concern in a roundabout manner: "It's true, the idiom 'Any port in a storm' but much better a dignified setting is a helpful place to be when one needs to bare a portion of one's soul."

Corley, ever attentive to his older companion, instantly asked, "Is this when you will explain the real purpose behind your Northern Campaign seven years ago?"

"No, not so. That's too involved to tell in the evening. I think it needs daylight for clarity."

"Bravo, Father," noted Agnes sourly. "What is it that needs and fits into a pleasant evening you want to talk about now?"

Lee doubted her interest but her grumpy attitude registered on his fatherly heart more than on his intellectual bearing. He looked at her, not defiantly nor lovingly but perplexed about her exact motive. It was a prolonged pause before the old man spoke again. He didn't know exactly how to make intelligible his reaction to what had happened to him well over quarter of a century previously.

"Significantly it's a pleasant situation, Agnes, a sterling setting that is needed to talk about an unpleasant possibility concerning life or death." Yet his statement showed some sign of avoiding the depth of the problem.

Wiggie astutely realized he had something stashed away. "Are you in severe pain? Are you too ill to go farther?" She cared; she really cared, though she was ill, too. When suffering confronts suffering, oft times it blows up as a severe form of self-criticism in both parties.

Her father did not answer those probes. She simmered at his restraint though nonetheless felt sorrow for him in the same instance.

"What is wrong, Papa? Tell me. Please."

"What can I do to help, Sir?" muttered Corley.

The old man interrupted his pausing, hanging his head and softly said, "I'm sorry to have distressed both of you. I am not trying to be melodramatic. Forgive me for being obtuse, difficult to understand."

"Well what is it, then, Father. Please?" Another prolonged pause followed. *Is he setting a stage for something out of the ordinary?* Agnes wanted to shout, which would have embarrassed her father, ending the story before it began.

Even while breathing noticeably slower R. E. Lee needed to compose himself in order to speak. *I've only told the necessary military officials years before of that particular episode and then my wife Mary in an intimate time,* thought the sick old man, getting sicker by the minute. Of course, he had recalled it various times after returning from the Mexican-American War 1846-1848, staying mum about it nevertheless. *I probably shouldn't have begun this matter. Even with Agnes and James.* One of the residuals of war is its silences, that masks or mutes the living as well as all the dead; horror is best held in silence.

Then reluctantly below a whisper he said, "I was nearly—killed." A rasping cough caught everyone by surprise, the old man included as he fought for a breath of air.

"What, Father? Speak louder."

"I was nearly shot to death."

"When, Father? Where? In battle? At the college? When? What are you talking about?"

Corley wracked his brain trying to remember if Lee was referring to some incident during the war when his commander was under fire. Nothing came to mind.

The silence when he would not, or could not, speak was unbearable. Silence can also hurt.

With a soft rustling of words like wind over some dry leaves on the ground R. E. Lee finally finished, "By one of my men..."

"*What?*" boomed Corley, breaking into Lee's words. "In what battle? What are you saying, Sir? Where did this happen?"

Wig stood horrified, and covered her mouth with her right hand to stop any inappropriate words or stem the flow of bodily fluids that began welling up in her throat.

"By one of my own men. During the Mexican-American War." And he clammed up. *That answer will settle the matter,* he miscalculated, promptly falling silent.

The answer no way settled the matter for Agnes or James. They leapfrogged over one another to get the story.

"You mean one of your men tried to shoot you in the back?" asked Corley in a thick off-putting voice.

"Why would a soldier shoot you?" rushed in Agnes.

"Was it a duel with a fellow officer?" posed Corley just as fortissimo.

"Was the assailant drunk, Father? Out of his head? Sick? Or a Mexican? A spy maybe? Someone opposed to the war with Mexico? What was happening?"

At that point Lee was dumbfounded because he had thought nil of the possibility of being assassinated. And Agnes' catalog of assaulters was a deluge of fear and compassion, making it too eccentric, too implausible to respond one by one.

A further torrent of questions came. Where? How? Why? What did you do? Who was it? Which battle was it in? Not a Mexican? A spy? A disgruntled soldier? Repeated several times by both daughter and friend in different sequences with increasing frustration, Lee's continuing silence aggravated them all.

The old one remained silent, but stood up after several minutes. Next he walked around the sitting room, the space separate from the two bedrooms father and daughter were to occupy. His movement of seeming independence from the discussion irritated both the daughter and friend even more. The emotional atmosphere was bulky: lots of anger, a blot of fury, a trace of unbelief, and a heap of annoyance in an amalgam of foulness irritated all three.

"What is going on?" repeated James Corley. The redundancy impaled R. E. Lee straightaway because he would have to detail the situation.

Forced by his own lulls of silence, yet an honest need to complete what he had begun, the former officer of long-gone-years began reciting faintly the incident.

"In my early forties another tempest stormed over me as had the first one when my father deserted the family. With hair-raising intensity and searing physical proximity it confronted me with my own personal death."

Of course he paused again.

Wiggie turned away from her father, moving as if to depart by picking up her shawl and purse, then stopped all movement. She wanted to escape, but less so than she wanted to know the reason someone had tried to shoot her father.

"The danger was so stark that afterward one can imagine the jet-black night terrors that emerged violently, attacking me in bright day as during the burnt umber of sleep or the reddish aggression of sleeplessness for months later in the War with Mexico," he volunteered, becoming surprisingly loquacious.

As one would expect, he paused. He brawled with himself whether he should continue the story or if he were emotionally able to continue with it. He delayed. Delayed speaking. Delay often is a Hell self-induced, whether to justify an action or condemn it.

Corley coughed in anger and unbelief, then said a simple, "And?"

Confused, Lee all the same exhibited a defensive attitude so couldn't back away from his story, and said somewhat scoffingly, "And I didn't dwell on the shadowy ordeal for several days after it happened. Nor did I mention it to other army comrades. Perhaps not mentioning the event was that it didn't happen on the killing fields in Mexico as we Americans invaded their country."

"Why were we there at all, Father? What did Mexico do to provoke America?"

"You've asked a powerful question; a virtuous one, Wiggie. It was due to Texans. But that's not pertinent to my story. True, the event had overtaken me in wartime—in the American war before the 'civil' one. The young Abe Lincoln had strongly opposed that war, a criticism that cost him his re-election bid for the Congressional House of Representatives.

"War costs are copious, umpteen and diverse in number. Death. Destruction. Desertion. Military and civilian costs are effectively diabolical on friend and foe alike. Everyone is scathed somehow by war."

Lee didn't want to dwell on his shadowy ordeal yet he had to set the event in a proper perspective. Perhaps the reason for his seldom mentioning it in twenty-five years or so is that it didn't happen on the massive killing fields.

"The Mexican-American conflict had been a war of choice. America's choice," he declared. Yet multitudes of Americans in all states of the Union openly and broadly opposed it. Others saw wealth and new lands. Discord was rampant across America on all economic, social levels about that war. "It was a terrible time," Lee stated, looking into his hands and not at either companion. "Former President John Quincy Adams viewed the war as a naked land-grab by America. Dauntlessly, on the floor of Congress, he proclaimed that war to be evil." Now Lee looked to one then the other companion as if for support.

Corley joined in as a reader of American history. "The war with Mexico was so bad that Ulysses S. Grant, a lieutenant brevetted two times during that war, often told various people it was an unjust war waged by a stronger nation against a weaker one, noting it was a republic mimicking European countries wanting only to gain territory."

Lee humbly said, "Amen and amen," clearly in agreement with his former foe's evaluation.

Corley, seeking additional approval, noted, "Bad wars are 'badder' when good nations initiate them; they have the 'baddest' consequences."

The popular name for the conflict was "Mr. Polk's War." President James Polk had glamorized it as a way to expand the nation westward to California and southwestward to Texas. Supposedly those lands were part of America's "Manifest Destiny" to fill the continent.

"Manifest Destiny was a fiction to gain a new frontier. Other nations rejected the fiction," chimed in R. E. Lee. "Not one other nation agreed with American aggression."

Lee had served in this war, an adventure for him, exciting. He grew in wisdom and strength and in favor with his commander and fellow officers. Courageous and skillful, he was always in good report with Commanding General Winfield Scott, whose high estimation of Lee continued throughout the general's life, present even fourteen years later when Lee rejected his oath as an officer of the United States Army, resigning to serve another master.

In the course of the American invasion of Mexico, Lee faced something about himself that only grew clearer with time: he was not doomed to die an early death nor to die in war. It was a kind of revelation; some colleagues thought it was just bravado, but Lee knew it to be a moment of self-discovery, therefore "sacred." At least semi-sacred when he was totally "scientific" about himself.

That sacred condition surfaced again six years later at the death of his decidedly impressive mother-in-law, Mary Fitzhugh Custis. He was affected with more than sadness; he had loved her as he had his own mother. Ten years later still, the condition emerged again at the death of his military alter ego, Thomas J. Jackson, called "Stonewall." Now another seven years more it resurfaced on this vacationing trip with a daughter, a few months before Lee's own death.

The frightful event during the Mexican War was reported by the most intellectual of American military officers, called "The Pen of the Army," Ethan Allen Hitchcock, grandson of the Revolutionary War hero Ethan Allen. What Lee could recall of the official report, he told his companions. In its entirety, the later-to-be Major General Hitchcock wrote in his diary on 20 March 1847:

Capt. R. E. Lee, one of the engineers and an admirable officer, had a narrow escape with his life yesterday. Returning from a working party with Lieut. P. T. Beauregard, he turned a point in the path in the bushes and suddenly came up on one of our soldiers who no doubt mistook him for a Mexican and challenged, "Who goes there?" "Friend," said Captain Lee. "Officers," said Beauregard at the same time, but the soldier on guard duty in trepidation and haste leveled a pistol at Lee and fired. The ball passed between his left arm and body—the flame singeing his coat because he was so near.

Recalling and reevaluating that event took the adult Robert Edward Lee back to the times as a boy his famous father, Henry "Light-horse Harry" Lee, had shared his Deist religious values with his family. Deists contend God created the world and imprinted it with laws to run on its own without godly intervention. Thus, things happen outside God's purview, range of authority or control; things are not ordered by God.

One of those Deist values came into action after the shooting: Captain Lee did not want the soldier punished. His commander was abashed. Simply put, Captain Lee understood that accidents do happen in the Universe and no one is rationally responsible. Things happen. Period. Exclamation point!

Captain Lee had reacted calmly to the shooting, expressing compassionate consideration for the soldier. His immediate superior would not hear of it. No one knows what self-assertive Beauregard thought by pulling rank of "Officers" contrary to Lee's congenial "Friends" answer to the soldier's dutiful questioning.

Doubtless Lee felt something profound or he would not have intervened on the trooper's behalf. How could it be that he did not express negative emotion? Something way out of the ordinary had happened to him. Death passed between his arm and his breast. Three, four inches to the left and his heart could have been hit. Lucky? Then again, would "blessed" be an exaggeration?

Perhaps Lee was saved by an act of grace from a loving God. Possibly. One can believe what one wishes. Yet, it is the case that *finite* human beings cannot know with absolute certainty how an *infinite* Being acts.

For some other people the incident was pure happenstance. A twist in time? A wrinkle in the fabric of space? Possibly. One can suppose what one desires; to know is seldom a certainty, often even for the human beings involved in dire situations.

Still others could interpret it as a portent of what was yet to come in life. Whatever the case, the incident was bewildering: Lee shot at close range, near the heart, still alive, unshaken. From appearances the situation and his undoomed condition must have sunk into his subconscious mind. He was an "undoomed warrior" through war and peace.

Briskly Captain Lee in the American War with Mexico relied on what he knew best—duty. Clear as the hair on his face, R. E. Lee was the personification of Aristotle's *Nicomachean Ethics* summed up as: "We are what we do repeatedly." Excellence in life is not a single action but the habit of a lifetime. Lee was duty personified—but living in a society-become-lackadaisical.

Robert Edward Lee's default position for everything was duty. Duty to God. Duty to others. Duty to self. What we do repeatedly is what we are.

CHAPTER 19

"War would end if the dead would return"

When old men in their remaining years weep together, it is typically offhanded and fleetingly about their physical maladies. More is meant in their word-heavy years than meets the ear. The tears of old men trickle down time-eroded cheeks from beholding the glory they encountered, then treasured, in life with other old men, but they go no further. It is well with their souls, though they have no solution to life's gravest issue.

When old women in their remaining years weep together it is from the depth of pity human beings bear for others. They go on, as daughters, sisters, friends, wives, mothers, grandmothers, clearing the way for the next generation. It is well with their souls because they face the gravest issue.

The glory of both women and men in old age is gladness and a security springing from understanding... that is, *standing under*... receiving the full impact, the weight of the gathering of a totality of values from those who behold their depth.

As a poet phrased it:

When old age shall this generation waste,
Thou shalt remain, in midst of other woe
Than ours, a friend to man, to whom thou say'st,
"Beauty is truth, truth beauty," – that is all
Ye know on earth, and all ye need to know.

Beauty and truth... the first, an emotion, the other, an intellectual virtue... arrange and order human existence more than human-made codes, laws, and systems which have their day and pass away. Beauty and truth fill up the corners and rise to the heights of human existence in old age, although often unacknowledged until later.

Old men weeping together behold as well the depth of virtue, the permanence of love, its fixity, its eternality. Their tears are liquid that tumble with their passing years, cementing virtues together to make way for coming generations.

So it was that two such old men were photographed on a porch in sunny Savannah in 1870.

Lee and his two fellow travelers had visited various "friends" and found the visits pleasant yet not consequential. Of course the social calls were much, much better than the southward-bound railroad stop intrusions. The old master noted to his two traveling companions who dropped him off to visit his old friend from their military academy cadetship together, "Most revisited memories do not hold all the meaning people think they do. Most revisited memories.... Most revisited memor—"... and then stopped. The former cadet who became a Superintendent of the Military Academy was unable to avoid feeling a homesickness for the Plain, the parade ground at the Point which caused vivid images of splendid pomp and circumstance to process through his head. "The few memories that do occur are ever so precious because some have gone to their long home either in war or peace."

The ancient traveler longed for much while in such a splendid place as Savannah. Yearning was an interlude for Lee, waiting for an uncovering, a revelation. Many a time such aching for the past occurs to resting minds, pausing hearts. To bide one's time creates an opening for augmentation, a veritable snowballing of personal extension, spawning growth, more than just sinking into oblivion.

So it was for former classmates, comrades-in-arms, generals, friends, losers; they met one another. Their time had come. Lee visited Johnston at the latter's home. Johnston visited Lee at the same time, the same place—their hearts. Tears evident in the old photograph, and the erect posture of the two old men on rocking chairs on the front porch of Johnston's home embody familiarity, respect, fellow feeling, humanness.

Robert Edward Lee and Joseph Eggleston Johnston were born in 1807. Both graduated West Point in the Class of 1829. Both served with distinction in the West while in the United States Army. Later in the War with Mexico they distinguished themselves again. Both became Confederate generals, Lee from Army colonelcy to brigadier general in the Virginia militia, then lieutenant general in the Confederate States Army. Johnston from Army brigadier general to lieutenant general in the C.S.A.

"We've come together to do truth and beauty, *for* beauty and truth after all these years," blazoned Lee with a genial salute. They followed with a handshake lasting minutes, left arms gripping one another, forming a statue missed by a great sculptor. Johnston reminded Lee they had wept together during the Mexican-American War in 1847 when Johnston's nephew was killed in battle. Warm tears mingled as their heads touched, for seconds become minutes. Old men love old men because they are survivors blessed by one another.

Johnston could not do less than a handshake, did not want to do less. He literally grabbed Lee around the shoulders, drew him close, and bear-hugged him while whimsically venting a soft Southern uncontaminated purr rather than words.

Both men stood face to face, heart to heart. Laughter arose neither had heard in years. They were youthful again. Two newly minted second lieutenants bursting forth with joy, shaking their heads affirmatively. Long in tooth in 1870, yet short in energy, that day each "undiscovered self" discovered itself anew with the added boon of discovering ever so gently each the other's self. They became comrades-in-life... for eternity.

Scoring points is not a realistic option in old age, unless one is in second childhood. Neither needs to prove his self or her self to a world that doesn't much care any longer. Probably never did. But they stand sharp, clear against the horizon.

"Bare but honest. Robert, my newly discovered self meets everything in life that matters, whether of excellent report or not, from whatever source or sources. Being true to myself I am not false to anyone—nor to what is Real, to God," avowed Joe

Johnston. The unadulterated enormity of the war in which each had been a notable part, could not be lackadaisically tossed over the fence, or be forgotten. Or prayed away.

When seated comfortably on the porch and served a large tumbler of spearmint tea and a few chips of ice, R. E. Lee thought they would talk tid-bits of their lives since the war, much as he had done visiting the other friends in Savannah the days before.

Lee was unsettled rather austerely. *Johnston is speaking something deep, maybe dark about himself, baring his soul.* At that point Lee shuddered. *Who am I to investigate another's soul? What am I doing?*

His posture shifted noticeably. By a hand gesture, and leaning head and shoulders toward Johnston, he showed he was open to dialogue. Additionally, widely opened eyes invited a reaction Johnston could not fail to observe.

At that point Lee waffled, mentally. *Or maybe he's thinking about the present status of our friendship,* a point which he had previously anticipated. *Or even ordinary gossip, comings and goings of mutual friends,* he imagined to fill their time together. *But not of the war with the North. Not that, I trust.*

Always late to speak about himself, R. E. Lee awakened and the master strategist unveiled his inner self also.

"Face to face and purpose to purpose I've engaged that Real, too. Knowing what I do about your relationship with former foe, William Tecumseh Sherman, I have found something singular and exceptional in you. It must be the case that it is within, an undiscovered self deep-seated. You've discovered *soul*."

Now it was Johnston's turn to wait, to listen before speaking. And there was a lengthy period of minutes of typical "Lee-silence"... standard shifting movements, clearings of throat, fading sounds and nervous coughs, commonplace false starts and expressed excuses.

Looming large was the question how well it was, or was not, with their inmost beings, their souls. They had been through so much in the grisly fratricidal war, a war that almost destroyed a whole nation, a war that caused each of them to order thousands of men and boys to do battle. In like fashion each man brooded, ruminated, agonized.

150

Lee thought of the horrors encountered in fighting Indians in the Southwest, then of Mexicans in that contrived war, then of fellow Americans in the recent war, causing him to say, "Sherman is right. Hell it is, not figuratively but literally. War *is* hell."

Johnston surged, "We made a covenant with death and with hell... we made lies our refuge and under falsehood we hid ourselves, as Isaiah the Prophet thundered against wrong-headedness. Old Sherman but echoed that biblical complaint. War uses mankind's best to do mankind's worst. Two armies fighting one another is really one army committing suicide." Johnston remembered only too well the campaigns around Atlanta, Georgia, between his army and Sherman's "March to the Sea" where they could never cautiously hop, skip, and jump enough to ward off that dreaded Union army march and his own loss followed then by a spiteful and ignoble removal from command by Jefferson Davis.

No wonder there were still dried tear marks on each man's cheeks when the photograph was taken. Tears not from nostalgia; not from regret. Rather tears from the overall tragedy of stupidity, hot heads who started a war by violating the Constitution of the United States of America. Hoarsely Johnston cited the constitutional illegality of the Southern position: *No state shall enter into any treaty, alliance, or confederation under Restrictions upon Powers of States.* "What did we do but violate our own law? And then we lost. Lost the war. Lost the cause. Lost thousands of men and boys and civilians we needed to be a whole part of the Whole United States of America!"

Then R. E. Lee reasoned, *Thank God!* And was serene in his heart.

Joe Johnston waited. And waited. Waited still more.

R. E. Lee then realized more than he thought—and spoke up, "Thank God." Embarrassed he had waited so long to do duty as an American and Christian and human being, he needed to speak his truth in a more complete way. In that instant he recalled the powerful words of his greatest sub-commander, Thomas "Stonewall" Jackson: *"People anxious to bring on war don't know what they are bargaining for; they don't see all the horrors that accompany such an event. War is the sum of all evil."* That statement alone won the discussion more than anything either had said.

The day was won once again—by "Stonewall."

In supplemental discussion they went beyond the politics of war by discovering other dimensions of their personally discovered selves. Heartbeat to heartbeat, face to face, purpose to purpose, and a simple glory in the other. A simple glory in which they engaged the everyday Real of their lives in old age up to the Absolute Real, God, and beheld now easily in the other man's discovered self.

"In a world turned topsy-turvy, the discovered self realizes that humans are made for each other," Lee continued.

Post haste Johnston added, "Human beings do not exist alone but find themselves in others as they sort through their selves, known or unknown, to become self-discovered. We are more than we think we are."

Lee thought to say *Amen* but instead said, "It sounds easy," expanding Johnston's thought, "but is quite involved since people seek something else entirely. People want and seek happiness. Yet that is fallacious thinking. Happiness is not a condition apart from some other value, some other virtue. Happiness is found in doing the right thing, plus doing it for the right reason."

To the astonishment of Joseph Johnston, Lee moved upward in moral thought, beyond happiness to its grandest origin, saying, "Even with the dead, we discover that love is the purpose of life. Living with love and for love, for God first then love for life, then others, and last for one's self. There are so many dead, particularly in war, who died with valor, with dedication, with grandeur, truly with love. They show us the way to re-union in this world and fulfillment in the next.

"We loved so much—but not so well. We did not need to go to war to behold love in dead soldiers; we could have as well beheld it in their labors, in their preparations for the future, their commitments to their communities, their families, their homeland—all of it South and North—and to our God.

"And war against brothers and sisters is not the way to solidify freedom in a nation, for everyone, black and white, rich and poor, blue and gray. 'War *is* the sum of all evil' as Stonewall Jackson proclaimed.

"We need to find love for one another, to love our neighbors as ourselves, if we are to have grandeur in our nation—now more than ever before—*A New Order of the Ages,* as the Great Seal of the United States of America proclaims it," Lee averred.

Johnston needed no repeat convincing. *That man should occupy the Executive Mansion in D.C. before he dies. He should walk in Washington's footsteps as president of more than a college.*

Lee and Johnston; Johnston and Lee found exhilaration late in life as they laid bare their own undiscovered lives... serving two purposes... as discovered souls.

Both former generals confronted the massive original transgression of humankind.

War is by far the towering evil in human existence. It is the gravest, most malevolent, cruelest crime, heinous horror, staggering sin that human beings commit—war against their own kind.

CHAPTER 20

Joy and sorrow. Sorrow and joy

Savannah had been nearly an unending round of joy, remembrance, friendships created and friendships retouched like old masterpieces. Everyone seemed to like the elder Lee and he seemed to like everyone he met—old, young, civilian, and ex-military.

His two companions delighted in the attention. The salt-and-pepper bearded man kept on introducing them to earlier friends or former colleagues, and when acquainting them with new people he'd recently met, he made particularly sure they talked to his daughter and their escort Corley.

"To detail the many friends visited, meals shared, evenings entertained would take an entire notebook to write home to mother," voiced Agnes, "but I wish I could have a picture of all the wonderful people we met."

Corley confessed, "I'll remember all the fine cigars I smoked at the scores of places and homes we visited—so many that I started collecting them. I'll have enough for a week to take with me to my home in Charlotte. And I thank you, Sir, for the two you passed to me that someone forced on you."

"I was going to crush them and throw them away," Lee replied, "but I thought it would embarrass the men who gave them, mortified they forgot I never smoke the filthy weed." And then they laughed.

"Do remember, Sir... I always smoke in moderation."

"Oh?"

"Yes, indeed. Absolutely, Sir. Positively." Corley then anted up his punch line, "One cigar at a time!" Smirking in self-satisfaction, Corley swaggered his hips and began to moo like a sick cow, "One... at... a... time."

The old man retorted, "Only a jackass laughs at its own joke."

Poking fun at grown men is not only a gift for a woman to capitalize on but Wig's next action affirmed it was a woman's right. "Two winners in your burlesque," she hurled at father and friend, then lulled them into masculine self-congratulation. Seizing their smugness, in a very loud nearly shouted riposte, she burst out, "And... two losers, you two!" triumphantly.

Both males were caught off guard, their faces turned pink. Agnes couldn't help herself; she just had to poke fun at her father. "And look at him," she said pointing to Father Lee, "The red of his cheeks spotlights that black and white beard."

Old R. E. Lee, aghast, experienced boyish heebie-jeebies, collywobbles—or name them what you will—and choked back a half-formed response that he knew instantly was useless against his daughter's sortie. He gulped. Sometimes it's better to swallow one's attempt at humor than to lay oneself unprotected from a bombardment.

Somewhat younger James Corley must have realized that "truth" about bantering humor back and forth. Said not a word nor did he utter a sound. Instead was outright happy she had not picked on him.

Chivalry dictated that Lee... or any male... not retaliate publicly when tackled by a woman. For that reason alone quietude filled the air. Agnes was on Cloud Nine, bobbing her head up-and-down, up-and-down in grandmotherly fashion giggling, "Ain't it funny the way things does go? Ain't it funny, funny, and funnier the way things does go."

In such a serio-comedic manner the trio departed Savannah. James Corley headed back to Charlotte, North Carolina. Fond farewells were difficult to swallow, for friendships had ignited. Wiggie was weepy for she found Corley to be a strong person to rely on, easy to talk to—a friend. Bygone comrades-in-arms face to face, slowly saluted one another deferentially, then hugged as brothers with a respect verging on reverence.

Father and daughter headed not back to "old Virginy" but continued southward into Florida to a sad but necessary place.

Andrew Lowe, their Savannah host, joined them as a "tour guide." Lee wrote home to his wife Mary back in Lexington. "Lowe thinks Agnes and I are unable to take care of ourselves." In point of fact it was true; Agnes had fallen ill the day they were to head southward so the trip was delayed four days until she fully recovered.

Off the shore southeast of Savannah lay Cumberland Island. R. E. Lee had visited one time as a young second lieutenant in 1829, and wanted to do so later during the Rebellion in 1862 when he was in charge of Southern coastal defenses of the Confederacy but could not find time away from military duties.

So it was the new trio boarded the steamer *Nick King*—a "slow boat to China" between Savannah and Palatka—on the shore of the Saint John's River in northeast Florida. The steamer made a satisfying living for Captain Horace Bell and his wife Mazie, chief cook and bottle washer with a Creole's sense of humor. Captain and cook made the trip satisfying for all and any passengers, including oft sorrow-filled R. E. Lee.

At Brunswick on the mainland, people turned out to see Lee but made no demands upon him, so he stayed "hidden" on the steamer, to his delight.

The party was joined by William Nightingale, grandson of General Nathanael Greene. Greene had received Cumberland Island as recompense for his Revolutionary War service back in the late 1700s. Nightingale was successor owner of Dungeness, the estate on which "Light-horse Harry" Lee had died when returning "with his tail between his legs" from self-imposed exile and escapade in the Caribbean islands.

Father Robert told daughter Agnes that Grandfather Harry Lee had become seriously ill on the Caribbean return and was set ashore at the closest spot when incapacitated beyond shipside human assistance. That spot was Cumberland Island where "Light-horse Harry" disembarked, ill as ill could be. On the island lived the daughter of Harry's Revolutionary War commander, Major General Nathanael Greene. It was this daughter who took him in and cared for him at Dungeness.

"Light-horse Harry" died shortly thereafter and was buried on Cumberland Island, alone, far from home. Far from his Caribbean haunts, as well.

The *Nick King* tied up at Cumberland Island. R. E. Lee, Wiggie, and Lowe went ashore to the burial ground. "Agnes decorated my father's grave with beautiful fresh flowers," Lee wrote to his wife, and added simply, "I presume it is the last time I shall be able to pay my tribute of respect. The cemetery is unharmed and the grave is in good order, though the house of Dungeness has been burned and the island devastated."

What Lee did not know was that his own daughter had brought along an old prayer book of his father's along with the discarded spur she had kept from childhood to remember him by. Agnes handed her father the book and asked him to read a prayer, then lay it on the grave.

It was terribly difficult for the old man to leave his father's prayer book on the grave site, but his daughter had asked him to do so for religious reasons.

He did as asked, silently praying his own prayer-filled thanks to God that the stormy shadow of abandonment by his father was erased with compassion from both his father's then his own soul. Son Robert Edward Lee reached back in time to his father's desertion, then loneliness, then pain, then illness, then death apart from family. R. E. Lee's pain was not to be recalled even in his own darkest sick days yet to come.

Lee looked at his daughter, smiled, and nodded his head. "You are brave, as brave as was he."

Wiggie rose up from her kneeling position, threw her arms around her father, kissed his forehead and then his lips, and began to weep. They were tears of sorrow yet... gradually... dissolved into faint laughter as she felt a union with her father and grandfather whom she never knew. It was a consciousness she had never felt before. Nonetheless permanent, it became a daily consolation.

CHAPTER 21

Almost Florida-bound

Walking down the steps on Cumberland Island to board the *Nick King,* Wig stopped, turned, and faced the two men following her. Without delay they stopped, too.

"What's up, daughter?"

"Why the halt?" said the other.

She addressed directly their new companion, Andrew Lowe, so he would know she too was important to her father's health trip. "I've never been to Florida but I've heard wonderful stories about the weather, the hardy people, bright fruit, many cattle, and rich grasslands... but mostly about the ocean for swimming or wading, or boating. I've never been in the ocean. I want to have a happy time, now that I feel better."

Both friend and father laughed at her enthusiasm. Lowe said, "We won't interfere. We'll relax and let you pick fruit, soak up the sun, swim or sunbathe—and chase after calves," and then he let out a slight rumble of laughter that lasted an inordinate amount of time. Some people get a kick out of themselves, particularly if no one else does.

Her father didn't guffaw but squawked somewhat like a sea gull, which surprised Agnes for she had only heard him imitate horses back home or that mule back in Savannah. He got a kick out of himself, too.

"Some people... bah humbug!" Wiggie threw in for laughs.

As the three walked up the heavy plank to board the steamer, there was Mrs. Bell, "Mazie," greeting everyone with a husky, "Welcome aboard, friends." Then she reached to a small table behind her that held her wares, recipes, products, and gave each person a Creole cocoon cookie. It was slathered with pounded, ground sugar similar to the kind confectioners use. She repeated to each of the various passengers, "These are Creole, not Cajun. They're country cookies not city cookies: Creole not Cajun. Homemade. Their mine and now they're yours."

"May I have two?" asked the college president. "Waiting has made me hungry," he added and then blushed beneath his beard for being pushy. No one could detect pinkness this time, however, behind the salt-and-pepper beard.

"Sure—if you want to spoil your lunch and supper of old time Creole food. Remember Cajun food is made with love... but Creole, old time Creole, is made with spices and pepper. A mouthful you'll never forget."

"What all is in it?" asked Eleanor Agnes.

Mazie let forth a spiel as if she were a barker at a circus tent. "Spices, spices. Spices galore and more spices are Creole cooking. Like the *rouax,* gravy which must be just the 'right' color and is easily burned. The big one, 'Mr. Important,' is cayenne—or red pepper—plus black pepper, dried in hot areas, a room in the house or a shed. Strung up whole, it's dried, seeds and all. You better be careful not to get your hands near your eyes. They'll burn!"

And then Mazie paused for a deep breath of air. "But people juice up the mixture with dried sassafras leaves from the only plant that has three different leaf shapes: egg-shaped leaves with only one lobe, mitten-shaped leaves with two lobes, and trident-shaped three-lobe leaves.

"In late summer people go in the woods carrying cotton sacks, and literally fill them with sassafras leaves. They take them home, put them in a dry, hot room sometimes piled waist deep, and stir them regularly until they are properly dried. Pounded into powder after the stems have been removed, and stored, sassafras adds to the sauce a distinct but puzzling flavor, spicy and perfumed at the same time. Many folks get addicted."

Andrew Lowe spoke out loud, "I think I'm looking forward to either lunch or supper. Not both."

Dragging his heels, so to speak, Lee sounded a timid, "I am, too," not convincing anyone, even Mazie.

Agnes was enlivened only a degree or so, wondering how eating Creole gumbo would affect her stomach and all-around health.

Mazie's assistant, Captain Horace Bell, slapped his right thigh and let out a doltish "tee-hee, tee-hee," mimicking a purposely silly woman. Then like Peg-leg Pete the Pirate, he limped off to the wheelhouse of the steamer, and tooted the whistle three times for departure. The *Nick King* was Florida bound.

CHAPTER 22

Something happened for the lone time

The steamer entered the Saint John's River in Florida proper, anchoring at Jacksonville late afternoon to discover a gathering awaiting. "General Lee is aboard the *Nick King,*" must have put them on the alert. A crowd emerged in a flourishing attitude of personal friendship for the arriving personage. It seemed to both Lees a repetition of the disturbing events on the way south, the same as the railroad trip from Richmond down to Savannah.

It would be the same mini-disaster for the old man—or so he thought. Increasing numbers of joyful well-wishers converged into a multitude ready to burst. A formal committee with Mayor of Jacksonville, Peter Jones, greeted the elder Lee, making much ado about his presence in the Sunshine State. As if that greeting were not enough, a huge group of ordinary citizens scrambled aboard the steamer to the extent that the boat practically flooded with water. It did not swamp because the citizens soon realized the precarious situation and self-organized an orderly line around the deck to shake hands with R. E. Lee and daughter plus Andrew Lowe.

Lee was silently impressed, and smiled. Seizing upon that shipshape action, Captain Bell directed the citizenry to depart the boat. He was an old codger, eccentric to the hilt in full white uniform and a bright yellow sash crisscrossing his chest; his white cap had a black visor lettered CAPTAIN in China-red sewing thread, and Western cowboy boots made from Florida alligator skin brightly colored green, making him a sight to see.

There he stood in his uncomplicated pomp at the gunwale ushering people ashore.

His wife Mazie was doing her part in the rear of the crowd urging the citizenry ashore, "Go, please. Go." Floridians were compliant and quiet while waving goodbye to the visiting party of three, causing old man Lee to think, *I'm glad this boat didn't capsize in the mud,* which had seemed imminent several times.

Captain Bell, in his adornment, also shook hands with each exiting citizen, and invited them to travel northward back to Savannah on his steamer... not forgetting to mention the return fare would cost only two-thirds. Captain Bell was an entrepreneur American style: when the sun shines one makes hay.

That's how the South will recover, Lee thought with an audible belly laugh.

Wiggie was a shade dazed at Captain Bell's undisguised commercialism but without delay thought, *He's full of himself as a tick sucking blood on a horse's rump. But that's the way of the world.* She let go a chuckle of her own and felt good about it.

While shoreside, others could not reach the boat so someone called out to Lee senior: "Why don't you go up to the captain's deck and address the crowd?"

Lee, however, simply edged through the remaining people to the side of the boat and stood motionless. Silent. Unperturbed. He would not be talked into public address. Did not attempt to speak. Did not doff his hat, as he would sometimes do if the spirit moved him. Almost on cue, the on-shore crowd quieted down. A few coughs and fewer subdued sounds steadily vanished as if an order had been given.

The crowd faced Lee; Lee faced the crowd. No movement at all, except several children altered the scene for a few moments then seemed to sense the crowd's stillness. They too fell into silence, immobile.

Breath-taking silence and unbelievable motionlessness reigned on shore. No one knew why. *Parents, too.* What was it? Admiring reverence? Was it inappropriate to cheer? Would it be discourteous to shout greetings? What was it about that old man which changed the whole atmosphere of the assembled crowd? How did he do that? What manner of man is this?

On the *Nick King* complete silence, too. *Unbelievable,* Captain and wife thought.

Everyone was transfixed. There's no other way to describe it. A moment in time frozen. Agnes shivered in surprise. There wasn't intrusiveness like those previous railroad stops; none. There weren't calls of "Lee, Lee, Lee," either. Nor probings, nor touchings; none. Silence alone reigned, on land and on the boat.

There was, nonetheless, exclusively serious eyeball to eyeball contact, intense looking... some would call it *staring*... others *searching*. Constantly, fervently, respectfully, they stared at one another—the crowd at Lee, Lee at the crowd. Each with a searching heart. They beheld him flesh to flesh, heart to heart, soul to soul; he beheld them raptly, keenly.

It had never happened before to any one of them including the old man, old general, or old college president himself. R. E. Lee was positive his heart was growing warmer and warmer yet he was without fear that it might combust and he'd die. He thought, then, of his ancient biblical hero, Job, of a thousand losses including all his children, all his livestock, all his wealth, all of all gone. Except Job's pestiferous wife. Lee also felt everything was gone except a loving, not a pestiferous, wife who had brought him through many an earthly hell.

Lee's thoughts became an unalloyed vertigo of images. What was happening to people in the crowd no one left a record; it was too precious and would be too difficult for anyone not present to comprehend. Later at eventide, R. E. Lee strove to recall what had happened to him, to the multitude, what had honestly precipitated the silence, the immobility. Memory failed; it was as if he had been present at a non-eventful event. Then he sensed a tremor running from his scalp to the bottoms of both feet, strange jerks and shots as if jabbed by pin pricks. Nevertheless he could recall only somewhat yet without any distinct identification. Uplifting but lacking clarity he thought what he could identify as his own might not have happened, that he was dreaming, hallucinating. It was a mystery. Probably unsolvable.

Lacking lucidity he thought the non-event event would be murky, yet there wasn't murkiness; there wasn't concealed dishonesty of any sort. There was just "something" and he could only conceive of one thing—a *virtus*, a power, a wonder-working power of some sort, very seldom encountered in human communication. The old man had nothing else to characterize what was happening—or not happening.

Then he, the daily Bible reader, pondered more than ever before about a hill far away, an emblem of suffering and shame. It came to him in focused image with words clarion clear as if someone in front of him were speaking: *"About 3 o'clock on a Friday afternoon in a small Roman province at the eastern end of the Mediterranean, atop a skull shaped hill... silence fell. Except for two thieves on either side of the image who heard a whisper, 'It is finished'."*

Robert Edward Lee had no other category to "explain" what was happening in Jacksonville, Florida. It was not a religious conversion of any sort but rather an affirmation by countless lives through the centuries of a single Life well lived among humanity. A Life standing erect with them, before them, and in the presence of the Eternal Creator of worlds without end, of life, of lives, of the True, the Good, the Beautiful: a mystery unsolvable.

Human profundity requires the unorthodox, the abnormal, the exceptional Alone. Erect. Waiting silently. It's as good as any other explanation for what happened... or did not happen. When it happens to one person it is a mystery; when to a crowd it is an utterly profound mystery.

A *Jacksonville Union* newspaper reporter noted in 1870: "The very silence of the multitude spoke a deeper feeling than the loudest 'huzzas' could have expressed."

Much deeper, never again experienced in this world by R. E. Lee, he had "heard," he had "seen" into Eternity. He had witnessed ethereal in the silence of God's children in this world. "Silence tells us secretly everything" is as true as science tells us. R. E. Lee—rational mathematician and engineer—could not make clear sense of it. Neither rational nor irrational at best it was trans-rational—in, through, and beyond reason or rationality. At the same time in the same place it was all three states of being. Nonetheless that experience made a difference in the last months of his earthly existence.

Agnes couldn't make sense of it either. *Father must be really happy. There's no noise to disturb him. They did not drive him to distraction.* Remaining silent way past the steamer's departure, she did not speak to anyone else on the boat. *I feel better, too.*

Andrew Lowe, their new travel guide, only guessed; he didn't have any intellectual category in which to pigeonhole the experience. *Lee is a popular hero.* He never thought of "tragic hero," and probably never thought of Job, thereby missing the "patience of Job." R. E. Lee's patience, also.

Given the alternating capture and occupation of Jacksonville during the late war by Union troops then Confederate forces then again Union forces with multiple black soldiers occupying the town for four years, some Rebellion sentiment in the locale provided a civil unity. Since the "stick togetherness" of community interest was not virulently Confederate, an unruffled feeling may have influenced the quietude of the crowd when Lee was there. Such an answer may be too modern though, too rationalizing to explain what happened with that unique crowd. How does one explain silence? How does one explain humanness? How does one explain respect? Worthiness? How does one explain a person like Lee who had put on Job's mantle?

Deck yourself now with majesty and excellency, array yourself with glory and beauty; cast abroad the rage of your wrath; behold everyone that is proud and abase him; look on everyone that is proud and bring him low; hide them in the dust forever. Then I will confess unto you that your own right hand can save you!

Such an experience had not happened before on Lee's trip for healing. But heal it did, although it did not cure him of physical maladies.

It served as a balm, a balm in Gilead without any unguent or salve applied to his person, or even thought of.

Telling tales out of school, it did not happen again on his later trip northward back to Virginia by a different route through Georgia, South Carolina, North Carolina, and homeward bound for Lexington and Washington College for what would be only one more academic year.

It remained, however, a lodestar of his life, in daylight, in the shadowy night.

CHAPTER 23

At last, colorful Florida

The event/non-event at Jacksonville so intrigued folks, the authorities wanted the Lee party to remain, at least overnight. But true to his nature if he had created a schedule of any sort then he was duty bound to keep to his plan. Over and above that fact there was a former comrade-in-arms, a citrus grower whom Lee planned to visit in Palatka drawing him to discover more of the Sunshine State.

Palatka had a fascinating history due chiefly to its name. Lee's interest piqued, it galvanized him to inquire of various sources. He would not miss going farther into Florida for its novelty as well as his desired physical health recovery.

Lee discovered, by asking questions about the Indians of the area, they contrasted with what he knew firsthand of Indians in the American Southwest when he had served in the Federal Army. While a commander in the 2nd U.S. Cavalry—with two squadrons of troopers at Camp Cooper on the Comanche Reservation along the Brazos River in Texas—his command had been tasked to round up the ever mobile Comanches. They'd break out of the reservation, melt away into the hills, caves, and canyons populated with rattlesnakes... and wolves. He wanted to know about the sedentary Timucuan Indians of Palatka, Florida: *Were they like the Comanches?*

Palatka was on the banks of the Saint John's River about sixty miles south of Jacksonville, but a trip by boat took considerably longer than by carriage. An ancient and fairly docile tribe of aboriginals, the Timucuans were renowned cattle herders.

The word "Palatka" meant "crossing," describing the place where Timucuans crossed their cattle through and over the river at shallow spots. The aboriginals were an intelligent people who took advantage of the year-round abundant green pastures of vine-like grasses. They didn't have to work strenuously driving cattle, who were intelligent enough to realize they were going to satisfactory places to eat and laze, and eat again. It was a symbiotic relationship between human and animal, pleasing both species.

On the waterway to Palatka the Lee trio was much impressed with landscapes that suggested peace and repose. The elder Lee dozed more deeply than in most hotel rooms and all the time on the noisy steamer *Nick King*.

Several times when her father awakened, Wiggie sang to him, slightly changing "Brahms' Lullaby":

Lullaby, and good sleep, the sun sinks deep;
Now may its golden beams, fill you with dreams.
Close your eyes, and rest,
May these hours be blessed,
Till the sky's bright with dawn,
And you wake with a yawn.

One time the old man said to his daughter he thought he heard his mother Ann singing, which brought copious tears to his eyes. He couldn't determine whether he was asleep or awake when it happened. All he could do was wipe the moisture and listen, listen for echoes. A mother's lullabies last a lifetime.

Agnes wondered what had happened but was sensitive not to carry out an inquest, and returned to humming. He closed his eyes, yielded to reveries of his mother and slept the sleep of childhood.

Shortly after he woke it was time to go to a local hotel for a night's rest, which their new traveling guide Andrew Lowe had engaged when the steamer *Nick King* docked overnight. As well Lowe had sent a note to Lee's friend and former comrade stating Lee was now close by.

In the morning Lee's Chief of Commissary of the Army of Northern Virginia, R. G. Cole, greeted him and ushered the Lee party to his plantation. It was a typical Florida day, warm, comforting, and one that took the edge off the long inland voyage of the previous day.

The old president insisted on walking among the orange groves and taking in the colorful fruit, ranging from green to pale yellow to vivid orange when mature. It was a delight to his eye and tasteful to tongue, eating citrus for the first time right from the branch. He made much ado about the full tang of the fruit while soaking up in a handkerchief the excess juice he had splattered on his clothing in his eagerness to taste.

Former colonel Cole asked, "Would you like to taste, or just see, other kinds of citrus grown in Florida?"

He knew what the answer would be and led the party to the south side of a processing barn, the sunniest, therefore warmest side. There grew a few other citrus trees of varying greenery and foliage.

"On the left are lemon trees," Cole said, which the Lee party easily discerned by the bright yellow color. "They grow in groves south of here, on the other side of the Peace River which is about halfway down the peninsula, whose waters ultimately run into the Gulf of Mexico to the west. During the war, the Peace River divided Northern forces on the south side from Southern forces on the north side, much as at Gettysburg where our Southern forces attacked from the north and the Northern forces defended from the south," Cole added.

That quip caught Lee off guard, stinging him with twitches and spasms. The old man stopped abruptly, stood silent then instantly braced himself on Andrew Lowe for a time until he could steady himself again.

Lowe seemed surprised and could sense shivers coursing through his old commander's body. He was gentleman enough to give no indication of his former commander's fettle.

Of course the others noted Lee's reaction, and Cole, to redeem himself promptly pointed to the single lime tree, with small pale green fruit. "Limes grow farther south, even out the 100-mile long Florida Keys where they are much prized."

Given the present circumstance of Lee's condition, no one was much interested.

Cole forced his luck a bit and pointed to two trees, still on the sunny side of the barn. "These are grapefruit trees with large fruit, often a spotted yellow but much larger than lemons."

I'll tell Cole he shouldn't take offense at my reaction to his Gettysburg remark. He couldn't know my loathing of battle talk about the late war. With dispatch he turned to Cole and repeated aloud the sentiment, thereby putting the others at ease.

The *Nick King* departed that night in the wee hours—3:00 A.M. It headed back to Savannah, leaving behind the Cumberland Island grave, the Palatka Indian crossing, and Cole's assorted citrus fruits and wide ranging stories.

Agnes told her father, "You beamed beneath your beard from ear to ear whenever our host talked of the colorful Florida fruit."

"Cole raised but God gave," announced the old man.

During an extended quiet period from Palatka northward, Captain Bell told a story the older Lee had never heard. The situation occurred the first year of the war, according to Bell, when a Georgia farmer-businessman contacted President Davis of the Confederate States indicating there were enough swine in southern Georgia and cattle in northern Florida to feed all the South's armies for two years if a railroad would be built to transport them to central Virginia for allocation.

R. E. Lee's heart sank as if the *Nick King* were sinking. He speedily questioned Captain Bell who could not give more, nor specific, information. Primarily Lee remembered agonizing over his army in 1865, having to surrender because his troopers were starving.

President Jefferson Davis had spiked the idea forthwith including its good points. First there wasn't Southern industrial production available in 1862 to make 700 to 1,000 miles of trackage for a railroad. Even if there were iron mines to provide ore, there were so very few factories that could build locomotives (only three engines were actually built during the war in Southern factories). As well livestock cars to transport cattle and swine were non-existent, somehow they would have had to be built. Countless bridges as well would have taken more steel from war needs. The plan was no way practical. Jeff Davis scotched the idea.

Furthermore, at the beginning of the war there wasn't money to pay for the project. And there never was enough money to do so. The only central governmental agency that showed a profit during the war for the South was the Confederate Post Office. But it would have had to print millions of ten-cent stamps to pay for the project—and there wasn't enough animal hide glue in all the South to coat those stamps. Chances are no one could have found farmers who would kill horses or cattle to make animal hide glue because of a cockamamie scheme.

But for extended moments R. E. Lee did think, *What if?*

Then without losing a stroke he discerned such questioning after the fact can make people emotionally ill. He said so to the steamer's Captain Bell, thereby relieving both Bell and himself from further ado.

The *Nick King* chugged slowly northward leaving a repose he'd not forget.

CHAPTER 24

With the Savannah MacKays

Back again in Savannah, the Lees were treated ever so kindly, especially by the loving family of his bosom West Point comrade, "Jack" MacKay. The two MacKay sisters were visiting the homestead for Spring housecleaning. Lee and Agnes stayed with them overnight and had a trying time, for different reasons.

The elder sister talked at length with the elder Lee because they were the same age, born in 1807. She was Mary Cowper MacKay Elliott, wife of a physician and mother of another, causing Lee to ask questions about his physical problems and search for something his own physicians may not have informed him concerning his health; the information gained was of little avail though.

Despite that fact, interesting conversations ensued about lifespan, physical being, welfare and longevity. Which of the two valued the other more was difficult to ascertain, for they, like other MacKays, were interesting conversationalists.

The somewhat younger sister, Catherine MacKay, never married. She didn't mind being called "Old Maid" since she provided for a young guest, the orphan child of a dear friend. And the youngster kept repeating, "Old Maid. Old Maid. Maid Old," to the discomfort of each of the adults other than Catherine herself. Catherine was patient, quite forbearing in order to keep the youngster in the MacKay firmament.

The child, perhaps nine or ten years of age, was a package. A bundle of mischief and likeability wrapped together apparently topsy-turvy or higgledy-piggledy, the youngster was as close to a perpetual motion machine as one could imagine. Constantly moving from chair to chair, lap to lap, room to room, person to person—and a mouth that moved still more. She pranced, not walked, and PDQ gave a nickname to each adult, relishing in doing so. She somehow understood at an early age that naming another person gives a sort of control or ascendancy. And control meant power, power a child normally does not have.

The child—not to be named—went about the MacKay home singing, "Hairy Monkey, Scary Monkey, Hairy Scary," for bearded Lee.

Knowing he should not do so, Lee resented both the remarks and the repeated prancing. In fact he did not simply dislike the girl but resented that she was more often than not the center of attention. "Youngsters need to be taught manners," he retorted and turned away from the child, who trailed him droning a tune like a bee buzzing around a bush. The old man thought of a paddle.

"Come on, Bobbie, she's wet behind the ears," opined Mary Elliott, Lee's age.

The youngster then turned on her: "Mary Contrary, Contrary Mary, Quite Contrary," which made two adults simper and smirk.

This distressed Mrs. Elliott since she had tried to side with the youngster.

Then the young one turned on Wiggie, having heard the elder Lee address his daughter Agnes with that byname. "Wiggie go piggie; tee legged, tie legged, bow legged Wiggie."

"The lilt was amusing but the content unfriendly," her adult consort, Catherine, replied. "You'll hurt people by making fun of bow legs."

"Cathy go bathy, tee legged, tie legged, bow legged Cathy," snapped back the youngster.

Without announcement Lee got up from his chair and headed to the bedroom assigned him, brooding to himself. *I wonder whether or not we'll meet such spite again homeward. If so, I'll leave, walk out.*

Agnes followed suit though she needed to be directed to her sleeping quarters.

Both MacKay sisters drooped their heads in dismay. No one bid "Goodnight."

The youngster asked, "What's wwwrr-ong? Wadda I say?"

"Too much," indicated Mary MacKay Elliott. "Way too much."

The next day was bright at six o'clock in the morning. The Lees ate breakfast with the MacKay sisters, engaging in hushed conversation so as not to awaken the youngster.

The sisters had a fine time together in the kitchen, and prepared their mother's family recipe of mush and milk—corn meal boiled in milk from cows or goats then served with goats' milk. Following breakfast porridge, the guests were treated to thick slices of bacon and corn pone bread with blackstrap molasses. As a side dish each received a large plate with two goose eggs fried easy-over which completely covered their plates. Agnes had never eaten fried goose eggs but the sisters remembered that Bobbie Lee had liked them, way back decades before.

Sister Catherine asked the elder Lee if he remembered their mother, Eliza Anne McQueen MacKay.

"I certainly do," he replied. "This was the kind of breakfast she prepared for Jack and me many times back in '29 and '30."

The sisters teared up. They thanked him for remembering and acknowledging their beloved brother and mother.

"No, no. I thank you," he replied.

Agnes repeated the same words. She rose from the table and kissed each lady. Three ladies then teared up. Tears tell much; they water human body and human soul to keep both from being scorched and wilted: a dried out, prune faced, empty being. A good cry, for example, often saves a marriage.

After last cups of coffee, juiced up, strengthened with chicory included in Southern style, father and daughter made a lickety-split departure before the youngster could enter their new day.

They were off for the railroad station in a cab, a different kind of transport with space for six or eight passengers and drawn by two horses, not one mule. They left trailing heart-felt, "God be with you till we meet again," restated in turn by the sisters, the last time they would ever see one another.

Wiggie pursed her lips and gave forth a lively whistle with a merry intent. *I'm skipping along mentally, to get away from that imp. It's such a minor victory it doesn't deserve a big hurrah of any sort so I'll whistle instead.*

That minor encounter with the youngster was the single bad experience they had coming to or leaving Savannah both times. The elder Lee actually shook his shoes when he stepped off the MacKay property. No one noticed his act of rejecting the youngster's impolite words; he felt both good and bad about his action. He never did remember her name. Why would he want to?

At the railroad station there wasn't a farewell crowd, large or vocal. There were, however, groups of people who recognized and bid them farewell. It was ever so agreeable to be free of much-ado-about-nothing farewells. It was peaceful; he was grateful. Wiggie felt the same, smiled broadly, and waved goodbye to no one in particular with both arms swishing through the air. R. E. Lee doffed his hat and laughed. Laughed at himself!

The experiences in Savannah the first time and at several places in Florida contrasted vividly with the first leg of the trip southward from Lexington *et al* by railroad, persuaded Lee to take a different route homeward. Thus they would travel the coast line proximate to the Atlantic Ocean north from Georgia through South Carolina then North Carolina and into Tidewater Virginia.

Lee knew they were taking a chance, particularly because there wasn't a "tour guide" as James Corley and Andrew Lowe had been to direct this venture. Both had interceded for them in many ways, protecting him in particular along the way, motivated by love, only love. Both knew travel was mildly risky since Lee and his daughter were struggling with illnesses. Each "tour guide" realized he had done a human kindness; life-long each felt he had been blessed to be in the presence of the old man. Agnes was a lovely bonus.

She didn't much like the choice of a different route homeward. Notably because she had not been consulted. She stood rigid when her father told her of the new plan. Yet she didn't want to upset him so stood silent, fuming slightly. She didn't want to upset herself either; her own physical condition was weakening though slower than her father's. *There won't be a James Corley to console us.*

Two strikes against R. E. Lee already as they headed homeward: the nasty youngster in lovely Savannah's MacKay homestead; and to boot, Agnes' non-involvement in decision making which crept over him like a noxious odor in the cab going to the station when she said not a word to him. Not a mutter, nor protestation. He knew something was wrong. It took him a while. Maleness and old age can be delimiting factors.

"Possibly I made a poor choice," he noted. Then not a word more.

Nor a word in the railroad car, either, for hours traveling from Savannah.

Silence was just as well, thought Eleanor Agnes comfortingly.

CHAPTER 25

Flowers, everywhere flowers

The mid-Spring days of the trip through the northeast corner of Georgia into the Carolinas were delightful with flowers, their colors and pungency, their numbers and fragrances, in myriad places. Agnes thrilled effortlessly. R. E. Lee also was in an enthusiastic state of mind amidst such delight because he was basically pain free; it helped Wiggie who was alive with joy, at least for each day-by-day junket.

That area of the Southland in mid-Spring 1870 looked as though the world was only hours from first creation... God's recreation. Out of nothing—out of no thing—except possibly Love. Father Lee imagined, *Such splendor must have given rise to the ideal of Beauty so important to us human beings.* He visualized vast areas of flowers covering Creation, not only Earth but the moon, the planets, even the stars. His state of mind expanded vastly within him until he saw splendor increasing around every tree, every bush, every rock, every stream until he was overwhelmed with beauty all around.

The mature man thought he was in the "Garden of Eden West."

A violet by a mossy stone
Half hidden from the eye!
Fair as a star when only one
Is shining in the sky.

He so astounded himself he had to pause: pause scrutinizing, pause thinking, pause appreciating, nearly pause breathing. He became overwhelmed with splendor. He dreamed in the daylight that beauty was all around, glory above, and God within. Then... thought it simply a dream. A daydream at that!

The latter thought quivered, wobbled him side to side. He couldn't possibly assume that he was adopted into Deity, one with the Eternal already. No, it would be a pantheistic thought, primitive and unchristian. He couldn't allow such an idea because it contrasted with the Judeo-Christian ethic of duty, always duty that was his life's style *in toto*.

R. E. Lee was so close to a spiritual mystery it pained him, yet he knew not why. He would not allow himself the spiritual luxury of the Christian pilgrim's song through these present fair lands of Paradise here and now wherein Life and Love and God are veritably One. For him, Beulah Land, ultimate reality, the Kingdom of God remained a goal not a fact. He was living for victory, missing the grandeur that "the well-lived life is Beauty" already revealed.

All around him the beautiful flowers of Spring bloomed, coloring more than earth. The elderly one thought of a childhood ditty his mother Anne Hill Carter Lee had sung for him, then his wife, Mary Custis Lee, sang to their children:

How many kinds of sweet flowers grow
In an English country garden?
I'll tell you now of some that I know
Those I miss you'll surely pardon.

Mothers Lee would rattle off a baker's dozen, changing kinds from time to time: roses, tulips, orchids, lilies, daffodils, marigolds, lotus, dahlias, sunflowers, gladioli, carnations, chrysanthemums, camellia. The mothers changed the order sometimes, or added other kinds and subtracted usual ones. In his present rail travels northward through the South the old man assured himself he saw all of those flowers each day, and if not the actual ones, then others as bright and beautiful.

In the meantime his concept of mathematical precision as a trained military engineer interfered with a creator's accomplishment of spiritual faith that Life and Love and God are One, here *and* now, from the beginning, to the future *fait accompli*.

Agnes was exuberant, giving the impression of being incapable of calm. She began to whistle. Her father was caught off guard, remembered vaguely that her brothers had mocked such efforts when she was young. Now she was whistling Beethoven's "Ode to Joy," or at least the easy parts. Then she began to hum. Then began to sing softly what she remembered. Then fairly got loud about abiding friendship in the words of the poet Friedrich Schiller the librettist:

Friends, no more of these sounds!
Let us sing more cheerful songs,
More songs full of joy! Joy! Joy!
Joy, bright spark of divinity,
Fire-inspired we tread within thy sanctuary.

Thy magic power re-unites
All that custom has divided,
All men become brothers:
Whoever has created
An abiding friendship,
Or has won a true and loving wife,
All who can call at least one soul theirs,
Join our song of praise.

R. E. Lee was flabbergasted. His daughter Wiggie sang as if she knew faith was an accomplished fact not a process, salvation a successfully fulfilled fact, eternity a present consummation. Flabbergasted was a weak expression for his amazement; better, he experienced an implosion as one of the trains entering a tunnel on their trip, an implosion of sound and darkness and coolness that caught him unawares.

In astonishment R. E. Lee tapped his feet in front where he was seated, impressed by his daughter's singing. She went over to him, took his hands as if inviting him to dance with her. Of course dancing would have been much too much for his physical condition so he shook his head in the negative. Instead he extended his left arm, orbited it around and around indicating she should trip the light fantastic. At that point they devolved into laughter together. "Tears and laughter" are a mighty poultice of warmth and medication to heal the human spirit, the human mind, the human heart.

Eleanor Agnes cracked up so close-packed she had to plop down beside her father, causing him to dissolve into mirth, too. The young woman had not heard that form of enjoyment from him since childhood when he often played with her and her siblings at their games and actions... when he was home from military service. She took pleasure in his quiet humor now, in the present moment.

One time, at a rural rail stop at a water tower, cow herders in the area rounding up cows for afternoon milking and heifers for feeding time heard sounds from Agnes' lips who repeated moo-ing as if making echoes. As far as any human being knows the herders didn't know Ludwig van Beethoven's music nor Friedrich Schiller's text, but they appeared to make a rejoinder to her efforts.

Wiggie was taken aback soon realizing she was reading too much into the animals' sounds. She did think they were joyful creatures in their actions, discovering a magic power beautiful in its own way. "Someday they'll discover abiding friendships," she told her father. He looked askance, not disapprovingly, but wondering if it would be so for her.

Secretly R. E. Lee wished he had not lost the deep baritone voice he one time had. Singing was one of the things he liked about West Point when he was a cadet and later as Superintendent; in fact it may have been the only thing as Superintendent he cared for deeply, to build *esprit de corps*. Later in life he noted that he did not think one could have an army without music, both singing and playing. It bonds men more than yells or coarse curses, and when an enemy hears troops singing or playing music it tells the enemy what they are going to attempt doing is to destroy something deeply human.

Recalling that feeling, Lee did doff his hat to the two boys and two young men herding cattle, though they didn't know what that gesture meant. The young men waved back, and the boys raised their bamboo cattle control poles to salute the stranger watching them.

That evening Lee wrote home to wife Mary and bemoaned his sorry state—not to be able to sing when the whole universe awaits human participation. *"All life gathers where there is song. All things respond to the sound of rejoicing,"* he wrote, planting a kiss after his signature: R. E. Lee.

And then he drew a lily of the valley on the back of the envelope with white showing through the coral bells, and imagined he could hear them ring in his head. He kissed the envelope, too.

Wiggie asked, "What are you doing, Papa?"

He looked surprised, delaying his response to allow her to question her own question.

Daughter Agnes presently put two and two together... and got five... which is what love does, it adds value to everything. "Oh, you're writing home, a love letter."

"Yes and no," he replied quietly. "Yes and no." Pointedly, in a direct and unambiguous way he asserted, "I'm writing to my bride."

Agnes was open-mouthed. Never had she thought of her parents as bride and groom, nor as young lovers. Or that love stays young because people harbor it to last a lifetime.

Agnes wanted to say, *I'll receive it from my groom.* However she couldn't get past it to another thought, *How will it get past mother's wheelchair where she is stuck every day? Sometimes nights, too?* And then Agnes wept for what she had missed in her parents' lives as well as what she was missing in her own.

The flowers around them appeared to wilt. Curious, really, since the weather was beautiful and not oppressive or uncomfortable.

Father's love hasn't wilted! It really hasn't, even in old age. I'd love to have that love in my life now. Maybe someday it'll be so. Someday.

CHAPTER 26

Life is antonymous... thankfully

Sometimes—no, often—life is antonymous. It runs this way and that, and then it turns another way. Sometimes it runs the way we want it to go; sometimes the opposite. Sooner or later it doesn't run at all but drags on from minute to days, weeks to years, months to decades then millennia. You know the drill.

Some antonymous conditions are *graduated* in intermediate steps from one extreme to the other such as empty to three-quarters to full, intelligent to dull to stupid, bright daylight to evening darkness... covering all the ground, so to speak, from rock to sand to loam.

Different antonymous conditions are *complementary* but without a middle ground, such as forgotten or remembered, input or output, married or single. No middle ground, either yea or nay, no maybe.

Fewer times human antonymous conditions are *relational* such as buyer and seller, employer and employee, parent and child. Common ground whereon both conditions exist but neither as opposites or gradations.

R. E. Lee encountered all those conditions when he and daughter Agnes traveled beyond the wonder of Savannah—and the nastiness of the un-named youngster with the quick tongue but sluggish conscience at the MacKay home. Her lack of manners troubled Lee for quite some time, and caused him to feel children should be seen not heard.

It took him several days to experience the impressively beautiful life beyond poor manners and thoughtless relationships as well as railroad conditions throughout Dixie. The latter had been loud, sometimes wild, spontaneous celebrations around him. As well the splendid silence in Jacksonville and whatever caused it. All that splendor was supplemented joyfully later with multicolored trees in citrus groves... their hues, shades, or tints of green, orange, and yellow fruit... Lee's appetite was fixated on citrus fruit. Not on Creole spices though.

Overwhelmingly, the trip north through South Carolina and North Carolina was accentuated with positive meetings on occasions such as railroad stops, overnight accommodations, and well-nigh countless gatherings with former comrades-in-arms. Multiple homes were open to him and Agnes, as if they were family visiting from afar.

He hadn't remembered how amiable veterans are after the fire, smoke, shooting, wounding, killing are over... how peace bonds brothers as solidly as war, but with greater rewards.

And the memories, oh, the precious memories of companionship and valor, of manhood and spirituality when life is on the line to do one's duty: possibly sacrificing one's life for a greater good; *"Greater love hath no man than this, that a man lay down his life for his friends."*

That noble duty is so much more human than a line of work or business, or a line of scrimmage, or lining one's pockets with money. Dying at work, expiring during play or being wealthy adds exactly what to the human species?

R. E. Lee was happy to be with veterans for they are alive as he was alive. And together, *"bound in the bundle of life"* in a spiritual sense they keep alive their comrades who have marshalled at heaven's portals. As well abundantly, all the millions they saved by doing their duty. *The many forget the few more than the few forget the many,* was Lee's tribute and prayer for his veterans.

Very little, therefore, was obnoxious as had happened on the southward leg of their trip. Even so, several times he did feel spasms of sorrow for fathers and brothers and uncles and cousins in graves, not well enough remembered merely five years after the fratricidal conflict.

Lee did say on two occasions when meeting with former comrades, "Act with a determination not to be turned aside by thoughts of the past and fears of the future," to applause of his veterans. "The one past you and I had was inadequate. The two ways to your and my futures are either to live without fear or to live repeating that inadequate past." He appreciated the applause. "For defeat does not dim duty, dedication, honor, and virtue." He was inclined to repeat this position at meeting after meeting with former comrades-in-arms. Not because of the applause but because defeat is not bitter if one does not swallow it but rises above loss with love for those lost. Defeat has no power to defeat love.

These occasions experienced momentary hushes until the message sank in. Then applause. At one venue there had been a sustained ovation at a certain point in his talk where Lee picked up his hat from the table as if to wear it, studying it then put it on but quickly doffed it... and managed a broad smile that made his beard look shiny. Everyone laughed; R. E. Lee knew a good thing when it happened, so ended his talk right then—to heartier laughter, and clapping and foot stomping.

Wiggie was mildly surprised, approached him, and hugged and kissed the old man to his delight. The crowd approved with another round of applause, harder stomping while several youngsters called out, "More. More," as if at a wedding party.

At another place Eleanor Agnes did cheer him up, sensing he was tired or morose. "This is such a charming vacation, Father. Maybe we should have come this way on our trip southward from Lexington."

"True," he declared, "and we would have missed the tribulations and trials of travel. Yet experiencing these courteous, gracious meetings convinces me there are other dimensions of human encounter than the negative reactions of dislike, gloom. I'm tired; yes, but no more than the first week. I still want to go home, Wiggie; don't forget, please.

"Although I've encountered cloudy times, I've also seen, to an extent, bright times in and after Savannah, and Captain Bell of the *Nick King*, and Mazie his wife and her interesting cooking.

And I've drunk the fresh ambrosia of the gods from the orange groves. I've seen both sides, Wig.

"The first part of the trip disarranged things. Maybe arranged them in an order I did not comprehend. I'm not sure. It did set us up for all these Carolinians we've met recently. Maybe we were whipped into shape for these friendly... glorious... days. What do you think, Wig?"

"Oh, I haven't evaluated yet, Papa. I've been so busy meeting people, enjoying people, lovin' how deep their Southern drawl is, and amazed by their cooking. I feel better than I have the whole trip," she revealed, smiling brightly.

Her father continued, "For my part I didn't recall I had so many friends down here. I knew about former comrades but I forgot numerous distant relatives. There are Lees all over the place."

"Now, now, Father, you've understated the facts. You've named just about every pretty Southern woman a cousin. No wonder you can't recall."

"Possibly. No, probably so, Agnes. But it's your mother Mary who has my heart. And always had. Always had. We'll call it even, Wiggie. Right?"

Eleanor Agnes simply rocked her head side to side.

The old one didn't pay attention.

There was, however, an unpleasant encounter at one railroad stop in South Carolina. A middle-aged man, who would not identify himself by name or location approached, declaring that there were blunders at the victory at Fredericksburg, Virginia, and wanted to know who was to blame. All the old ex-general could remember was the horror of war at that victory and asked the man, "Why open wartime's memory rather than grow with the new South?"

Lee received a sharp answer. "Because we won many victories yet lost the war."

To Lee that answer seemed terribly inadequate. "War is not like a sporting game where you keep a cumulative account and the higher score wins. It is a deadly event where one defeat at a strategic place and a crucial moment determines the victor. It's not a ball game. Real men and real boys die; it's a lethal venture. Far more detrimental than beneficial."

He had met such gloomy dissent a few times post-war and had refused to argue. This episode seemed more rude, even nasty, possibly because it was in striking contrast to the predominantly encouraging outlook he found many places on the trip in and after Florida. He realized there were pockets of virulent opposition to the Northern victory all over Dixieland who wanted to fight again—and grasped the reality the South would lose another time with far more awful repercussions and be more markedly impaired than at present.

Lee was bowled over that the unknown man did not accept as reliable evaluation the South would fail again. Sometimes failure likes failing, then one can bitch since bitching is a blunderbuss weapon spraying shot all over the place, seemingly hitting some error or truth to satisfy only the shooter.

But failure also prepares one for success another time if one studies failure honestly. If, on the other hand, one rationalizes—justifies—the causes for failure it generates perverse "reasons," setting one up for more future failures.

In reality, the majority of people enjoyed or purposely helped entertain him and Agnes. And, when traveling to meet friends of friends who were escorting them from place to place, Lee was ordinarily left in thought. This time he reflected openly that they should count their blessings.

That notion kindled the same response in Wiggie who sang in tranquil tones:

God moves in a mysterious way his wonders to perform;
He plants his footsteps in the sea and rides upon the storm.
Blind unbelief is sure to err, and scan his work in vain;
God is his own interpreter and he will make it plain.

One of the grandest stops on their homeward excursion was Charleston, South Carolina, since it had been a city which suffered much destruction in the Rebellion and was on a citizen-determined rebuilding program, a community effort of the highest magnitude. *The Charleston Courier* was insightful in describing Lee's presence:

Old and young, the gray beards and sages of the country, the noble, pure, honorable, poor and wealthy, with hardly an exception, were present, and glad to do him honor. Stately dames of the old school, grandmothers of seventy, and a long train of granddaughters, all flocked around the noble old chief, glad of a smile, of a shake of the hand; and happy was the girl of twelve, or fourteen, who carried away on her lips the parting kiss of the grand old soldier.

If their many encouraging engagements had happened only in South Carolina, Robert Lee would have been suspicious and Agnes disenchanted. It would have been a conspiracy unworthy of even a defeated people. One might think that those citizens of the Palmetto State would have deserved defeat for starting the war, but they were citizens of a new state of mind worthy of their heritage and of the re-formed United States.

When the same adventures happened again and again as the Lees traveled homeward through North Carolina, the elder felt that his emphasis back at Washington College was 100% correct and noted: "Those young men are to put aside defeat, eliminate animosity for the North, and make their education work for them in a newly constituted nation." There was much more agreement with his sentiments measured by applause than the mute or tight-lipped reaction evident from diehard Rebels. Each chance he had when he mentioned his admonition to his students it was well received by the very large majority of Southern white male students who wanted to be Lee-like.

Times came when it was Wiggie's turn to boost her father's position. She clapped and clapped. On three occasions she thumped her father on his back in approval of his statements, to the surprise of the different crowds, stupefaction of some but familial wonderment of the old man himself. Whether because of swaying and seesawing actions of Eleanor Agnes a few but far between opposers declared she was some kind of fanatic, religious dogmatist, or just a weird duck out of line.

She really was having a good time—Savannah, southward of Savannah, back to Savannah, north of Savannah, Savannah through the Carolinas. Savannah was in Agnes' heart.

Each such event caused her to repeat, "The further north we go the thicker the Southern drawl becomes," and then laugh, especially while her father clapped in approval. It could have been that both father and daughter were in a "revival" or religious camp meeting mode. Yea or nay, both were in highly positive states of mind. And because it was small-scale exuberance and short-lived, no one was seriously offended. The question for them was, "Is it successful in rallying result for reconciliation of South and North?"

After one of those diminutive merriments the elder Lee asked, "How do you think the southern section of Virginia will be about meeting us, Agnes? Will the drawl get thicker?"

"Oh I hope not, Papa, but I'm not counting on it. Particularly with your sons, my two brothers living there. They, too, fought for the Confederacy, and that fact alone may make a big difference."

The old man reflected, puzzling how those sons may have— or not—overcome defeat and emerged American again. "I'm certain they both know what they're doing with their lives... drawl or not. They're not dummies or night-riders, Eleanor Agnes."

The future for his sons looked clear for R. E. Lee. He slumbered after such Carolina encounters, not just forty winks. Unbroken slumber typified a settling of emotions he did not readily diagnose, nor need to. He even enjoyed sleeping on train seats in this portion of his journey.

Wiggie never commented about her sleep after such events. Anyhow, she snored. Her father paid no heed.

The senior Lee did take on a task he needed to know because it had bothered him on the southward leg of his trip. Friend Corley had discovered that telegraphers had passed on from station to station that he was on the train, causing crowds to gather. The actual process, however, was unclear.

Lee decided to investigate. At the last railroad stop beyond Savannah in Georgia during the extended transfer to another railroad company heading northward to Virginia there was time to do so. He sought out the stationmaster who was also the landline telegrapher.

Lee interrogated the man so thoroughly he disturbed himself. He then expressed regretfully, "I'm sorry I'm pushing you but I don't know when the transfer to the next railroad will happen or be finished." It was a weak apology satisfying himself more than the stationmaster.

As so often happens in such cases the stationmaster replied, "That all right, I understand," to make a customer feel good about himself or herself.

Then the railroader went into a lengthy discussion of railroad telegraphy, noted that railroads all over the country use Railroad Morse Code, also called American Morse Code, over the thousands of miles across the continent. Also, he said something about how helpful it is and makes for safety that railroaders appreciate. Then he asked Lee if he wanted to see a demonstration. Of course Lee did; the stationmaster was happy to impress, and proud that he could serve the former general.

The man then moved to the apparatus with Lee in tow, sat down and explained about the Edison electric key. He began tapping electric impulses. Those impulses would be received by someone somewhere along the railroad line. Another telegrapher using another Edison product, would receive the impulses on a machine at the other place on the railroad line. The second telegrapher—with keen hearing—cleverly would hear the dots and dashes as alphabet letters forming words and write them on a paper pad. Or, would have the machine print the dot and dash sounds, called dits and daws, on a paper tape receiver using the form of Railroad Morse Code.

The telegraphing started with what seemed irritating noise. The sounds originated from a metal key point against a metal plate, generating an electric spark at the point of contact. The telegrapher's finger pushed a "key" down, released it, and then pushed down various times and different lengths of contact times. Words seemed to appear miraculously out of the sounds representing English language.

The stationmaster then telegraphed a message to another stationmaster up the line: where father and daughter would be heading:

daw daw dit dit—dit dit dit dit dawdaw dit dit daw dit

daw daw dit dit dit dit ___ dit daw dit ___ dit--dit dit ___ dit_
   daw dit dit ___dit dit ___ dit dit dit dit _ _ dawdaw dit dit
   dit dit dit dit dit did dit ___ dit dit dit daw dit dit--dit dit
   dit dit-dit dit ___

daw daw dit dit daw dit dit dit daw dawdaw dit ___

dit dit dit dit dit daw dawdaw dit daw dit dit_

daw daw dit dit daw dit____ dit—dit dit___dit___daaawww dit
   dit___

dit dit daw dit___ daw daw dit dit—dit dit___

dit—dit dit daw dit dit daw dit dit dit dit dit—dit dit___

daw daw daw dit

Lee remained annoyed by the staccato sounds and the speed with which the telegrapher audibly spewed out the message. He covered his vexation by saying, "Well. Well," which the stationmaster assumed meant approval.

"We'll have to wait a couple of minutes until Fred answers," he said. "A recipient has to read the print-out on the ticker tape machine or else if he is proficient—that is, very expert—he listens to the dits and daws, and from them forms letters mentally of the alphabet and mentally re-forms them into words and scribes them on a piece of paper for quick message transferal."

"What did you write to him?" asked Lee, not really interested in the procedure.

"Just that you were in the station and interested in how the Railroad Morse Code and apparatus of the system works."

"Thank you. I understand somewhat; my head is jostled a bit though."

A return message came crackling through a moment later in Railroad Morse Code.

dit dit dit dit daw dit daw dit dit___

dit dit dit dit dit dit daw daw ___

dit dit dit dit dit—dit daw daw dit ___ dit dit dit dit daw dit
   dit___

dit dit dit dit ___ dit___ dit daw daw ___ dit daw___ dit dit dit
   ___ dit daw___

dit daw dit dit daw dit dit daaawww dit dit daw dit--dit dit
  dit__
daw daw daw dit__dit dit dit dit dit __
dit dit dit dit dit daw dit—dit dit dit—dit dit dit daw dit
daw dit dit dit dit—dit dit dit daw dit dit__ dit dit daw dit
  dit__
dit dit daw dit__dit dit—dit dit daw dit dit dit dit dit dit
  dit__
DIT DIT DIT DIT DIT__ DIT DIT DIT DIT DIT DAW
DIT—DIT DIT DIT—DIT DIT DIT DAW DIT DAW DIT DIT
DIT DIT—DIT DIT DIT DAW DIT DIT __
DAW DAW DAW DIT

Lee was anxious to know what the reply contained but waited until the telegrapher turned off the power and closed the apparatus. Not able to contain himself the old man finally asked his host, "What was the reply?"

The telegrapher didn't want to say much about an unofficial service so he turned to Lee, shrugged his shoulders with a quick upward thrust, twitched his head and replied, "Fred wished you good traveling." Then he turned around and left his own office pronto.

R. E. Lee wondered whether what the other telegrapher had sent was so simple. More than he knew, he was right about Fred's response.

The old college president saw the telegrapher's handwritten note. And the last section was in capital letters. It must have been significant. The old man surmised something was askance but he didn't know what it was.

The station telegrapher realized from the telegraphed text some people love their sicknesses. And perpetuate them.

Fred was one of them. He was among those who swallowed their defeat. And suffered unforgivingly anyone who accepted defeat for a better re-United States of America.

All in all the trip homeward was not only exciting but a restorative adventure. Truly a grand time for President R. E. Lee tired from traveling but motivated to begin his last year serving Washington College. Daily new experiences with eager students, challenges of guiding astute faculty better educated than he, and the genuine warmth of wife and adult children would fill his days.

In the midst of such soothing notions there popped up an experience he had not had for twenty years or so. Lee thought of Benjamin Hallowell, his next door neighbor to 607 Orinoco Street, Alexandria, Virginia. The noted Quaker schoolmaster had opened a school next door to Lee's mother's home. Young Lee was excited beyond measure. Each male, young scholar-to-be and matured popular educator roused the other, creating a tiny cell of educated and educating learners at school, then friends in the evenings face to face and heart to heart.

Hallowell motivated the lad to live the life of the intellect, of a burgeoning sage rather than success in some other endeavor. He realized the younger man had the essentials to add to the world's store of learning.

Now the recollection of Hallowell escalated in Lee's mind a certain perspective the learned master had shared with him on several occasions decades before. The deep joy of the final leg of his "health trip" back home to Lexington in 1870 was not world shaking but it was galvanizing and he thought of sharing this remembrance with his students. The idea was rather mundane but the old man knew it could help students.

Punctuation! Yes, Punctuation: those tiny marks, seemingly scratchings, in writing that nonetheless have extensive consequences. Hallowell was a stickler for such particulars of exactitude in written communication and abstract mathematics, as he noted later in recommending the youth R. E. Lee to West Point.

Pedagogue Hallowell had contended that a question mark (?) at the end of a sentence indicates a challenge. An exclamation point (!) was a flare-up, a multiplication of possibilities. A colon (:) was an opportunity to say the same thing differently. The semicolon (;) a way to embellish a story another direction. The comma (,) a pause to keep things from merging. Quotation marks (" ") and (' ') tell someone else's story. And a series of dots (...) or dashes (---) at the end of a sentence each is a means to leave open either positive or negative connotations about anything. Finally, the period (.) stops anything and everything a writer or speaker wants to state autocratically. "Be wary of the period; it can stop thinking," Hallowell would admonish the lad.

The adult Lee was amused that out of the blue he had again thought of Hallowell's understanding of punctuation. There cropped up afresh in the former general the consciousness that language is the prime and prodigious human achievement separating human beings from other natural species.

In an instant he confronted himself bleakly: he had not always used precise language enough when giving military orders. Lee shattered himself. Near to the point of collapse he thought dark, foreboding judgments about himself precipitating aloud, "Woe is me!" two times, one with a cry of despair drooping his head to his knees in anguish. His face creased in gripping frown; tepid tears percolated streamlets down through his beard as he mulled dark in misery, epic torment of the hundreds, thousands, even ten thousands slaughtered Americans because of his imprecise use of language.

Benjamin Hallowell, peaceful Quaker though he was, could not have assuaged the old man's mighty grief.

Proving what? Proving that life truly is antonymous: sometimes it runs this way, sometimes that way. Thankfully. Period.

CHAPTER 27

Home again, home again, market is done

It wasn't home at Lexington, but it was home state—Virginia. Here he had come into the world; here he would leave it. Not immediately, nor intentionally. At his advanced age of sixty-three, it registered in his mind that his father had died at sixty-two, his fraternal grandfather at fifty-eight, while his mother's grandfather died aged fifty-two. Only her father had lived to seventy... and only he knew how ill he was.

Lee would not address the situation publicly. So, weak, yes. Tired, yes. Wearing out. "I want to get home, Wiggie."

Lee and daughter detrained at Portsmouth, Virginia, after traveling in North Carolina. They planned to take a ferry across the Elizabeth River bay inlet to Norfolk where he intended they would stay the night only.

Despite their plans, fireworks filled the sky across the bay in Portsmouth where father and daughter had neither scheduled nor anticipated anything special.

Someone had pulled the same trick as on his southbound trip. A celebration, a parade, plus general pandemonium... a din of iniquity and merriment strangely combined. Lee was back home in old Virginy.

The waiting crowds were loaded with enthusiasm, some also with booze. They had read about Lee's all-conquering days traveling through North and South Carolina. Portsmouth wanted to show off his home state's appreciation for who and what he was: the best ambassador Virginia could ever offer in 1870.

Seldom was he surprised; however now he was tired of train travel, noise, smoke, sparks, bumps, and jolts.

Then it happened.

Wham bam—Whammo whammo—bam, bam, bam. BOOOMMMMM! Boomaday Boom. The sky was partially filled with fireworks; the rest of it saturated with noise.

Cannon fire sounded Portsmouth's welcome with thundering toasts. Young men of the town had "appropriated" the cannons from fire companies and made steady use every five minutes.

"What's going on?" Lee asked Agnes. "Why's this happening? It's upsetting. I don't like it."

"Itta be a hot time in the old town tonight, folks," the conductor shouted above the explosions and noisy passengers leaving the train. Lee could have thwacked him over the head with his cap but resisted.

Numerous people provided the social lubricant—alcohol, including some home-made hooch. The latter was specially bottled and labeled, shipped out of Portsmouth to Philadelphia, New York, even Boston as fitting "reward" for their winning the late war.

Agnes felt better than her father at the change of events. The clamor seemed to awaken feelings which had hung wearily around them during the lengthy trip north. Exhausted, inwardly she felt pins and needles jabbing her to find out what was next in Portsmouth. She wanted action, excitement, a change of pace; not knowing what was next complexified her. Agnes became seriously anxious even in the Old Dominion State.

At first sight everything baffled the two as they looked out from their coach upon entering the dock-side trainyard. Complicated steel trackage formed a labyrinthine web, crisscrossing as if a monstrous insect had spewed toxins into a dirty miasma that ensnared parked locomotives, gondolas, boxcars, cabooses, and piles upon piles of steel plates for spikes to hold the rails to the cross-ties creosoted with black pitch in stacks two yards high and scattered over the railyard helter-skelter.

Everything, just everything was plastered with dark gray soot from the locomotives puffing out jack-sparks and grimy smoke raining crud on everything, including their coach. The scenery, obviously, didn't help Agnes feel better. She began to think begrimed thoughts, about dirty railroad yards—and the men who worked in them.

To top it off, while the artillery was periodically blasting away, a smartly outfitted man walked to the front of the waiting crowd, seeking to greet the old man. Former Chief of Staff of Lee's Army of Northern Virginia, Walter H. Taylor presented himself with a sharp salute, and then laughing, had to dodge falling jack-sparks before embracing R. E. Lee as if a long lost relative.

Awestruck, Lee hugged even tighter. Shaking Taylor side to side in a bear hug, Lee was surprised at his own strength. His mind raced: *Here's a soul of my old life. A fine example of manhood though we disagreed strikingly from time to time. He was my best deputy. Without him I would have lost more battles.*

The old commander slipped into a reverie of route marching, consultations past, victories, failed attempts. He had to hug Taylor or he would have collapsed in wretchedness.

Walter Taylor knew wholly what Lee was feeling. He was unable to help himself; he wept in love for R. E. Lee. The old general was moved likewise in response: two old comrades who had needed one another through hell and high water.

People in the immediate vicinity stood quiet and motionless, witnessing... then savoring... the *virtus,* the power of true comrades, desiring the two *not* pull apart, wanting such friendship to last forever in this world of fleeting human ties, passing affinity, lost friendships.

The same emotion riveted Lee and Taylor spellbound. Much as David and Jonathon in ancient Israel.

Eventually all disturbances dropped away. The two chiefs and Agnes walked to the ferry to cross the Elizabeth River bay and dock at Norfolk on the opposite shore.

All the time on that farther shore, rockets, fireworks, and Roman candles burst. Everyone was so anxious to greet him that the Norfolk United Fire Company began rapidly shooting its cannon even after the ferry had docked.

As Lee stepped on solid ground the mass of people cheered so much, so loud, so long that those back on the Portsmouth shore were sure the Norfolk greeters were trying to outdo them. The rivalry became permanent for several years, much talked about but never repeated.

The next day, faithful to his Faith, R. E. Lee attended worship services. His host was a physician, William Selden—with whom he discussed his health—and a daughter, Caroline, who accompanied Lee. They walked to Christ Church, an old parish of the Anglican/Episcopal Church, dating to 1637. Later in her diary Caroline chronicled the Sunday-go-to-meeting scene:

The street was lined with adoring crowds. For [a] block before reaching Christ Church we had to almost force our way through a narrow pathway [which people] seemed to have left for him. Every [man's] hat was [held] in air, but being Sunday the homage was very quiet. I well remember he held his hat in hand all the way.

Norfolk had reason to be happy; it showed its best side to the best of men.

On separate days receptions were held for the old commander, so the Seldens held one for Lee. To his astonishment, he met another old veteran—from seventy years before. This one had been of the renowned "Old Guard" of Napoleon Bonaparte, the famous French general and emperor.

Formally designated the "Imperial Guard" (*Garde Impériale*) originally it was a small group of elite soldiers of the French Army under the direct command of Napoleon, which acted as his bodyguard and tactical reserve. As general, Napoleon carefully used the Guard in combat. It was divided into staff, infantry, cavalry, and artillery regiments, as well as battalions of sappers and marines. The men in the Guard, itself, distinguished between experienced veterans and less experienced members: "Old Guard," "Middle Guard," "Young Guard."

Lee discussed with this "Old Guard" not tactics or war itself but honor and virtue, a soldier's strength and hopefully a citizen's as well. The Napoleonic veteran agreed and noted France was presently at war with Prussia (Germany) and needed another Napoleon. Lee wanted France to go to arbitration as prescribed in a treaty still in force. The "Old Guard" agreed.

Lee's great delight in meeting a peaceful "Old Guard" lasted the remainder of his days and he talked of the experience as a premier event in his life, not only his vacation health trip. Lee told Agnes, "A gift in old age is something unexpected, birthed as a miracle of love given when darkness is around the corner." R. E. Lee knew what was coming.

He continued explaining a miracle of love: "Similar to a partridge in a pear tree. Or three French hens, five golden rings, ten lords a leaping, twelve drummers drumming, and that daggum partridge always in a pear tree! It's peculiar, unlikely. It's highly inappropriate just like a baby in a cow manger... but joyous, bubbly... and merry!"

Wiggie went into a mild shock; nevertheless, she rejoiced for the comparison her father made. "This trip has some benefit for you after all, Papa," she told him. It jolted him in turn. They poked fun at one another. She twittered like a jester; he vocalized folklore like a Homer or Hesiod of ancient Greece. Both appreciated one another as more than daughter and father; their human to human relationship sharpened.

Meeting his former Chief of Staff of the A.N.V. revived his heart. Meeting the "Old Guard" of Napoleon's choosing was a premier event in Lee's life, unexpected in old age with history and dedication. It was another minor miracle that characterized his last year on this planet. Those two men would never know they'd regaled R. E. Lee's last months. However, he knew; he remembered. He knew he was blesséd.

Yet, unbeknownst to Lee, more surprises lay just around the corner in Tidewater Virginia. Richness not expected.

The iconic former general, now prescient modern college president, was being loaded with more grand values for his last year at Washington College.

And the last few months of his life on this Earth.

CHAPTER 28

Going home, going home
I'm jus' going home
It's not far, yes close by
Through an open door
I'm jus' going home.

More than he yearned or discerned, he was soon going to see family and friends at home. Inasmuch as home is where the heart is, some family and friends were close by in Virginia, not far distant as out in the western mountains of the Old Dominion. It was a reassuring feeling. And exciting—just as exciting as Portsmouth and Norfolk had been on the eastern shore. Or as lethal to him if his family down east might not be up to his drop in.

All the time R. E. Lee realized, if not the precise nature of his illness, his physical condition was a deadly serious matter. He understood, and accepted, how sick he was as well as emotionally needful of seeing family members in numbers, groups, homes, and situations five years after the war.

Compounded with those stark facts he felt older by the hour, feebler by the minute, done in by the second in physique, explicitly the main muscle of a human being: the heart.

R. E. Lee was living through his dying. Death was a fact of his life that he was observing, if not controlling... directing it out of a sense of duty to himself. Always duty.

Their Norfolk leave-taking had been quiet, much to his relief, and consequently to Wiggie as well. She did not hanker to console her father if commiseration was what he needed, for she didn't know the particular personalities of his wartime life. Instead, she held one of his hands to make sincere human contact—a warm hand, or if not warm, then a most comforting ministration.

The boat moved out of the Elizabeth River's bay, heading northward then inland northwest via the James River toward Richmond. Nearing home, Lee's mood lightened further. Agnes had nothing to say, and said it... to her peace of mind.

Engagingly, along that river route there were estates of family friends of years and decades, any number of which they could have visited unannounced. At the first stop—the Brandon Estates, of rich alluvial soils—Dame Isabella Harrison of Lower Brandon, an ancient acquaintance, welcomed them. She was a present they gave themselves. Lee was elated to be in her presence. He deeply appreciated there wasn't a swarm of people to greet him and zero social occasions to exhaust him. Not thinking the matter through he said to his hostess and his daughter Agnes, "This is a fine beginning that signals no more public displays until we reach Lexington."

"Don't count on it, Father. We have miles to go. Family to visit."

"Don't you be negative, Wiggie."

"I'm not negative, just realistic. We're a long way from Lexington." Then she rebelled against her father's optimism about a situation that had tormented him throughout the weeks and months of the trip. *He doesn't want to face the realities of travel. I miss James Corley and Mr. Lowe. There are too many miles, too many places, too many family members yet to see. I suppose I should pity not pester him, but I hate seeing him throw himself off balance.*

On another day they visited Upper Brandon and were met by a slew of friends, cadres of veterans, and onlookers galore from the neighborhood. It was a holiday in Maytime. Naturally on Sunday they attended worship services; he thought, *That pastor's sermon would have satisfied my students' souls because it was caring and informative,* telling the thought to Agnes who agreed readily.

Then he thought of himself, as the former condition of multiple meetings with numerous other people would persist on the way home. R. E. Lee practically bowled himself over like a tenpin. His stamina weakened.

Lee then turned to think about his daughter Agnes. He realized he had spoken to her sundry times in way too much haste, way too soon about her public displays of sentiment. He apologized overtly because they were alone. She kissed him on both cheeks through his dark- and light-colored beard. Old father thanked young daughter, bowing at the waist; she genuflected with a curtsey as each smiled approvingly.

The couple left Brandon and went to Shirley Plantation, on the north side of the James River, at a right angle crook in the river near Turkey Island. It had been the home of Lee's mother, Anne Hill Carter. Two years earlier R. E. Lee had announced he wished to visit Shirley before he left this world. Several reasons motivated him, none did he name. Now was the time. The visit was necessary, and now he would look back on Mother Ann.

In that mansion hung the famous portrait of George Washington by George Willson Peale, saddle maker turned portraitist *extraordinaire* of the American Founding Fathers. When Lee sighted the portrait again he fell into a conscious woolgathering state. Memories and impressions are the beaten path to the human heart; they form a cache of glory filling moments of quietude. They solidify one to meet life head on, prepared to take what comes and build fuller memories and impressions.

George Washington had been one of Lee's heroes all his life from boyhood to college presidency. His own father had been a personal friend and general with Washington during the Revolutionary War. It was demonstratively difficult for R. E. Lee to stand in front of the painting. More difficult to leave it, which meant leaving his father as well as Washington. R. E. Lee identified with both. Again the old memories, still blessing his father and instantly burning his own heart.

A daughter of the Shirley family recalled often after the Lee visit about his "great dignity; the kindness of his bearing." She cited his virtues, waxing lyrical about R. E. Lee the remainder of her life after that 1870 visit. Lee was the premier influence on the lives of young women and old women in mid-19th century Virginia, as he had been upon young and old men during the wartime years.

With all those perceptions, the eldest daughter of the Shirley Plantation family never quite realized the eminence of Robert Edward Lee, though her soon-to-be-spoken phrase outlasted her and reverberated through decades: "We regarded him with the highest veneration," she proclaimed often to the assembled crowd. And then at the fete for R. E. Lee at Shirley Plantation she blazoned for all to hear: "We have heard of God—but here is General Lee."

Of course in the religious South: God. Then more.

"But here is General Lee!" One seldom if ever beholds virtue enmaned in the flesh; nobility alive; amiability in the land of the living; gentlemanliness among the masses.

"We have heard of God—but here is General Lee!" she repeated.

Silence reigned in the house, movement halted, talk ceased, even breathing for some folks broke off in long seconds as they gasped. Yes, they had believed, but now... now they saw. In the flesh, an incarnation of honesty, of strength, of virtue... and duty, always duty.

The eldest Shirley daughter's statement was impassioned, so commanding the words were repeated in many minds; many guests nodded their heads in agreement. One male guest, minutes after things settled down, insisted aloud, "That declaration is so genuine I wish I had said it myself."

Slowly applause turned round and round in the large house, increasing in volume until it became a joyous clamor. R. E. Lee was startled then confounded. The social activity engulfed him as if by a fog. A billowing blanket dropped over him; he shuddered.

A revelation, a bolt from the blue had struck the hearts of the company. It baffled Lee, then floored him, so to speak. The near equation of God with himself unsettled him to the degree that he began to wiggle his head in the negative. Until it began affecting how he stood. He wobbled and leaned against a tall stuffed chair for support.

There he froze, stiff, erect. Unbelieving, he thought the phrase blasphemous. Then he got his tongue around the word and uttered quietly: "Blasphemy."

Lee's word was an emotional bomb. Several people experienced astonishment. Others were emotionally challenged and had to hold on to something or someone, shaken by the potency of his word. Some were stunned, whether at Lee's reaction or the original statement was difficult to discern.

R. E. Lee was more than a person; he embodied everything still of worth in the South. The presence of their past, present, and future. Even their religion. Now he challenged religious language.

Her statement electrified a small number of the people present. They clapped, stomped their feet, and chanted, "Lee, Lee; General Lee! Lee, Lee; General Lee!" A few joined arms together and marched three abreast in and through the ground floor rooms and onto the porches of the large farmhouse.

R. E. Lee was abashed, conscience-stricken, almost beyond words. Identical to his previous negative reactions to demonstrations of lesser magnitude he spoke: "But I shouldn't be mentioned in the same sentence as God. Never. It is blasphemous. Please, no more."

From an adjacent room Agnes heard her father's protestation. She promptly pushed through the guests solidifying as a mass and took him aside to a corner of the room. For admonition: the daughter to tutor the father. "No, no. Let them live it up, Papa. They are honoring you: who you are, what you were. You give them a hero."

Then she paused, remarkably balanced, thinking of another place, another time. "This is what happened at Jacksonville, on our trip into Florida. When the crowd stood totally silent before you. You gave them a hero, too. They responded with deepest respect, in silence. Here they are doing it with her words and their joyous celebration."

Wiggie paused; then touching both her father's shoulders, looked him straight in the eyes and said, "Here Shirley Plantation and guests are paying you the deepest respect. The people are celebrating you. It's the same thing. Both silence and celebration are worthy ways to approach God. As well as to you. It should make you feel better, make you healthier, Papa."

R. E. Lee had no rejoinder.

CHAPTER 29

Ending and Beginning are Beginning and Ending

Late in the trip a blurry, garbled situation emerged in correspondence between husband R. E. and wife Mary Custis Lee about when and where a previously planned end-of-the-trip meeting would or could happen at the home of one of their sons in Tidewater Virginia.

That son had been affectionately named "Rooney" because his proper moniker "William Henry Fitzhugh Lee" was a mouthful for old and young alike. "Rooney" sounded lyrical to Mother Mary, so Rooney it was and forever would be.

He lived at White House, an unincorporated community on the south shore of the Pamunkey River, a James River tributary—not to be confused with the American president's home in the District of Columbia, named "Executive Mansion." The White House Plantation of Virginia was over 4,000 acres of prime farm land inherited from Rooney's grandfather, George Washington Parke Custis, adopted son of President George Washington and also natural-born grandson of Martha Washington.

Rooney had been a major general in the Confederate States of America's cavalry. He was twice married, losing his first wife to death, as well as a son named Robert Edward Lee II, and a daughter named Mary Custis Lee after their grandparents. All three died at different times during the War of the Rebellion. "I was torn in heart," Lee lamented. "I wore a restrained, stoic composure when encountering officers and men who were facing their own brutal deaths."

R. E. Lee's own daughter, "beloved" Annie, also died during the war. The Grim Reaper, like a crazed harvester, rammed full blast into Lee on a dark stallion, slashing right and left, trampling the innocents who populated Lee's caring soul. "Death seemed proud, obnoxious and overarching. Unaccountable—to man and God," he noted.

To have encountered death of loved ones in the midst of the deaths of thousands of his soldiers was beyond belief, a millstone round his spiritual neck. Sorrow runs red as any battlefield. And Death is the conquering worm.

R. E. and Mary Lee had previously corresponded about this meeting at Rooney's during the last month of his trip. A date was not set because Lee did not believe she would remember, and if she did, she would not want to travel such a distance because of severe rheumatoid arthritis. For nine years, she had used a wheelchair he had designed and built for her. He was a jack-of-all-trades, and a master of several.

But on Wednesday, 20 April 1870, Mrs. Lee arrived in Richmond via the Kanawha Canal—first planned by George Washington when a young surveyor—then southward on the James River and lastly by train to White House. She discovered there weren't to be other guests, so her husband would be free to rest or play with their grandson, Robert Edward Lee III.

As often the case in marriage, the husband was wrong. There was Mary Anna Randolph Custis Lee at White House, just as she had promised. Wiggie rejoiced in the reunion; her health improved in some measure to celebrate at least another time of being all together.

Papa Lee had time to ride over to Robert's for a short visit at his plantation, Romancoke, which had belonged to Rob's former overseer. It was in poor shape and Robert was in the process of bringing back the soil as farm land. He noted, "When Father entered and looked around my bachelor quarters he appeared really much shocked." In fact the old man was mortified.

When the two sat down to eat, the elder Lee relieved his son's embarrassment by jesting about the environment. However, when the younger man presented food on broken china and cutlery, his father suggested that Robert might pay a small sum to better equip the "mansion."

Days later when in Richmond, R. E. Lee bought a set of heavily plated knives, forks, spoons, and such and sent them to son Robert, who showed them off for many years.

R. E. Lee made plans to visit doctors now that he was back in Richmond. "I am to have a great medicine talk tomorrow," he laughed. "Physicians and confabulations, pow-wows and headache powders... and 'Contact me in the morning.' I don't know what they can do for me."

While in the capital, Lee contacted the sculptor E. V. Valentine who was to make measurements for a bust of him. The old man told the artist forthrightly that the war had greatly altered his features... and his own pocketbook. He quipped ever so gently, "Artists ought not have too much money."

Valentine didn't know whether to worry or not about payment for his artistry.

Later, as the conversation turned again to adversity, Lee observed, "Misfortune nobly borne is good fortune," an ongoing theme throughout his life as soldier and as educator.

Now Valentine definitely began to worry about payment for his efforts.

At the time the sculptor thought the observation was original. Subsequently, while reading the *Meditations* of Marcus Aurelius, he discovered the sentence in that ancient Roman emperor and philosopher's book. In his own notebook Valentine wrote: "No more appropriate epitaph could be carved on the tomb of the great Virginian."

The artist at length finished his measurements and explained he would see Lee again back in Lexington to do the actual modeling. He gave no other reason for delaying the project. Yet it was obvious to the artist that Robert Edward Lee was cognizant of a fast approaching end of earthly life and wanted to see him again and again before his demise.

Thursday, 26 May 1870, the old man left Richmond for the last time. He had defended it often. Traveling homeward by way of Charlottesville on the old Virginia Central Railroad and then on to Lynchburg by the older Orange and Alexandria RR, he made his way back on the South River—formerly named the North River. War changes many things, geography included.

Few friends, if any, were present in Richmond to wish him "Farewell." At Lexington, however, there was a unique group singing a "welcome home," which he appreciated and doffed his hat the whole time.

In one of the migrations from Germany in the 1820s to Pennsylvania there were "plain people"—the religious Anabaptists of Amish, Brethren, Mennonite, and Quaker persuasions—who moved south to northwestern Virginia in the Shenandoah River Valley because farm land in Pennsylvania was too expensive to make farming feasible in the "Garden Spot of America." In Virginia they were pacifists and did not support the South during the Rebellion. These men and women, two and a half dozen believers, came to tell in their way that they respected R. E. Lee's pacifistic sentiment.

They sang a simple melody in *Pennsilfaanisch Deitsch*, almost a representative example of medieval *plainchant* used in liturgical church services in the Europe of the 14th through 16th centuries in Roman Catholicism. It was soothing to the human ear, totally pacific to the soul, besides. R. E. Lee was ever so appreciative that he wished he could speak Latin or *Deitsch* to thank them.

They sang; he hummed:

Ich waer so gaern, Ich waer so gaern.
Ich waer so gaern daheim.
Ich waer so gaern wu Yesus iss,
Ich waer so gaern daheim!

I would gladly be, I would gladly be.
I would gladly be home.
I would gladly be where Jesus is,
I would gladly be home!

Bald landen mir am Yorden aan,
Daer andie Stadt hie laift;
Wer Glaawe haelt, daer iwwerkummt,
Des Wasser selbscht ihm weicht!

Soon we'll land at the Jordan River,
Which to the city flows;
Whoever keeps faith, he will overcome,
The water itself to him will yield!

Lee passed through land and the water, through Virginia, through where his greatest battles had been won and become the central scene of his life's drama: the water yielded. He passed through, the humblest actor in the drama.

He arrived at the President's House on the Washington College campus, Saturday, 28 May 1870, in the morning, two months and four days after his departure. His arrival coincided with the advent of a small rain. *To be expected*, he told himself. *To be expected.*

But only a drizzle and a dribble, only a sprinkle and a splash. Quite unlike his departure from Lexington in a downpour and a drenching, under a March cloudburst and torrential rainstorm, heading south to sunny Florida and citrus joys, then north homeward with human joys stop after stop after stop.

Job's "small rain" he could take this happy day back home.

And then raining ended.

As later so would R. E. Lee. In Lexington, Virginia. In the President's House of Washington College. In a downstairs makeshift sleeping arrangement, not in his own bed upstairs.

Patrick Henry's second choice awaited—as it does, always.

CHAPTER 30

The Past Awakened: Life-Long Dream Realized

R.E. Lee was dying. Dying matters because death matters. Lee knew those realities.

Death *per se* is an absolute unknown. We realize we only hypothesize about death; often that's all it is: assumption, conjecture, a frail will-o-the wisp. More likely, it is our uncritical belief about some state we've talked ourselves into. One way or another the human "death" state is unknown though much is assumed as actual about it. Death as such remains an unknown; we have only imaginations.

Peculiarly, death matters so much to those not dying. Yet, no one knows for absolute certainty whether it matters to a dead one, or ones. And there isn't a way to communicate with them.

Contrariwise, human dying matters, peculiarly to dying persons with aches and pains, damage or disease, abnormalities or infirmities, illness or accident, defects or troubles. Then again simply through old age, decline, and deterioration, people wear out. Bystanders may or may not suffer about another's dying.

On the other hand, human dying matters extraordinarily to those dying as they go through a process, an "undertaking," a sorting out of the facts about living and dying.

Truly a leap into the dark, dying is not an invalid, nullified condition but an affirming process. Dying is a valuable process honored in the centuries-old Christian Church prayer: "Good Lord, deliver us from sudden death," wherein there would not be time for the process of dying. In this, R E. Lee contended unreservedly the education of a person is never completed until dying is ended.

Such ruminations were among many Lee employed to remain in the land of the living as a vibrant participant. Endings always entail the possibility of new beginnings. For example, if a person has two cows, sell one and buy a bull. The result will be offspring—new beginning.

He'd had no time on the tiring trip south to sort through his life. Now he had place and time to do so. He needed to re-evaluate who and what he was as a human being. He needed to look, himself upon himself... fully, honestly.

The need was huge. He was old and ill. The keenest tool available was to reminisce, to cast his mind back to what had sustained him life-long. It would not be nostalgic dewy-eyed romanticism but duty to himself, which then would entail duty to others, and duty to God.

Now it was necessary that he think the noblest and act the best so as to stay vigorously involved as a sentient being. He needed to remember, to evaluate his purpose in life as his last days advanced.

A hymn he'd heard in the Northern Campaign in '63 when attending the German Reformed Church in Chambersburg, Pennsylvania, resounded in every fiber of his being:

Jesus, I live to thee, the loveliest and best...
Jesus, I die to thee, whenever death shall come...
Whether to live or die I know not which is best...
Living or dying, Lord, I ask but to be thine...

Lee did not consider himself a human failure. The military cause of Dixie was the huge failure physically, politically, intellectually, socially, and spiritually. Certainly spiritually, for biblitarian, fundamentalist South mistook words for the Divine itself.

Knowing he was rich, emotionally, Lee determined to use his emotional wealth to recall his past, the non-military highlights of his life story. He would summon post-war high points where treasures abounded by the score. He purposely would recall positive points of life's personal victories since the disastrous

Rebellion. He wanted to look in a mirror and not see an enemy peering back at him. He desired the reflection to be of one who seeks Truth and Beauty and Goodness.

Amidst his age and physical malady he resolved still to live a flourishing, expanding human existence. His memories by the dozens would help him celebrate life and liberty, faith and freedom, opportunity and duty: Truth, Beauty, and Goodness.

***

One poignant first memory was being devoid of money upon his return from war. No longer living in Arlington House, Mother Mary Custis Lee's parental home, they were houseless therefore homeless. Impecunious to boot. Throughout the War of the Rebellion they had rented dwellings in Richmond—paying in Confederate money, now worthless, including bank accounts.

The Federal government at war's start had "appropriated" Arlington House across the Potomac River from Washington, D.C., for use as a cemetery for Union soldiers and sailors. Mrs. Lee resented bitterly that her home had become a graveyard, hating the Federal government all the more.

After the war the Lee family expressed a deep need to leave their rented quarters because Confederate-destroyed Richmond was a doleful, even harrowing place to live. In whatever way possible the Lee family left downhearted; glum in fact.

However, there was nowhere to go.

For decades, Lee's deep desire had been to have a small Virginia farm where he could work the soil and be close to nature. Good for his health; much better for his soul than the slaughterhouse of war. Yet where to go?

Would he farm in fertile Pennsylvania he'd seen during the Northern Campaign? Of course not, for memory of Gettysburg would cause consternation at least and monstrous trouble at the worst. Try Maryland? No, for the same reason because of the loss at Antietam/Sharpsburg. The only viable option was Virginia, the Shenandoah River Valley where they could hopefully live surrounded by kindred folks, many of whom were rebuilding after heavy war devastation. If they, the Lees, had money, of course, of which there was zilch.

Then from out of the blue, an invitation. Almost a summons, almost a subpoena, the family had received an invitation. Once more divine Providence intervened. Or so it seemed.

Help had come through Mrs. Elizabeth Cocke of Oakland, Cumberland County, a widow of substance and station, who invited them to visit. She owned a smaller property eastward in Powhatan County, about fifty miles from downtown Richmond, which she wanted to show them. "Derwent" became a live option for the Lee family, unknowingly but gratefully.

Near the middle of June 1865, son Custis rode Lee's steed Traveller and visited with Edmund Cocke, a veteran of the Army of Northern Virginia. Near the end of the month the family— mother, father, son and two daughters—took a canal packet boat up the James River and Kanawha Canal and landed near the Oakland mansion about sunrise. There awaited a pre-arranged robust eye-opener.

Little blessings many-a-time result in sumptuous eating in which food is devoured, gobbled up, plowed into, wolfed down, polished off, masticated, munched, snacked, stuffed into one's face, even nibbled. No one should wonder we human beings have many names for eating times: breakfast, brunch, lunch, lupper, supper, dinner, banquet, feast, even tea time.

The Cocke family had been enthusiastically pleased to see the Lees eat the hearty meal; the guests were delighted as well to eat so much good food they hadn't seen since pre-war days.

After a week-long social visit both families backtracked two miles to visit Derwent which Mrs. Cocke willingly bestowed on the Lee family as long as they wanted to stay. Rent free. Among friends. A little blessing that loomed large. A silent fulfillment for R. E. and Mary Lee.

Derwent was modest, or less so in some ways. It was a cabin-type building with porches on two sides and two rooms downstairs and two up, a kitchen in the backyard and another smallish building as an "office" outdoors. The room for eating meals, strange to say, was in the basement.

Derwent had been Mrs. Cocke's slave-overseer's quarters pre-war. But it had the possibility of actualizing Lee's life-long desire, at a most favorable "cost."

For the Lee family, Mrs. Cocke unusually furnished the house with movables from her Oakland home, giving it a livable feeling. The cabin was situated in a small grove of oak trees as shade, a welcome feature in hot summers, and a snow-break in wintertime. However, the soil around the cabin-refuge had not been well cared for during or after the Rebellion.

Folks from Oakland Mansion and new neighbors frequently supplied baskets of fruit and vegetables for the Lees. Gladly given, they were thankfully blessed, expressly presented as God's gifts to the Lee family and reverentially received by them.

Remembering riding Traveller to church services on Sundays and venturing afar on weekdays into the country made him smile. He stopped to talk to local farmers in their fields about farming in the area, thereby becoming an instant success for his humility and interest in their day-by-day existences.

He'd reasoned good neighbors would help him make Derwent's fields good again with advice, with aid... and with manure. Always manure to replenish depleted soil that had been a war-torn, over-tilled, neglected piece of God's green earth, cattle manure, horse manure the best, sheep, chicken, even rabbit manure. Farmers know how to keep the good earth green and alive.

God was merciful through his earthly children around Derwent to the modest loser and his family.

Then another bonus. In fact, and now in memory. Lee's older brother Carter lived within easy riding distance. They shared childhood memories and future prospects for both of them in old age, plus laughter and tears. Farming, though, was Topic Number One.

Once Robert told brother Carter of his desire to write about ordinary soldiers' valor, endurance, and powerful humanity under wartime conditions. Carter made the mistake of saying, "Everyone says 'the publication of Lee's history of the war would bring $100,000!'"

R. E. was shocked that money would be made from America's bloody four-year-long strife over slavery and politics. With over 600,000 dead soldiers plus countless thousands more civilians slaughtered, it seemed cruel to Lee that money could, and would be made from writing about animosity, bloodshed, death, destruction. Defeat, too.

Five years after the war R. E. Lee's life-long dream of having a farm had become a reality back in early summer 1865. It was a minor miracle he cherished and delighted to reminisce about. At fifty-eight years of age, property-less and money-less, Lee had settled in eagerly at Derwent.

What wasn't to like about that environment: farming, relatives, sturdy beneficent neighbors, and a gracious proprietress? Derwent was a little gift and a great award... even if one might not exactly love it.

Remembering that "gift" of a little bit of land five years earlier revealed something else Lee had not understood before: Things have a dark or negative side as photographs have a negative or dark side before being printed.

On the far side of good things in life there is another as well, at times bad. Something lurking, lying low, skulking. Something shadowy concealing something to be revealed later.

It had been so at Derwent.

While the Lee family was rejoicing over their good fortune to have a house, to be able to make a home, the shadow of a tall, burly man on horseback was sliding over Powhatan County.

The horseman was searching for someone. He probed with a question. His shiny black suit made him look official, even somber. Folks wondered if he was a Federal parole officer seeking errant ex-Confederate soldiers.

The shadow slowly sidled along.

"Stranger. The way to R. E. Lee's house, please?"

R.E. Lee had not known he was the object of a shadow's search.

Briefly now he thought of the horseman and felt his chest tighten and his breathing quicken as he recollected. He thought, *"Another time. I'll visit that memory another time. Let me now be at peace."*

Diverse times on his health trip he had expressed one continuing emotion to his daughter Wiggie. He'd spoken it in unnerving episodes southward, in the mysterious silent greeting at Jacksonville, Florida, in delightful times among citrus trees, during a glorious time in Savannah northward, and homebound through the Carolinas into Tidewater Virginia.

One sentence, over, and over, and over again: *"I want to go home. I want to go home."*

Now he was home, remembering.

Peaceful, lost in memory.

And thriving... living his dying.

CHAPTER 31

The Past Awakened: Post-War Ennui

"We couldn't move so quickly today as when we moved to Derwent back in the summer of 1865," R. E. Lee joked to himself, remembering how astonished his family had been about that swift move, swift because their need was immediate.

They'd had few possessions but the pressure of moving from place to place was heavy then, its memory still heavy now. He deemed that memory irresistible in powerful feelings but necessary to understanding, as some memories are. There is sweetness and stinging in memories, both making heavy emotional demands.

He still felt the past weight of knowing he'd have to find employment in order to support his wife and family of three unmarried daughters, and, possibly, one son. A continual stream of visitors often impinged upon the family's time and limited resources then. That, too, added weight.

Visitors to the Lee house, almost to a person, had been poverty-compromised in various ways after the war. They often evinced a freakish combination of damaging poverty and emotionally disturbed temperament. Plus elevated hostility; possibly due to the fifty miles or so they had to travel to capital city Richmond just to grumble and complain, seeking redress for some flaw—or perceived flaw.

He tried hard to push past recalling that early on he had not yet established himself as a farmer. Wishing doesn't make anything so. Though it is true a wish is a blueprint of a dream, it still needs nuts and bolts, 2" x 4" lumber, frames, concrete, tar, shingles, paint, hammers, and nails to make a house into a home.

Wishing to be a farmer had not made him a farmer. Still, he mused, "Home is where the heart is and a house is where the pulse begins. My heart was there from the start. And my pulse quickened."

Lee brooded about the awful post-war conditions at least a full week, hearing comments in memory so vivid he had a hard time believing they were in the past.

The war had been lost on battlefields and by ineffective politicians in Richmond, yet a spirit of rebellion lingered in some nooks and crannies in Southland. And lingered on.

He'd heard: "What a pain in the arse," unfailingly, most days for months after the South's surrender. Numerous times and diverse places people grouched: "All we do is diddle around; where's that gittin' us? How much back-talk and sass do we have to take from their black soldiers patrolling our streets and country roads? We're becomin' nothing but lap dogs to Northern blue bellies—with either black or white faces. We've become straw men and couldn't pass muster if we had to. We're dead but won't keel over. We couldn't drive nails through a snow bank— we're a sad spectacle!"

And, "Yeh, but how about some sad-sister-Sue belongin' to a church that cooks noontime meals three days a week for anyone, friends or neighbors, blacks or white, even folks just passin' by."

"I hear that in our port cities and towns there's cotton already sold, just waitin' to be sent up north or across the ocean, so some people are 'gittin rich'."

As well, "There's always the western pioneer states, if we're brave enough. My brother-in-law joined the Army to fight the Injuns out there in the far west."

"We shouldn't gloat over a piece of good news elsewhere until we have good times a rollin' right here in Powhatan County. Gripe. Gripe, is all we do!"

Endlessly, then, in most every community, at the drop of a hat, Southerners questioned with temperamental heat the issues of defeat, recovery. "What is it to be American again in a brotherhood of states?" Little agreement about solutions prevailed throughout Dixie; Powhatan County no exception.

He wondered whether or not people were finding answers.

"We were wrestling with the same issues," he recalled. "We were part of the 'Great Flood' rolling over Dixieland: *ennui,* a listlessness that nothing really mattered anymore. Everything was dull as dishwater and people felt dirty for being nullities, zombie-like. Stale. At best murky and sunless."

Looking back Lee could reason that the deadliness of the emotional disease of the spirit shocked many people, not into the appalling Black Plague of the European Middle Ages, but, rather, into a featureless dreariness. The South was losing its soul. It was like monotonously waiting for Santa Claus as if he were the fourth member of the Christian Trinity, but with faded costume, musty and fusty, and beard filthy with shreds of food stuck here and there. Defeat had been a disaster for many Dixielanders.

"Will the South ever rise again?" He heard the words spit from his mouth of their own volition.

"It's still post-war. People still are depressed, much worse than their overworked soil, some of which is useful only if one needs to pick dandelion leaves for a salad. Souls, not just attitudes, still are deteriorating among grown women and men. Youngsters are growing up deprived of positive role models.

"Truth is being twisted, beauty faded. It seems like goodness shows itself primarily in music. More often than not bursting out from black churches, though also from a precious few white ones scattered across Southland. Southern literature is going to develop lop-sided, despicable characters and sinister families—plus bitter politicians who'll be hated bitterly by their constituents.

"There has to be a way to thwart crushing poverty, to repair wide-spread destruction, to outsmart limited resources, and to stem the effects of advancing age pestering all and immobilizing many. The South has to be better than the North in all those sad situations or it will cease to exist as a culture worthy of the name in the re-United States of America.

"Who will do something about it?"

He remembered having asked the same question after moving to and settling in at Derwent. And hearing no answer.

But there had been a personal answer of sorts, one on its way to him at that very past time of questioning, though Lee did not know it then.

The sturdy, unrelenting rider continually moved o'er the landscape of the two counties' back roads, main roads, lanes, paths asking the same question over and over.

He had traveled on his appointed task from the Blue Ridge Mountains farther west in Virginia searching through the countryside west of Richmond.

Steadfastly he inquired, seldom getting an answer: "Stranger! The way to R. E. Lee's house, please."

Some adults turned fearful; most didn't know because they hadn't heard the news about the newest family in the area just several weeks previously.

Youngsters walking the gritty roads to a swimming hole or a fishing pier, waiting for school to re-open sometime soon, would pepper him with questions: "Who you? Where y'all from? You a Northern parole officer? What's y'all want Lee for? He lives in Richmond. We don't know."

A bright girl purposely spoke up, "The Gray Fox is hiding in hunting season."

R.E. Lee smiled with the image the memory provoked. He, himself, had not seen the horseman, just had heard tales after the fact. Likely, he'd have been a bit scared if they'd met on horseback, if truth be told.

He smiled again, remembering what happened next.

CHAPTER 32

The Past Awakened: A New Vocation and New Puzzle

There he'd stood, the stalker. The bulky, beefy man in black. As big in R.E. Lee's memory as he'd been in the Derwent cabin in 1865.

The searcher from the hill country had found his quarry. He'd been looking for the defeated general; in popular opinion, the biggest loser in the Rebellion: Robert Edward Lee.

He'd towered disproportionately in the doorway to the Lee's small sitting room. No longer was he a shadowy figure, menacing silhouette, nor tracker. He was a statue of a man swathed in an obviously new black suit for the occasion. A statue leaning a bit on the doorframe for support.

"It cost fifty out-of-pocket dollars... United States of America currency, of course... raised by passing the hat among my fellow trustees," he announced, unquestionably bewildering to the Lee family as he stepped inside. Dumbstruck, pinned, as it were, to their spots in the small room the family wondered his purpose.

A gold-lined riding cape partially covered his shiny black suit seeming to stretch over his frame as if to fly. Mother Mary was cuffed into wide-eyed silence, mouth agape by the image, clothing, demeanor, and words with its one hefty, mysterious assertion. Two daughters on the perimeter thrust their hands backwards against the log wall to steady themselves out of anxiety while the third got the creeps, shivered, and plopped on a stool.

Lee's mind held a vivid picture of the man in black—*he was a queer old duck: He'd wanted to ask a question of me. I remember he said, "Just one."*

Yet he didn't start talking that way, with an interrogation. He was clever; I thought him a roguish salesman of something or the other as indicated by what he said next: "I'm from Lexington, Rockbridge County, in the Shenandoah Valley."

Then he paused and took a few steps toward the center of the small room while he scanned the remainder of the downstairs living quarters. We thought him nosy. All six of us Lees present were mortified at his audacity.

Before we could recover we heard him say, "I'm here to 'bribe' you!" Lee spoke the phrase aloud to hear how the words sounded in this present year: *"I'm here to bribe you."* The words sounded hollow to his ear.

He patted his knee with his right hand, laboring to remember what happened next.

Oh, yes, that Hell's Belles declaration of Custis. The Hell's Belles he changed to Hades ladies! Everyone got the real meaning, including the intruder.

The word bribe shocked to life any parts of us that weren't awake. What followed was a verbal grenade. Mrs. Lee's breath was an updraft followed by a blustery wheeze, a gush of air accompanied by faint rushes of sputters and coughs from two daughters.

Eldest daughter Mary stifled her physical reaction. She looked wooden. Then, "For heaven's sake!" she petitioned. "What could you possibly mean by bribe, Sir?"

At that recall R. E. Lee rose and hightailed it to the kitchen. He was hungry. And he knew why.

He peered into the dark of the icebox, found what he was looking for, made a sandwich, ate it, and washed it down with homemade root beer.

Bringing the memory to life, he mused as he returned to sit in the rocking chair he'd occupied that morning of remembering.

He sat. He closed his eyes and leaned back, propping his feet on the chair rung so the rocker would stay tilted backward. It made for more comfortable napping that way. *Now, where was I...?*

Ah, yes, the bribe: He had a twenty-three pound, eleven-ounce home-cured Virginia ham, hand rubbed weekly with sea salt to buy my vote, he said. He looked like a jolly Saint Nicholas in a Charles Dickens Christmas story.

"I believe we met one time, Sir," he'd addressed me.

And I replied, "I can't recollect immediately."

Lee's memory trailed off. He could recall only bits and pieces of the ensuing conversation and happenings. And he was sleepy from the ham sandwich that had overfilled him. He remembered the stranger had said something about peace and a pumpkin but he couldn't quite put the scene together.

In fact the stranger had told them, "I was one of 131 Peace Commissioners in 1861 from all 33 states of the Union seeking to head off civil war and the dissolution of the nation."

The Lees were caught off guard. They felt twisted emotionally, in opposite direction from where they had been, each in a different way and to differing degrees.

"To enhance my bribe," the man had continued, "for Mrs. Mary Custis Lee I have a three feet, six inches straight-neck pumpkin that would have grown to four feet in another week, straight from Lexington, Virginia." And then, opening a burlap bag, he'd set the pumpkin on the floor, positioning it upright.

"What is this?" Lee had inquired. Thinking *trickery* or *flimflam* he'd followed with, "What's behind this display of presumption?"

Family members all had caught the reticence of their family head. The stranger, though, had paid no attention to Lee's restraint.

Lee remembered that eldest daughter Mary, detecting a degree of honesty in the visitor's approach, quietly repeated his question, "What is the meaning of this?"

"Mary's keen and intuitive," the words tumbled out of Lee's mouth between half-snores and sighs.

Unbeknownst to the Lees, the stranger was one accustomed to frolicsome play. Realizing his approach of sharp-wittedness had upset the family he'd taken it upon himself to announce, "I am Judge Brockenbrough, the Rector and vice-president, of Washington College in aforementioned Lexington."

"What?" asked Mother Lee.

Lee remembered Mother Lee's surprise: *Her voice had squeaked.*

"I am Judge John White Brockenbrough, from Washington College in Lexington. Our Board of Trustees, as of 4 August in this year of grace 1865, has elected General Lee the President of Washington College, named for our first national president... and after whom your oldest child, George Washington Custis Lee, here is actually named... who decades ago provided a benefaction to help the college survive."

All six Lees were speechless. Each one went null. Void to boot. What to say immediately escaped each Lee present.

The family studied each other for some word or help, any word, even a grunt or cough might be of service.

Sister Mary Lee had the first dawning, a most positive idea. "Out of the blue—employment, at a college, no less! A new start for an old man. Not believable, but here it is. Right in front of us!" At the time Lee thought he'd never forget those words and the promise they held.

A new start. Lee woke from his napping with those words seemingly in front of his face. He remembered then Judge Brockenbrough's making a softly-spoken apology for his unique approach to the serious matter. *"I thought telling General Lee he was elected without having been informed or even under consideration for the position would be a shock of sorts so I decided to appear incognito to break the ice for the good of our young male students back in Lexington."*

Mother Mary retorted first, "You almost got yourself kicked out of our new home here at Derwent."

The Judge had quickly replied, "Well, then, you'll be happy to hear that the Board has authorized a new "President's House" with all kinds of modern features including indoor toilet facilities for our new president's family and an attached stable for your husband's horses."

"Amazing!" Mother Lee had exclaimed. And everyone had joined in response, relieved and positive.

Except for Lee. *I was fuzzy about the concept. I hadn't liked being Superintendent of the Military Academy at West Point in the 1850s so being head of a private college didn't promptly seem to make sense. I was leery. And I certainly was clueless to a high degree.*

His mind's eye saw Judge Brockenbrough take a paper from a satchel and read formally: *"As Rector, Vice President of Washington College in Lexington and member of the Board of Trustees, I present this invitation to Robert Edward Lee to become President of Washington College, who was elected unanimously on Friday, 4 August A.D. 1865."*

Surprise of surprises! Without having asked me or having told me I was summarily elected president.

At the time he'd felt surprised, but, as well, conflicted, usurped but thankful, woozy but excited, questioning and pondering... all at the same time. He'd been about to say "No" on the spot, then realized that action would be as arbitrary as the vote. Instead, he'd pressed his tongue to the roof of his mouth, purposely pursed his lips together tightly, and slowly opened them. *"Aha!"* he'd said, rocking his head up and down like a disoriented mule not yet in harness. *"Aha."*

"Aha," Lee said now, years later, leaning forward in the rocking chair. His head shot toward the ceiling, toward the resounding "Oh?" he thought he heard. The "Oh?" like the one Judge Brockenbrough had responded.

I remember changing my Aha to "Oh?" and then back to Aha! again. Impulse, I guess, to match the judge. But right impulse. For some reason the words still sound concordant, the sentiment similar, even matching. Those simple words, that simple emotion, solidified a firm relationship between us, one that lasts. One that began even before I'd made a commitment to accept the position.

I remember asking, "There are other stipulations, are there not, Your Honor?"

The judge had told him, "Oh yes, but not many. We want a president who will lead us out of the nightmare of the last four years of war. We will depend upon your Superintendency of the United States Military Academy at West Point which you led for three-plus years."

Mrs. Lee knew her husband had disliked the task of Academy Superintendent because of the strict regimen of student courses then current in most American colleges. As her husband, she realized a graduated Army officer is still to be broadly educated in order to serve adequately a multidimensional country; a narrow curriculum hardly met that criterion.

"The requirements upon you would be to administer and lead the school as a 'collegiate' entity. Second duty would be to follow the example of our former presidents and teach philosophy courses. You will receive for all duties $1,500 a year salary, a home, a garden, and a proportion of each student's tuition."

Anyone not present would not believe at that point R. E. Lee arose from the sofa where he was seated, started to walk, and stumbled. "Teach philosophy? *Philosophy?* My goodness, Sir, I am not competent to teach philosophy."

Lee's memory instantly grabbed hold of the stipulation—I *was to teach philosophy but I wasn't a philosopher.*

The judge had replied, "Why, yes. Yes, you are well educated as well as broadly experienced in mathematics, leadership, and public relations through engineering projects you led in Savannah and New York and St. Louis... plus you know something of world systems and human beings' outreach to all that is knowable."

"But I'm not certified to teach philosophy, Judge Brockenbrough," R. E. Lee, a jobless ex-general not a jobless academician, had opined.

The Rector and Vice President of Washington College took the ex-general to task. "Philosophers are not certified like tradesmen or apprentices or even physicians or lawyers. Rather they are adjudged by their ability to philosophize, to analyze words in connection with other words to determine whether or not there is a proper rational relationship between them. To do the same with ideas, to determine proper rational relationship between and among ideas. How they function together is of crucial importance. And that words as spoken ideas attain a new, a fuller relationship among themselves and with the real world around them. And you do that quite well, Sir. You've led men to do more than load muskets and pull triggers."

Lee was puzzled that one could be competent at philosophizing without having a prescribed, definitive body of knowledge to illuminate, to depict, to expand upon such as chemistry or mathematics or engineering.

Judge Brockenbrough, about R. E. Lee's age, suggested, "I've actually told my students at Lexington Law School that the law is to generate in the mind of the student a taste for the study of law as an enlarged and rational system of jurisprudence, and to imbue them with the *philosophical* spirit which pervades throughout all its extensive ramifications; to teach them to regard law as a noble and refined science, and not merely as a crude collection of arbitrary precedents, and philosophy is of the very same warp and woof."

R. E. Lee had hesitated. A dim light seemed to emerge yet intellectually he moved only laterally. "But there will be so much to restore at the college after the war damage," he'd challenged. "So much to do to determine what to repair first. And I imagine, to recruit more students than the few from last semester during the war." Standing and rigid, as if to challenge the judge, he'd continued, "Plus, if I'm right, there also would be professors needed to supplement present staff."

Judge Brockenbrough admitted there had been only four professors and forty students the last year.

"Aha," Lee had replied. "Ahaaaaaa!"

The college Rector decided to keep his mouth shut.

Thinking he had scored points in the short debate, Lee spoke forcefully, "I'd have full work for hands and head to do for students on each of those levels as well as all levels at one and the same time. No, I would not be equipped to study in philosophy or philosophizing. At the same time management and administrative duties with you as Rector/Vice President. Recruitment of student body and possible faculty recruitment will be capital efforts post-war. No, I think I cannot accept your offer..." The old man's calm voice quietly trailed off. "Sorry, Your Honor. I think at my age I cannot do all that is required to help Washington College. Nonetheless, thank the Board of Trustees for judging me worthy of such an honor."

Years before, Lee had heard about this judge and his experience, but had not met him. Brockenbrough then sat perfectly still for at least five minutes—maybe six, seven, or even ten—as if he were in a courtroom analyzing a legal case turned over to him for arbitration. Of course thereby he dominated the non-spoken conversation from all Lees present.

The judge knew what he was doing. He neither sighed nor coughed, nor hid behind a handkerchief. Did not change position on the chair. Did not look at the ex-general one time. He was loading up a reply.

As a gentleman, Lee was outmaneuvered; he dared not interfere, although it was on his own turf at Derwent.

At last, the judge rose from his chair by a window, moved over to the front door, stood purposely as erect as he could raise his bulky body and expounded his truth with what amounted to a quick dramatic statement. "But you are an exact example of the brilliant German philosopher Immanuel Kant's description of the moral human being. You, whose moral faith is of the ever-striving and ever-seeking kind. The kind that can be embraced and lived victoriously in doing one's duty, day by day, person by person, event by event as you have stressed from your early years to today. Doing your duty above all else. That's the philosopher Kant's position."

The judge picked up his riding cape as if to leave with a melodramatic urgency that puzzled the ex-general.

"You do your duty," he continued. "Like Kant, you know theologians are wrong: there aren't metaphysical laws of nature. But there is the moral law within oneself. *'Two things fill the mind with ever new and increasing admiration and awe,'* Kant said... *'the starry heavens above and the moral law within.'* The person who obeys that inner law of not only a will but a good will rises above the fluctuating senses, impressions and enters the realm of reason leading to human freedom.

"If you view yourself objectively, Robert, you know what emphasis you place on a good will by which to live daily that then increases admiration and awe of living the human experience. You live *duty*, Sir. You have a duty to yourself, first; and you know that fact. Then you have a duty to others, realizing that fact as you seek to provide for your family and then help others also as you did with your troops in the Army. Ultimately you understand you have a duty to God, which you have lived for decades. You follow the Kantian philosophical script almost entirely... without realizing it."

Then he paused. For effect.

"Kant wrote three deep philosophical critiques. These critiques lead the way to a masterful insight beyond their contents: he entitled it 'To Eternal Peace' for life in this world. His position sparked his major point: 'Reason makes the state of peace a direct duty.' Peace is the logical human attribute, and highest consequent of his whole philosophy. The goal of true philosophy is peace. Peace, Sir: Peace.

"And you, Robert Edward Lee had sought peace in wartime by formal proposals to a higher political authority but were rejected two times, in 1862 and '63. Peace has always been your goal even as it was for Immanuel Kant.

"Sir, you know first-hand seeking peace. In your Northern Campaign of 1863 when you sought to proclaim peace not battle on the 4th of July, Independence Day for North and South, while in Pennsylvania—but were thwarted by the totally accidental battle at Gettysburg. Peace was your goal up North, not combat, and you stated that fact in your official report to the Confederate War Office. Or in 1862, weeks before battle at Antietam/Sharpsburg, Maryland, you asked President Jefferson Davis to send a peace proposal to the North. He rejected your effort. The reasonable thing would have been to make peace the South's direct duty.

"What other battlefield commander ever had the audacity to request a proposal of peace from his political commander-in-chief as the highest reasonable duty a human being can do?

"You see, Sir, you are philosophical, philosophizing about what really matters—peace. You exemplify Kant... and could teach philosophy if you would will to do so."

Lee remembered being stuck after the judge had completed presenting his case about teaching philosophy. *I knew it inevitable I'd have to review Brockenbrough's evaluation of me and my abilities, my desire for peace, plus the deal-breaker, teaching philosophy at Washington College.*

He remembered watching the judge hang his riding cape back up on a peg and hearing the judge say, *"Robert, you, philosophize about what really matters. You philosophize by actions!"*

I thought my position sound because I had never conceived of myself as philosophical, just dutiful. But I gave a weak answer in that awkward situation: "I will talk it over with my wife Mary. With our young people, too. I will then inform you shortly by postal mail of our decision." I muddled through.

I wonder how Judge John White Brockenbrough knew at that point to back away, knew I'd decide in favor of the college. He wasn't troubled nor hostile and didn't push for an instant answer.

Wider awake now than directly after lunch Lee urged his feet to move the rocking chair vigorously while he pondered, *What is nagging at me?*

All of a sudden he stopped rocking with a jerk. *That's it! Sister Mary's secretive smile. And buttermilk.*

He'd remembered correctly. Sister Mary, eldest of the daughters, had been smiling secretly to herself. Innocently she previously had done something unplanned that might have farsightedly enabled her father's possible college presidential status. She never told that story until decades later after all members of the family had pre-deceased her.

And daughter Eleanor Agnes had taken it upon herself to offer everyone the buttermilk their mother had made the day before as it was her Papa's favorite beverage.

I gave a rousing Amen to the serving of buttermilk. The group probably saw that like the laughing a jackass does when it gets fresh water in the morning.

Then John White Brockenbrough had bid the family, "Farewell, Lees. The Eternal Father keep you in the hollow of his hand." Instantly one other Lee knew how she would vote if father and mother included offspring in decision making. Two votes were now secure for Washington College. And the judge left

Derwent convinced he knew Lee's answer would be positive. Old age has insights all its own.

Some trustees back in Lexington who heard of the conversation later reckoned, "The judge knew Lee's answer logically." Others said, "Intuitively." Another trustee noted, "The Judge caught Lee in his own trap." One wag put in his own two cents worth, happily noting, "Lee and Brockenbrough are two peas in a pod; it must have been an affable sparring match—but I'd never want to go up against that backwoods judge. He's got too many cards in his deck."

Back in their cabin where the Lee family lived sparingly there was quiet appreciation and time to plan ahead for their good fortune. On his part Lee had known about philosophy's history for it had a long story line in Western nations ever since ancient Greece. Also, he remembered its place in Western higher education, including most American colleges. But the idea of teaching philosophy had circumscribed him tightly.

He'd sought help from a local Episcopal priest and one of his ex-officers concerning Immanuel Kant: his writings, stories, mannerisms, scuttlebutt, honors, virtues, weaknesses, anything about that philosopher who was born in 1724 in Koenigsberg, East Prussia, and died there in 1804, two years before Brockenbrough's birth and three years before Lee's.

Kant's philosophy had swept European and American philosophy, and now it flooded over Lee. He let himself appreciate the deluge. He came to understand he could have philosophized, although it might have been one-dimensional.

When Judge Brockenbrough returned to Lexington he was so absolutely certain Lee would accept the challenge as president he pled a cause with the Trustees of Washington College. The Board acquiesced in his recommendation to print handouts and newspaper advertisements to publicize the Autumn Semester. They were mailed across Virginia and as far as New Orleans in Louisiana, Atlanta in Georgia, St. Louis in Missouri, even Baltimore in Maryland, Philadelphia in Pennsylvania, and New York City, but not Washington, D.C. Many small town newspapers additionally received it using all the copies of the ad.

The Trustees passed a motion that the ads not be published until Lee had accepted their offer. Brockenbrough as a Board member acquiesced. He was astute as educator, lawyer, judge, and college Rector/Vice President. He had 100 copies printed for distribution then 15 more for good luck. All were used.

WASHNGTON COLLEGE
A non-sectarian Christian college
Lexington, Virginia
R. E. Lee, President

Autumn Semester 1865 and Spring Semester 1866
2 October to 22 December 1865 and 1 February to 12 May 1866
Late start available Autumn semester only. Graduation 13 May 1866.

Degrees granted: B.A., Bachelor of Arts; B.S., Bachelor of Science

Tuition $300 per year; 15-18 credit hours per semester. Some financial aid available. Room and Board; cost varies by availability.

Courses offered on two and three year cycles for 120 credit hours towards graduation.

Courses of Study:
Agriculture, Animal Husbandry, Art, Athletics, Biology, Business, Chemistry, Education, English, French, Geography, Greek, History, Industrial Arts, Latin, Law & Government, Literature (American and English), Mathematics, Music, Natural Sciences, Philosophy, Physics, Social Sciences.

Apply to: Rector, Washington College, Lexington, Virginia

(Signed) Judge John White Brockenbrough
Rector

Some facts of those early days of becoming and being President of Washington College lay too deep in memory for Lee to retrieve. Close to the surface, though, was this thought: *It's a shame I never taught philosophy at the college. I came too late to that realization.*

The judge and educated college trustees had known it all along. They knew students missed beholding a giant human living life in full measure, a happening that would have helped them abide victoriously after the South's political defeat. They sorrowed, at the same time, that R. E. Lee missed one of the most exceptional opportunities an educator at any level can have. He missed the joy of sharing with students directly, personally, intellectually, and spiritually in changing the future and exalting the past at the same time in the present.

Lee missed what a philosopher wrote about his contemporary Immanuel Kant:

> *Kant may be said to have been always clear and attractive. He conducted, one may say, an* experiment *before his audience, as if he himself was <u>beginning</u> to meditate on the subject.*

Another philosopher, a former student, pronounced the famous evaluation of Kant as a top notch teacher:

> *His open, thoughtful brow was the seat of unfailing cheerfulness and joy; the profoundest language fell from his lips; jest, wit, humour stood at his command; and his instructive address was like a most <u>entertaining</u> conversation... always coming back to the disinterested study of nature, and the moral dignity of man[kind].*

Judge John White Brockenbrough and the college Board of Trustees told Lee he could have been an American Immanuel Kant, professor extraordinaire. They lamented the world would not know him as philosopher, as well as army general.

Lolling in his rocking chair Lee moved between contentment and discontent. He had not wanted to be an American Kant. He'd never wanted to be anyone other than Robert Edward Lee, a man. *But maybe it is a shame I never taught philosophy at the college.*

This thought preyed on his mind and puzzled him: *Perhaps I ought spend some of my remaining earthly time with philosophy.*

CHAPTER 33

Duty Awakened, and Doing It

There was no *perhaps* about it. R. E. Lee recognized the new duty that had surfaced was for him to carry out.

I'm tired, I hope it's the last duty to arise. Tired, tired, much of the time. I could have, yes, should have, philosophized with the college students. That opportunity is gone. It seems a duty to myself remains, though.

Lee rose from his desk chair, straightened his back from its bent-over stance and moved around, gathering this, gathering that, returning to place all on his desk.

I'll put every book and paper I have about philosophy and history and politics here on the desk and have a go.

He sat back down, sharpened the nib on his pen, stretched his mental faculties and began work.

Then, just as quickly he stopped. *I can't write without opening these books and rereading some of what I've read before. I'll read this morning, write this afternoon.*

He rose again, extracted from the mound of books the titles seeming to offer the best first challenge, then moved for better light while reading Socrates, Jesus, and Abraham Lincoln heavy in his hands.

He read all morning long in his office under the chapel at Washington College.

He ate lunch, took a half-hour nap, and then began to write. In the past, writing ideas always had led him to new understanding. He trusted this time would be no different.

In bold script he wrote on the top of the left-side page of a leather ledger-type journal:

"Socrates, Jesus, and Abraham Lincoln, wise men"

And on the right-side page he wrote in bold:

"R. E. Lee, myself"

Across the centerfold of the ledger he wrote:

"What We Hold in Common"

And beneath the left-page heading he added:

The wisest of philosophers, Socrates of Athens, condemned to die, easily could have avoided that penalty. Friends had bribed the jailers, and, with their assistance Socrates could have escaped prison. But he persisted in his truth, and freely drank the deadly hemlock. Had he walked away from death by the State he would have given the death sentence to his own life of seeking the truth at any cost. Dying by the hand of the State he lives.

Jesus of Nazareth, could easily have avoided the Temple Guards and Roman Legionnaires. The night before his crucifixion he could have escaped out the back entrance to the Garden of Gethsemane free when they came to arrest him. But he persisted in his truth and freely went to crucifixion. Had he walked away from death by Religious and State complicity he would have given the death sentence to his own life of seeking to live truth at any cost. Dying by the hands of Guards and Legionnaires he lives.

Abraham Lincoln, accosted by a stark, thoroughly depressing premonition of his own death, easily could have avoided public assassination. He could have remained home and not attended a play at Ford Theatre. But he persisted in his truth of all Americans being free and so went about in public freely. Had he walked away from being open to the public who supported the Union he would have given the death sentence to his own life of seeking to live his truth at any cost. Dying by the assassin's bullet he lives.

Beneath the right-side heading he wrote:

I could have avoided rejection by Northerners who judge me traitor for abdicating military allegiance to the United States of America. Some of my fellow Southerners adjudged me traitor to the "Lost Cause" because I surrendered my army to the United States of America and then counseled comrades-in-arms against guerilla warfare, "night riders," and the KKK.

Had I walked away from serving small, war-torn Washington College of forty students and four professors and accepted leadership at a proffered larger, more affluent and prestigious college, or had I taken the $10,000 per year job as president of an insurance company whose officials had said, "only for the use of your name," well, then I would have given the death sentence to my life-long foundational principle of duty and seeking to be honorable at any cost.

Now, five years after the War of the Rebellion I am ill and dying. Pain cloaks me often, and other times envelops me in spells of silence. Death no longer conveys the idea of time ending, but rather Life's fulfillment. Life forever. Truth enduring.

Lee, of course, could not know he would become second to Abraham Lincoln as the most written about person in American history. Nor could he know the honor of paragon military icon would go to him, a positively non-victor, a decided loser.

Among military heroes Lee is the iconic American general. Not George Washington, not Winfield Scott, not "Rough Rider" Theodore Roosevelt, not General John J. "Black Jack" Pershing, not acclaimed, and self-acclaimed, General Douglas MacArthur, nor even General Dwight Eisenhower, leader of the most massive invasion army and navy ever, stand above him in American history. Lee is the person representative of military genius and heroism.

It is Lee who is the very embodiment of the motto of the United States Military Academy at West Point: *DUTY, HONOR, COUNTRY*. The loser Lee had been outstanding as a student at West Point, later became Superintendent of that Military Academy, then the father of the outstanding student of the very highest Academy standing, higher than his own, his eldest son, George Washington Custis Lee.

Lee began a new entry across both ledger pages:

There was always something more for Socrates, Jesus, Lincoln, and Something or Someone more for me. For all of us it was more than an idea of grandeur, more than a belief in greatness, and more than a perception of being predestined—there was Something or Someone. Certainly for me there was something more than living a life and fighting battles toward the purpose of pomp and circumstance. There's been more than just my personal earthly destiny at play; I've been part of something larger that future generations will tell or sing about. So too it was with Socrates, Jesus, Lincoln.

They lived something more, something other than such emotional traps as legends, sagas, epics, romances, adventures, even history or simple chains of events. Their stories are preternatural, unprecedented, mysterious. They are not history as an objective recall of empirical events but a *Heilsgeschichte,* a progressive self-revelation of Infinite Reality, of God in and for Life and Salvation when needed.

I will say the same for myself. I imagine that in their lives, as in mine, there was the unveiling of Something humans keep discovering for our welfare in this life as well as beyond: Something that inspires. At times, even leads.

Heilsgeschichte can be a stumbling block. That the Infinite Being, Creator and Ruler, out of the whole Universe should have chosen this galaxy, this star system, this rocky planet, a particular nomadic tribe at the eastern end of the Mediterranean Sea which escaped centuries-long slave captivity, then wandered forty years in a desert, finally formed a kingdom, then while some followers accepted one individual man as savior they trusted with full earnest their prophetic idea of the Infinite Being's universality for the welfare of all humankind in order to accomplish its Divine Will is a completely amazing life-sustaining ethic for millions throughout human history.

True, a stumbling block, yet indeed, Rock of Ages, or Cornerstone of the Universe in this Milky Way Galaxy, in this Solar System, on our planet Earth: *miraculum et lamenta.* Miracle and Lamentation.

That message coincides with the paradoxical, existential nature of human life, dovetailing particularly in importance with the sanctity of individual human beings yet the impunity with which they treat one another disastrously.

Yet, stumbling blocks sometimes are stepping stones.

Origen, of Alexandria, Egypt—a Greek scholar of the second and third centuries A.D.—wrote about a stumbling block becoming a stepping stone:

> *When we see in him some things so human they appear to differ in no respect from the common and some things so divine that they can appropriately belong to nothing else than to the primal and ineffable nature of deity, the human understanding with its narrow limits is baffled and struck with amazement at so mighty a wonder, knows not which way to turn, or what to behold or what to hold to. If it thinks of God, it sees a man, if it thinks of man, it beholds one returning from the dead with spoils after vanquishing the domain of death.*

R. E. Lee, a stumbling block himself, admitted vanquishing the domain of death... meriting spoils of respect, of honor, of esteem. Before he faced the mystery of death head on he declared, "I can only say that I am nothing but a poor sinner, trusting in Christ alone for salvation."

Still, Lee purposely sought to live a deliberate life to the end as a completed education. He exemplified words of a famous Northern Ireland/British scholar: "Aim at heaven and you will get earth thrown in. Aim at earth and you will get neither."

Some few humans stand out and above others as saviors of one sort or another. Lee knew it to be so about Socrates, Jesus, Abraham Lincoln. He did not know history would place him securely in the company of those sages.

"Sometimes a gorgeous Tragedy does sweep by... where more is meant than meets the ear!"

CHAPTER 34

Prompts from an Unknown Philosopher

R. E. Lee looked hard and long at the piles of books, loose papers, newspapers, and pamphlets he'd arranged on his desk. He'd made "topical" stacks: History, Race, Redemption/Reconciliation, Things to tell Corley, Unknown Philosopher.

How am I to do this last duty I see? It's not enough to identify how far away I am from the mark of Socrates, Lincoln, and Jesus. I'd certainly have had to do more than that had I taught philosophy, done philosophy, with college students.

Where shall I begin? It seems a daunting enterprise to think about my thinking, to reason about my reasoning.

He answered his questions by picking up a sheaf of loose papers from the pile he'd labeled "By An Unknown Philosopher."

How did I come by this work? He struggled for an answer but memory would not come to his aid.

"Human beings are distillers," began the first page written by that unknown philosopher.

I agree with that statement, thought Lee. *I'll start here.*

Then, except for prolonged periods spent considering how what he read fit with his reasoning and experience, he read until the stack was half its original size.

"Human beings are distillers," the philosopher repeated. Then he expanded: "Each of us brews a heady draft of living. At any particular instant we blend whatever comes into our *physical-intellectual-spiritual* being with what is presently ___e. All we encounter at birth, and, definitely afterwards, makes potent tipples of the hard stuff of human experience.

"We distill whatever comes in through our five senses, our skin, our brain. We carve, squeeze, concentrate, shape, condense, sculpt, cleanse, refine, crystallize, magnify, filter, mold, purify, expand, deform, develop, or re-form *without exception* anything and everything incoming to our very *physical-intellectual-spiritual* beings. The reason is simple: We see things *as we are,* not as they are, in and of themselves. We distill all incoming information.

"Whatever we grasp we distill into human 'wine.' Sounds become ideas, needs convert to aspirations. If we boil oats to make wallpaper adhesive, or if we browbeat with accusations to make declarations of war, or if we purify purposes to make them into creeds of faith or pledges of allegiance, we've been distilling these items into something more, something else than they were alone.

"Put another way, we've been making our own selves in our own ways in our own worlds.

"As we mature, nearly from the instant of first breathing, we begin another process that involves a grander distillation. It is an amazingly rich process: we perceive that other *physical-intellectual-spiritual* beings are something, are selves much like our selves, and we incorporate them in our distillation.

"Without realizing it, the truth of wholesale distillation extracts the essential meaning of something and makes it ours, too. Such extraction of meaning from relationship is the beginning of *community*, that is a sodality, from the Latin *soldalitus*, a *companionship* of like entities.

"When full-grown a grander distillation matures and results in a still grander reality: *communion.* The *'common union'* is a common unity of shared outlook, shared purpose, shared action. As 'common unity' it performs a simple (not simplistic) act, and rewards by expanding us, thereby adding to Nature.

"When one analyzes it, history is one of the prime building elements of humanness with overwhelming 'thatness' and/or 'whatness.' <u>That</u> something is, exists at all, then <u>what</u> it is as something in particular. Thatness becomes a whatness meaning something, existence... that something is... always precedes essence... what it exists as.

"We are a species which has massive assets; we name those assets as 'that' story or another 'that' history. All told and all tolled, human beings have a history. A more precise way of describing us might well be 'We are a history.'

"Other species of life have a history imputed to them, a given history. They do not exemplify, detail a history *per se*, nor put on record past events or future possibilities—as far as we know. If they do so exemplify, they give no evidence of it to others, such as our human species.

"Our nearest natural relatives, anthropoid apes, may have a history, but they give no evidence of knowing and analyzing their ancient forebears or descendants beyond the welfare of their own progeny. They live by instincts; instincts help preserve their lives. Their domain is, *rightly*, their life in *toto*, no more and no less.

"Human life on the other hand is our own *and* our ancestors' (by attribution and remembrance) *as well as* our descendants (by attribution and aspiration). We three are bound in the bundle of life, that is, we are the present, the past, the future.

"War interferes massively in human lives. It radically destroys much of present, much more of the past, and conceivably future living human beings. War mutilates our ancestors while doing so to present human beings. Yet who knows how many will not possibly live, well-nigh blanking out future heirs.

"Then unplanned—but perversely—our wars do the same to other species, species that did not start wars, nor fight them, nor win or lose them. Such broad exploitation by war is un-natural, so irrational, so unfair to non-participants and to the planet. What other species wages war over the planet without taking other species into account?

"It well could be humanity has a peculiar, a freakish task: destroy itself to save this planet for the trillions of other species on it."

R. E. Lee read the document a second time before pondering its implications. He called to mind the setting by a brook that bubbled idea after idea in his head where he wrestled for half a day with life's magnificence. He began to consider how he perceived human greatness in the academic setting of which he was a part, human greatness in intellectually-minded people there, faculty, students, students' parents. He went on to reflect on human greatness in his own family.

Then he deliberated what, in his point of view, constitutes human greatness. There was no contest among concepts when he considered himself: Deep Faith was his answer.

His own deep Faith visualized human beings as God's caretakers of this life, this earth, this Eden, the physical and spiritual all around us, a garden of virtually limitless resources.

There welled up in his being John Milton's discerning poem about Divine Providence from two centuries before:

Let us with a gladsome mind praise the Lord for he is kind:
He with all-commanding might filled the world with light:
For his mercies shall endure, ever faithful ever sure.

Human beings are distillers: Lee knew full well he had realized in himself a deeper, or higher, or broader Faith: "When Life and Love and God are One." He was more than male, more than soldier, more than Confederate, more than academician, more than American, more than white, more than Christian, even something more than human. When Life, a spontaneous creating action, joins Love, also spontaneous and creating action, they merge with God, the monumentally awe-inspiring Creator. That blending originates a New Being: as One, a perfect Unity.

This is what I want remembered of me, he thought. He took up his pen, opened the ledger journal to a fresh page, and wrote the same bold heading on both left-side and right-side of the journal:

"Philosophic Truths Realized"

When he finished writing about how the philosopher's distilled points had led him to conceptualize Faith, Lee sighed deeply with relief.

But it's not enough—that thought came quickly. *It was necessary but not sufficient,* he concluded. He smiled at how quickly that *necessary but not sufficient* philosophic term had come to him: *Maybe I am a philosopher.*

But I have to work with war. And peace. He closed the ledger as he thought, *Another day. I'll consider sufficiency another day.*

It was not long before another day for reflecting and philosophizing arrived. R. E. Lee was at home, too tired to attend to academics that day.

I will consider war today, from home. I don't need the books piled on my desk at the college to prompt my reasoning about war, or about peace, he thought. And so he began.

As there had been a growing sensitivity for peace before and during the War of the Rebellion I asked the sitting political powers to seek peace. They would not have it, so I slowly became pacifistic. Albeit, I am a provisional pacifist: if and only if one, or one's homeland... adjudged a veritable Garden of Eden... were attacked. "That still holds," he heard himself speak aloud.

My struggle leaves me with a poisoned present and a disillusioned future when I contemplate the Franco-Prussian (German) war in Europe. France and Prussia had previously signed a treaty to arbitrate issues before going to war with one another. Nevertheless they warred.

Paper fades or shreds. Intentions weaken. Willpower diminishes. Stupidity increases. What is known as stupidity makes room for hatred and the worst stupidity—killing people kills both ideas and ideals.

The ex-general seriously suspected the Prussian War would lead to other wars that would lead to still others.

Lee opened the ledger and wrote these thoughts to evidence a bit more philosophic sufficiency:

America is not involved in Europe's alliances and wars but I have been disillusioned about the future. So disillusioned I informed my college faculty of my provisional pacifism. My eldest daughter Mary is embracing my stance as well. He would write more later as he deemed his philosophical musings to become more sound.

CHAPTER 35

Redemption: Is it Possible?

Over and over again R. E. Lee questioned: *Is my personal redemption possible?*

He had been interested in religious questions, historical and doctrinal, long before and long after he had become Christian in the Anglican/Episcopal tradition. He'd been instructed in the Episcopal catechism. However, interest and instruction in religion and self-examination of a spiritual kind that pertains to said religion are two different entities.

Self-examination usually is irritating. For Lee it was awfully irritating. Scrutinizing himself post-war centered on inaction, non-lighting of the world by his *inner light.* He had not followed Jesus carefully: *"Let your light so shine before men that they may see your good works and glorify your Father which is in heaven."*

On 17 July 1853, at age forty-six, Lee had been formally and properly catechized, confirmed in the Christian Faith, during a worship service in Christ Church, Alexandria, Virginia, alongside teenage daughters Anne Carter Lee and Eleanor Agnes Lee.

It had been highly unusual, though not wrong in any sense, their sire's confirmation with them as young people. All three kneeling at the chancel rail to join the Christian Faith was a moving sight. Two teens and one adult of the same family, two callow girls and one battle-tested veteran, side-by-side joined in religious communion of the Christian Church. It was an atypical event for the congregation, though a beacon accepted readily because it was R. E. Lee.

Lee's mother-in-law, Mary Lee "Molly" Fitzhugh Custis, had died April 23, 1853, a mere three months before his acceptance of Christianity. Presence of a religious life disappeared dramatically for R. E. Lee upon her death. He often told people, "She is the most Christian person I ever knew."

It's possible, maybe even likely, that by example she led R. E. Lee to the Christian Faith that bolstered him the remaining seventeen years of his life. It's possible her life was so overwhelmingly noble it influenced him to join with his daughters in that unorthodox activity of religious communion that stayed with him every day thereafter.

Mrs. Custis' record of Christian love for blacks and whites was *nonpareil* in a racist, capitalistic culture. It was unrivaled for everyone who knew her, in a time when it was a crime in Virginia to educate Negroes to read, or for them to marry legally. Both offenses could result in financial penalty or jail. Nonetheless, Molly Custis loved and provided for all God's children.

And Lee loved her. Lee adored her, held her in the highest esteem of all human beings he knew, including his own mother. Mother Custis' death expedited his conversion; he didn't want to miss her faith that was Life for her. Nor miss her joy. Mary Lee Fitzhugh Custis, though dead, lived in the lives of the least, the last, the lost around her. The true and brave also: Robert Edward Lee included.

The idea of personal redemption had become more ominous and challenging for him as he grew older, the more distant he was from the battlefields of his career, figuratively and literally. Beginning to think of his deepest thoughts as philosophic enough to record, he wrote in the leather-bound ledger, "I am bothered deep-seatedly by an exchange view of redemption—that some error, sin, could be redeemed, bought back, the wrong or wrongs of human life negotiated away by beliefs in Christian virtues. I find the concept artificial, too mechanical, too man-made.

"If redemption means someone else will pay the price for my errors—and everyone else's—I find it opposite common sense which does reason's spade-work... and never should be shoved aside.

"If redemption is a concept only, a mental construct, without any explanation or rationale I find it off-target, unsound.

"And, if one does not have a concept of redemption at all, it is plain stupid because there definitely are, in this world, corruptions and crimes, errors and fallacies, injustices and sins, villainies and wrongs. They do exist. In multiples, too. They need to be rectified. But how? *En masse*; worldwide? Or a wordy profession? A creedal formula?

"I find it honest and necessary that the Christian Faith deal with reality, with the *need* for redemption."

"Woe is me," in some variation was Lee's daily lament and ledger entry concerning personal redemption.

The more he pondered the matter the more convinced he became that an answer was necessary, yet, conceivably impossible to attain. If the latter case existed, humankind would be doomed; there is no exit from impossibility. "Woeful is humankind."

Chiefly, R. E. Lee's own conscience had bulked-up massively against him after the close of hostilities. He would not visit the fields of battle where he failed to win, but, as well, even those fields on which he was the victor. Trying not to think of either way proved to be unsuccessful effort in the post-war world.

He knew full well his faulty choice of a military strategy of offense had not conserved lives but had marked him as audacious *in extremis*. His authentic casualty rate was higher than Union commanders, higher than his chief opponent General U. S. Grant who was considered by Southerners a "butcher." Although actual numbers of Confederate casualties were lower because Lee's armies had fewer troops than the Union forces they faced, his rate of casualties was higher; "audacious slaughter" it was labeled North and South.

Those tens of thousands killed remained in Lee's heart. He recalled them daily. In fact, the tens of thousands of Federals his army killed heaped so high he would become infamous for having killed more Americans than anyone in the world, ever.

With such a record how can I be redeemed? he mused. *By stating an apology? By repentance? By prayer? By remaining silent, as if the spiritual terror would vanish, be forgotten in time?* Neither philosophy nor learned religion lessened his daily questioning and angst. It was a righteous struggle, and right for him to struggle.

He wrote in the ledger, "How can losing a war redeem a person? How can one clear oneself by living in the pristine environment of a college campus? Does a lost cause come with a free pass justifying tens of thousands of men and boys ordered into death's jaws simply because grieving will cease and their names forgotten?"

Lee had persisted in his military battlefield tactic of repeatedly attacking, attacking, attacking. Sacrificing, as he considered his troops were doing, with so little overall effect. Or to no avail at all. Starvation finally laid waste his army more than battle, so what rationalization could he conjure for continuing warfare?

How did he sleep at night? On the battlefield? At Derwent the summer after the war in free digs? On clean sheets in the President's House at Washington College? How could he live with himself? R. E. Lee fought his private emotional, legal, spiritual war of *Lee vs. Lee* while at the same time living for peace.

Is honor still important post-war? How important is duty? Lee asked those questions of himself daily. He answered the duty query. Duty was important because it takes at least one virtue, such as obedience to duty, to assess oneself as human—although too often duty is only what one expects from others rather than what one expects of oneself.

He was carrying out the newly arisen duty to look at himself philosophically. Did he still have other duty to himself? To others? To God? He wondered and obsessed about those things.

He wrestled, particularly, with his new involvement with a post-war group making excuses for the "Lost Cause" of the Rebellion. To console Southern pride the group expended much effort promoting the misbegotten and misleading Lost Cause across the former seceded states. It flourished from Virginia to Texas, Missouri to Florida. It championed Southern leaders like nobles of King Arthur's Roundtable, Southerners for being united in support of the Confederacy, Southern women for being stalwart supporters of "The Cause," and Confederate armies for not being out-fought but out-gunned by Northern factories and then overwhelmed by armies comprised of immigrants and blacks.

Mostly the "Lost Cause" significantly held views that slavery was a congenial institution for slave and slave owner alike. Benevolent masters supposedly treated slaves warmheartedly. And *Uncle Tom's Cabin, Or Life Among the Lowly*, written by Harriet Beecher Stowe was a lie. "A downright despicable lie," echoed and re-echoed throughout Dixieland.

The group emphasized "states' rights" as the chief cause of Secession and Rebellion, not slavery. However slavery had been the very "cornerstone" during Secession as pronounced by Vice President Alexander Stephens of the Confederate States. He had made clear before and during the war that everyone could see equality of blacks and whites was false doctrine:

> *Our new government is founded upon exactly the opposite ideas; its foundations are laid, its cornerstone rests, upon the great truth that the negro is not equal to the white man; that slavery, subordination to the superior race, is his natural and normal condition. This, our new government, is the first in the history of the world, based upon this great physical, philosophical, and moral truth. This truth has been slow in the process of its development, like all other truths in the various departments of science.*

Stephens changed his racist tune somewhat after the war. Then he, too, cited violation of states' rights, not slavery, as the cause of the Rebellion. When one lie doesn't work, human beings readily use another even though it is still a lie. A lie is a handle that fits all evils.

Lee had joined the group because his values were aligned with those of Lost Cause. He was aligned, but conflicted in his alignment.

How can I hold Mother Molly Custis in such high regard for her love and equal treatment of all God's people and believe as I do about the equivalence of black people and other breeds not colored white as the majority?

At least once a day he reached into his jacket pocket nearest his lapel and unfolded a piece of paper on which he'd copied lines from that unknown philosopher:

The first delusion we human beings have about the human condition is what the wisest of philosophers, Socrates of Athens, named misanthropy, the hatred of humanness. The second worst delusion we have about the human condition is hatred for branches of the human family other than ourselves, which is called racism.

"I may not hate branches of humanity but I do not think them all equal," Lee ashamedly wrote in the ledger.

He shivered as he read the remainder of the philosopher's words before he re-folded the paper and returned it to his pocket:

Hatred for a segment of humanity is deadly in the long run as it easily sneaks into hatred of all humanness by human beings. Second place always labors to become first place.

Darkness does not know it is dark since there is not light to show it to itself. Lee was trying to get to the light, his folded-over note reflected the light, but never in his lifetime was there fully successful meeting.

Attempting to relieve the pressure he felt about not being redeemable, R. E. Lee compelled himself to uncover what he really knew about his belief system.

He moved back in his mind to the first emotional storm in his life, at six, seven years of age. His father had deserted the family for the Caribbean.

Then another man, one related to his education, filled a bit of the void.

That man, Benjamin Hallowell, lived next door and had opened a school there. *He devoted extra hours and days to me as an adolescent boy,* Lee remembered. *That little gift of time and attention turned into a mighty endowment, as many such gifts do.*

Hallowell, a Quaker, a member of the Society of Friends, would write about R. E. Lee later in life:

Robert Lee entered my school in Alexandria, Va, in the winter of 1824–25, to study mathematics, preparatory to his going to West Point. He was a most exemplary student in every respect. He was never behind time at his studies, never failed in a single recitation, was perfectly observant of the rules and regulations of the institution; was gentlemanly, unobtrusive, and respectful in all his deportment to teachers and fellow-students. His specialty was finishing up. He imparted a neatness and finish to everything he undertook. One of the branches of mathematics he studied with me was conic sections, in which some of the diagrams were very complicated. He drew the diagrams on a slate, and although he well knew that the one he was drawing would have to be removed to make room for the next, he drew each one with as much accuracy and finish, lettering and all, as if it were to be engraved and printed. The same traits he exhibited at my school he carried with him to West Point where, I have been told, he never received a mark of demerit, and graduated at the head of his class. [Actually second in class standing.]

Lee remembered how gentle Hallowell had been and that he'd shared some of his Faith in the leisure times they two had together evenings and weekends.

He rummaged next through what he had heard about Christianity from the Christ Episcopal Church pastor so dear to his heart, William Meade. Content eluded him, but his memory produced an event of significance:

Rev. Wm. Meade, church rector, and, afterwards, the venerated Bishop of Virginia taught me the Episcopal catechism. Many years later when I passed through Richmond, as army commander, I heard he was on his dying bed at the house of a friend in that city. I went to see him.

I was told that the Bishop, in his weakened state, said, "I must see R. E. Lee, if but for a few moments." When I

approached the bed and asked, "How are you to-day, Bishop?"
he replied, "Almost gone."

His voice was scarcely audible: "But I wanted to see you
once more. God bless you, Robert! God bless you, and fit you for
your high and responsible duties. I can't call you General; I
must call you Robert. I have heard your Catechism so often."

I took the Bishop's emaciated hand and held it while he
asked me some few questions about the state of the country and
the army, showing, as he always did, the most lively interest in
the success of the Southern cause.

He pressed my hand warmly, and said, "Heaven bless you.
Heaven bless you, and give you wisdom for your important and
arduous duties." I returned the pressure of his feeble hand, and
then stood silent and motionless by his bedside for some minutes
before I left the room.

I remember Bishop Meade died the next morning.

Lee's time of remembering Hallowell and Meade, both
Christian of differing persuasions, cleared his perception. Now
he realized why the biblical passage about "letting your light
shine" so resonated and challenged him: *Redemption is being
faithful to the inner light, the key concept of Quaker teaching.*
That phrase, in Hallowell's voice, echoed in his memory.

More remembrance surfaced: *The inner light invites
seeking. It lights up the seeker's true life. The term "inner light"
has simplicity, clarity, direct given-ness. It is "being there"
already.*

But is remembering all that important? he asked himself.
Perhaps it's not enough.

Certainly what he had told daughters Annie and Agnes a
short time after his actual confirmation was not enough: "There
isn't reasoning or complex formulations of logic concerning faith
matters, about living a faith-full life, about the Christ, God,
salvation. Nor are rambunctious displays of religion what Faith
is about. I heard that from Hallowell before I went to West Point;
I saw it in Meade from my young years to adulthood."

I'll have to tell the daughters more–this, about the light.

*But the women have not sent thousands upon thousands of
men to their deaths, as I have,* he thought next.

I feel death by the thousands stalking me.

R. E. Lee could not redeem himself, no matter how much he thought about what he needed.

He'd already discarded the notion of "Leave it to the professionals," a new slogan of industrializing America. Some churches were becoming more and more professional, having college- and seminary-educated and trained clergy, adding to their advertisement of being Southern to note their separateness from the North. There now were Southern Baptists, Southern Methodists, Southern Presbyterian, many *Southern this or that!* Southern professionals could not offer him redemption.

As Lee's health deteriorated his personal need for redemption became accusatory. He saw in himself fault-line fractures separating him from true redemption.

Too many people had pronounced him "saint"; too many times he had been designated the noblest of human beings. Way more than enough people, more than enough times, both North and South, had pronounced him worthy of the highest office in the newly re-United States: President.

He did not succumb to that flattery, to none at all. Nevertheless, he reflected, *I know myself rather thoroughly, still, might those honeyed words be stuck somewhere on me?*

As he evaluated, Lee found himself unfree of sin. His own redemption demanded of him not so much a reexamination of his past as an evaluation of what he was now thinking and doing in post-war South. Deservedly he discovered the degrading power of sinning as he persisted in rejection of black people, thereby rejecting the possibility of God's good graces for blacks as well as whites.

Sinning, that is, continuing in sin, is the direst sin.

He struggled: *I voiced a restrictive rule that favored white people over Negroes. I responded to an invitation to appear before a committee of the United States Congress and contended that black people should not be allowed to vote because they are uneducated, therefore, unable to vote intelligently. But no one asked me whether or not white voters vote intelligently. Nor do I know how they vote. And there are no black students at Washington College.*

I am terribly weak on my beloved mother-in-law's belief that "all God's children" deserve respect in life. I fall way short of my intellectual devotion to the Christian Faith and to the grand model of Mary Anna Randolph Custis, unrivaled and unmatched Christian.

Lee held a deep perception of himself as servant: Servant of a dreadfully arthritic, wheelchair-bound wife; servant of several hundred young males in the college who needed help acclimating themselves to the *post bellum* nation wherein they were defeated underdogs. Those youth needed to prepare themselves to become leaders in the new America of frontier of gold, rapid growth, and thousands upon thousands of immigrants, to painstakingly repair everything Southern: agricultural, economic, intellectual, political, and religious.

Above both those practical servant-hoods he wanted to be a servant of the Eternal God for humanity's salvation. As easy as that condition seemed available with worship, biblical study, daily prayer, good manners and better intentions, it was the hardest of the three labors—wife, students, God—to accomplish.

Adding his failures at servant-hood to the burden of his military audacity that had caused thousands upon thousands of deaths, and his inability to recognize the equality of all people, he knew one thing—he could not redeem himself.

R. E. Lee gave up.

Only God could perform salvific duty from sinning. And it could happen only transcendentally, inexplicably.

But he was not certain. He brooded: *How can an act centered on a cross on a hill far away in a country at the far eastern end of the Mediterranean Sea almost 2,000 years ago redeem me? How?*

He thought it impossible... most of the time.

The *inner light* he thought not to be shining in Negroes and whites equally was not shining overly bright in R. E. Lee.

He riddled himself with conundrums, interiorizing them until the time he could forgive himself—if that were even possible.

The most significant: *Is my redemption possible?*

CHAPTER 36

Reconciliation is Possible

Robert Edward Lee did not feel himself redeemed, did not see himself redeemed, did not know himself to be redeemed.

Lee, unredeemed, was repentant nevertheless.

There were ten thousands by ten thousands of dead Americans for whom he bore responsibility. He repented every night. Every day, equally.

One cannot deny death. One is constrained heavily by tens of thousands of deaths. Often compelled. And impaled. Always in need of repentance.

He struggled: *What remains in my soul if redemption is impossible? What remains of my soul?*

Redemption for R. E. Lee, of course, was in the Eternal Father's hands, not in his, not in his wife's, not in his president's. His redemption was not even in his most godly deceased mother-in-law's hands. It was in the hands of no one at all. Save God.

God redeems, no one else.

But there is reconciliation, a Christian virtue, too. Lee knew reconciliation was necessary on the ground for America. He leaned heavily on the promise in the biblical proclamation: "God was in Christ reconciling the world unto himself."

He began to hear in those words that he could be returned to harmonious relationship with his Creator. *A new birth*, he called it. *A new birth like the one Abraham Lincoln saw possible for the nation.* "...That this nation, under God, shall have a new birth of freedom." Lee's reconciliation with God would be his singular birth of freedom.

In private conversations Lee would say, "The South had to lose the war. It was about perpetuating a faulty proposition that all men are not equal with some men having the right to own other men as property. Equally, we have to stay in the Union for 'stick-to-it-ive-ness' of our resolute values of family and Faith, morality and manners."

He would elaborate, "The North had to follow the South; the South had to follow the North so there could be a re-United States of America to fulfill pointedly the Constitution, itself, in the Bill of Rights, Articles 9 and 10: 'The enumeration in the Constitution, of certain rights, shall not be construed to deny or disparage others retained by the people themselves.' And, importantly, 'The powers not delegated to the United States by the Constitution, nor prohibited by it to the states, are reserved to the states respectively,' or to the people." The people, Yes. And again: Yea, Verily!

The American people reign by Constitutional order and may add to the "rights of man." They make expanding the rights of citizens into the fundamental human right for Americans, in a unique way. Unparalleled, Americans can and do create new rights for citizens. An example is the "Fifth Amendment," that an accused person does not have to speak, but has the right to remain silent if he or she claims that right.

When a nation, such as the United States of America, expands rights for its citizens it concomitantly expands them theoretically for other peoples, communities, nations for inspiration, and repetition. Thus expanding human rights is the fundamental constitutional right. And it is the reason the Founders placed on the Great Seal of the United States of America, *NOVUS ORDO SECLORUM*, "A new order of the ages," overseen by the "all seeing eye of God" and the blessing *ANNUIT COEPTIS*, "(He) smiles upon it."

Lee did not embrace same rights for all people because of his prejudice against dark-skinned people. However, he worked passionately for reconciliation between South and North after the horrible war. He sought reconciliation diligently from the beginning of his presidency at Washington College *post bellum*, primarily that students reconcile with the other Americans who were victors in the war. Interestingly, the college remained all white, broadcasting loudly Lee's less than perfect action there.

"I trust I am not failing man nor God in pursuing reconciliation," Lee often was heard to say. Perhaps his vocalization was to cover a not quite heartfelt embrace of total equality in reconciliation, a stance similar to his provisional pacifism. More likely his passion reflected his longing for personal reconciliation with God.

Whatever the source of his fervor, R. E. Lee's post-war actions contributed to facilitating the gradual way to recognition of human equality, to public awareness of the truth that a person's color in no way determines character.

Truth-telling must precede reconciliation of any kind.

R. E. Lee was learning that powerful lesson both personally and publicly through his remorse. As he desired, he was still completing his education.

CHAPTER 37

A Last Letter

After the exultant return to Richmond, Lee often longed for the easy—albeit sometimes challenging—companionship of dear James Corley. In these times he took refuge from loneliness by sitting with his daughter, Mildred, who ably assisted him in correspondence.

On one such occasion, as night-time approached, by the light of two candles at his bedside, Mildred captured the following:

President's House
Washington College

Lexington, Virginia
August 1870

To James Corley, Friend and "Tour Guide."
Charlotte, N.C.

The handwriting is my daughter Mildred's, called Milly for short, who serves as my secretary and takes dictation very well. Writing has become another difficulty for me .

When you toured down south Spring of this year with my daughter Eleanor Agnes and me, we spoke about various topics including the one that gives me grave concern. I usually avoided it: namely, the late war. I rarely talk of that conflict between North and South yet we co-travelers touched on it a few times as we journeyed by train south-eastward to Savannah, Georgia, on my "health vacation."

I kept ~~differing~~ *deferring the time to tell you about the Northern Campaign Summer of 1863 until "an appropriate time" which ended in*

269

failure at Gettysburg. I wanted to tell the rationale behind that peace campaign.

That time never came on our trip, or I forgot about it, thereby doing you an injustice. I want now to correct that missed opportunity by this letter. The one scruple I have is that you not publish it in my life-time. If you cannot accede to this request please destroy it before you die. Thanks, James; I'm sure you will honor my wish.

The first salient fact about our Northern Campaign into Pennsylvania the Summer of 1863 was "we did not intend a general battle... unless attacked by the enemy."

I wrote that statement in my Official Report to the Confederate War Office the end of July 1863. President Davis' writings confirmed it in a book he was preparing, "Rise and Fall of the Confederate Government."

As well I circulated an order to the whole army that if we see the enemy before they see us our army should NOT fire first.

The second fact is the day before the battle of Gettysburg began the chief clerk in the Confederate War Office in Richmond wrote:

JUNE 30 5 o'clock PM

The city [Richmond] is now in good humor, but not wild exultation. We have what seems pretty authentic intelligence of the taking of HARRISBURG the capital of Pennsylvania, the City of YORK, etc. etc. This comes from the flag of truce boat, and is derived from the enemy themselves. Lee will not descend to the retaliation instigated by petty malice: but proclaim to the inhabitants that all we desire is PEACE not conquest.

Proclaim PEACE the clerk wrote. PEACE!

Peace was the purpose of my Northern Campaign not combat, not conquest at all.

How, from those two statements, can history's gatekeepers and others contend that I was going to fight on Yankee soil a third overwhelming victory—a victory like the previous slugfest at Fredericksburg, December 1862, and the highly successful Chancellorsville battle in May 1863 where we out-maneuvered and out-fought a Federal army twice *the size of my Army of Northern VA?*

History writers use false statements entirely opposite mine and ink unused from my pen. Thereby they miss the fact the Northern Campaign was NOT about a great battle to win the war once and for all. Such writers persist spreading false theories; it's glamorous to do so.

Thus they make me out to be a liar! Rather in crazy theories one battle up north could stop the battle out at Vicksburg, Mississippi, and the battles down in Georgia, or overcome the every week greater tightening of the U. S. naval blockade of our seaports. And stop the food ~~roots~~ riots in Southern cities by army wives and mothers.

More so, even end the increasing desertions of troops from all our armies! Also, stem the lack of new recruits joining our armies because it was "a rich man's war but a poor man's battle." Only half of Southern white males of conscription age ever registered for the ~~fistll~~ first ever American draft. The other half? Deserters!

I am not a liar, James; peace was our objective, not combat and conquest. I trust history buffs and historians will correct their inaccurate views and not make me a liar. "We did not intend a general battle... unless attacked."

Battles are spectacular, you know that fact: they suck in the eye, the ear, the trembling body, the whole soldier. But they're not error free depictions of what happens in combat. Or even preceding hostilities.

Battles are comparatively easy to describe as movements of men and ~~material~~ materiel to the right places at the right times, or often the wrong places at the wrong times. Warfare can be easily explained because it's a massive response seen, heard, felt by most everyone.

Peace, on the other hand, is difficult to describe emotionally and intellectually, spiritually—even politically. There are elements at the same time involving ~~dabbl~~ damaged human beings who've done brave deeds on both sides of a fray yet are sometimes inhumane, unkind—shameful on both sides. Thoughtless acts, also both sides, cannot be justified but leave deep holes in human lives. So warriors want not to talk about them because of the nature of human evil, i.e., what human beings do to other human beings in war's fog and secret dugouts. There are un-reported horrors, countless of them, and usually denied. ~~Whenever writers~~

History's gatekeepers can quantify combat with numbers of troops engaged, casualty rates, ammunition expended, kill rates, financial costs, all sorts of data to justify the unjustifiable to following generations. But all are bunkum and balderdash. Not the blood and guts of valiant men. Not the souls of men murdering other men supposedly legally.

At the very same time, James, peace was afoot up North in '63. There was a huge peace rally in June 1863 in New York City to stop the war! Also a member of the House of Representatives of the Penna legislature proposed on the floor of the legislature that the state join the Confederacy!

In addition, Confederate Vice Pres. Alexander Stephens' peace effort with his friend Union President Abraham Lincoln to meet along the lower Potomac River for a possible peace ~~table~~ talk.

Also at the same time, my army moved north with a peace proposal of its own into lower central Penna.

Peace was afoot the summer of '63, James, but will history buffs recall those facts about my Northern Campaign?

Military tacticians observing my ~~toop~~ troop movements would easily note that I divided my army over a vast area rather than concentrating it for an all-out battle to end the war.

My troops were spread out along the Mason-Dixon Line between Maryland and Penna for 75 miles. Yes, 75! I divided my army in thirds: west, middle, and east. One doesn't divide one's army if one is going to fight a huge end-the-war battle. Do you not agree?

On the western flank Gen. Imbolden's cavalry division protected our flank out in Fulton County in case Federal troops arrived from Pittsburgh, while his Irregulars engaged in skirmishes causing our first casualties in the campaign.

In the geographic middle at Chambersburg, Franklin County, our main body moved northward—but I divided it, also. Half headed northeast toward Harrisburg, after collecting 60,000 head of livestock; cattle, hogs and sheep, horses and mules, some poultry to send back to Virginia. 60,000, James! At the same time the other divided-half of our main body I sent farther east through Gettysburg to York, then to "the banks of the Susquehanna," always of military interest to the South. There a massive one and a quarter mile covered bridge for railroad trains, included a tow path for dray animals to draw rafts and boats east or west in the river alongside the bridge, as well an actual wagon road inside the bridge for carriages and carts between Wrightsville in York County on the west and Columbia on the east in Lancaster County.

Then on my far right flank Gen. Jeb Stuart's raiding cavalry ran around the Union Army eastward through Maryland and captured 125 Union Army covered wagons loaded with supplies north of the area where the Susquehanna River joins the Chesapeake Bay, totaling a front of 75 miles!

If it were an invasion to fight a battle I never would have divided my army then sub-divided it so precariously. Never! Any careful study can see the difference between an army on the attack and one with something else in mind.

SELAH!

Dictation recommenced the following afternoon after father and daughter had amply recovered from their first attempt:

My first error was cutting off my supply line back to Staunton, Virginia, located 150 miles south in the Shenandoah Valley just five days before the accidental battle at Gettysburg! It was a major mistake. The ancient Chinese book The Art of War *by General Sun Tzu ~~Chan~~, newly translated from the French then read when I was Superintendent at West Point, wrote: "an army without provisions is lost; without bases of supply it is lost."*

President Davis' first error was that he did not support my request in early May for an "army in effigy," a dummy army led by high profile, Gen. P.G.T. Beauregard, to be parked west of Washington, D.C., threatening the Northern capital. It would have had the effect of slowing or stopping the Northern army from following my army into Penna on our purposely named "surpassing raid." Surpassing raid was propaganda as we moved into the soft underbelly of the North.

Deceit is the major point of The Art of War. *Mislead the enemy; that is, have his army at the wrong place for a battle, fool him one way or another. Thus two months before the battle I asked President Davis for that "army in effigy."*

The awesome Chancellorsville victory was due in large part because I used guidance from one of Stonewall Jackson's chaplains, who as a native to the area, then led Stonewall's troops on an apparent retreat but circled back around to fool the Federal army and surprise attack its right ~~wig~~ wing, all with amazing success.

That victory flooded Davis with work—the needless kind which distracted from the request for a dummy army to fool Northern generals.

Our president noticed after any Southern victory, on any battle-field, he was inundated with requests from Southern gentry (?) to be commisioned as "colonels" seeking his endorsement. No Southern gentlemen (?) applied to serve as privates. Even sergeants!

The joke in the Confederate War Office after victories was about forming "colonelcy regiments" there were so many requests. Davis could have used them for a dummy army to frighten Washington, D.C. The halls of Government House in Richmond would ring with doggerel verse:

Col. Fee, Col. Fye, Col. Foe, Col. Fum,
Retreating they muffle the drum;
Skedaddling before martyrdom.
Could not make a charge or take 'um.
Col. Fee, Col. Fye, Col. Foe, Col. Fum.

If it were the case that I had to call off the Northern Campaign then the Peace Movement up north would have passed; Vice Pres. Stephens' attempt to meet with Abraham Lincoln would have fallen through, as it did. Penna's collaborative move toward becoming part of the South would have been squelched pronto.

It was now or never in 1863 as the North kept growing its armies with new citizens—and loomed even larger in popular imaginations up North and down South. I saw biblical hand-writing on the wall:

MENE, MENE; TEKEL; UPHARSIN:
"Numbered! Weighed! Enemy at the gates!"

President Lincoln made two correct decisions. First, he named Major General George Gordon Meade, a native Pennsylvanian, new commander of the Northern army. And those people, Irish, Welshmen, Pennsylfannish Deitscher, English men all counted their soil as special, very special, holy in fact, because it's so highly productive. Wheat thrives almost without planting; oats and corn, pears the same; and countless apple trees stand galore on hillsides.

Foremost Lincoln insisted on a new military strategy: "Lee's army, not Richmond, is your true objective," he told his commander. It shook me to the core. I didn't want my troops to hear that bulletin.

My overall purpose was psychological and political; secretly military too. I wanted to isolate York County. Thus the huge Wrightsville-Columbia bridge had to be burned. Then I informed Gen. Ewell to have the Second Corps head up toward Harrisburg, the state capital, to block the bridge there and if—but only if—the town could be captured he may do so, though that was not essential to my plan. York County had to be isolated therefore the Wrightsville/Columbia magnificent bridge had to be destroyed to cut off Union troops from the east.

York was strategically important to us because it had been seat of the first American Confederacy! America first was a confederacy! The Second Continental Congress had moved there putting the wide Susquehanna River between it and the British army 90 miles away in Philadelphia. From 1777 to 1778 Congress deliberated in York as the nation's capital while Gen. George Washington was at Valley Forge.

In York, Congress promulgated and ~~disturb~~ distributed the "Articles of Confederation And Perpetual Union," the first constitution under which America lived for 11 years—11 years it was our national constitution— promulgated at York years before the 1787 Constitution under which America lived since.

Additional to that pivotal historical and political reason for going to York I had a personal reason. A very deep one.

My father, Gen. "Light-horse Harry" Lee, in 1814 opposed "Mr. Madison's War," that is, the War of 1812, over the impressment of American

275

sailors into the British navy. In Baltimore, Maryland, a friend of my father, William Hanon, was editor of the "Federal Republican" newspaper; it challenged Madison's War vigorously. Its printing office was attacked by a mob in favor of the war. In the days that followed, various other Revolutionary War officers opposed "Mr. Madison's War" and joined the embattled newspaper defenders' right to disagree with Madison's War.

On 27 July 1812, the mob attacked the printing office to get at the defenders. My father was severely beaten, molten candle wax poured in his eyes, his nose cut by someone stabbing him. He was left for dead upon the street. At the same time Gen. James M. Lingan of Revolutionary War service also operated a newspaper, and was murdered outright in the riot by the attacking mob because he joined several people present to protect the Baltimore newspaper and its editor.

My father suffered grievous wounds in the mob attack. Some friends picked him up, hid him in the shadows. Late at night they found a wagon and moved him to a safe place. The next two days carefully and kindly they transported him some 50 miles north of Baltimore to the small town of York, Penna. There, two teachers at the York County Academy, both physicians who taught science courses, nursed him back to health. Unnamed in history those Yorkers were Good Samaritans. My father lived. There he wrote his view of what ~~transformed~~ transpired that disastrous night in violation of basic human rights. He entitled it "Correct Account of the Conduct of the Baltimore Mob."

I have felt emotionally, spiritually, related to York for providing shelter, care, since I heard the story several times during childhood from my father.

York was a "balm in Gilead" for him on America's shore back then... at an in-land island of caring along the Codorus Creek, tributary of the Susquehanna River, onto the Chesapeake Bay, onto the Atlantic Ocean.

My crushed desire in 1863 to get to York contained my serious errors of judgment about battle before and during the accidental Gettysburg blood-letting, three days of hell for South and North.

In fact the Monday morning while in Chambersburg after I heard that Longstreet's spy had reported the Union army was ~~paws~~ pursuing us through Maryland into Penna I was in my office dictating a note to have an old blind horse which was seized illegally by my troops, returned to its elderly rightful owner. My presence was observed and recorded by a physician while he was in my headquarters. Dr. J. L. Suesserott of Chambersburg recorded in a publication:

> *I had never seen so much emotion. With Lee's hands at times clutching his hair and with contracted brow, Lee would walk with rapid strides for a few rods and then, as if he bethought himself of his actions, Lee would with a sudden jerk produce an entire change in his features and demeanor cast an inquiring gaze on me only to be followed in a moment by the same contortions of face and agitation of person.*

That physician realized I was undergoing something disastrous. Something cruel was happening to me.

Allowing for some subjectivity in the physician's account it's clear I suffered severely from knowing that my plan for the Northern Campaign to unveil a peace proposal at York on 4 July 1863, Independence Day, was thwarted. Meade's army marched to do general battle in the vicinity. My plan had failed before there was the accidental battle at Gettysburg. Failed before it began.

SELAH!

Mildred shook out her cramped hand and begged for a break.

Already tired from such extended discourse, the elder Lee acquiesced.

The following evening after dinner, the two reconvened for what Mildred heartily hoped would be the final installment:

Then unsettled, I made terrible decisions about troop movements. As a military engineer I failed before I failed in battle tactics! I had seven of nine divisions on the road to Gettysburg from Chambersburg over South Mountain at the same place at the same time. A bung-bled mess to say the least! A serious error to tell the truth.

I was negligent. I should have had a second in command at Gettysburg so I could have turned over the Army to him. The plan for a peace proposal was nullified, in fact impossible. It never happened on 4 July 1863: no peace proposal at all.

Then contrary to my explicit order Southern forces were not—repeat, not—to fire first, not to bring on a general battle under any circumstance. Yet that's precisely what ~~hearten~~ happened.

Capt. J.J. Young of the 26th North Carolina Infantry wrote the day after the battle to the governor of N.C. stating: "Heth's Division of A. P. Hill's Corps opened the ball and Pettigrew's brigade was the advance."

Some "ball" at Gettysburg! In defiance of a Commanding General's order not to start shooting and bring on a general battle!

Turned out Heth's small-scale beginning had the nastiest ending: Defeat all around, not just in that first skirmish but the whole battle was the beginning of the end of the Second Confederacy.

There were some glaring misinterpretations, anomalies and errors over those three days in July '63. The major misinterpretation was on Day One: I gave Ewell a weak order he could interpret as not needing to pursue and destroy the retreating Federal army on our left flank. We would have gained advantage on high ground eastward before the whole Federal Army was anywhere in full force. I was imprecise in my order to Ewell.

A major anomaly was what happened after the heavy fighting of the second day on our right flank. I did not think to include the two high hills, the summit's Little Round Top and Big Round Top in my plans. I overlooked two visible pinnacles! At first undefended by the Federals, then occupied and saved by the no-ammunition but-bare-bayonet stampede swooping downhill, the 20th Maine Regiment of the Federal Army won the day. That action and defeat left a sick-to-the-stomach feeling throughout the rest of the Army of Northern VA.

Since I, nor anyone in my army, thought we would do battle at Gettysburg, we did not study the field or ask locals for information about the locale. We were without clear information about the lay of the land. We were operating in the dark, so to speak.

As well, not only was I unclear what to do but one of my artillery commanders noted post-war: "I never remember hearing of any conference or discussions among our generals at this time as to the best formations and tactics in making our attacks, and our methods on this occasion struck me as peculiar." He didn't consider the planning top caliber.

Yet—and it is a monumental YET—there were five young men reared in the Gettysburg area, whose families had moved south a few years previously, who were members of different units of my army. In the surprising accidental meeting of the two armies their units' leaders never informed me of their presence. I could have learned from them of local conditions: geography of the area, land use, pathways, natural formations, wood-lands, farming areas, unique features of the topography of what became the battlefield. All kinds of pertinent material could have availed me better information than I gathered haphazardly. Any one of those five former Gettysburgers could have provided the kind of details we were able to use successfully at Chancellorsville in May when we routed the Federal Army overwhelmingly.

The five young men... Francis "Frank" Hoffman, Robert Hoffman, Wesley Hoffman were brothers three, and Henry Wentz plus John "Wesley" Culp... are barely known to history and were totally un-known to me. And Culp's Hill of the battle was named for his family.

Ben Franklin's proverb never has been more true :

For the want of a nail the shoe was lost,
For the want of a shoe the horse was lost,
For the want of a horse the rider was lost,
For the want of a rider the battle was lost,
For the want of a battle the kingdom was lost;
And all for the want of a nail.

Then at night a strange phenomenon, a stunner, occurred behind Union lines at Spangler's Spring, but not from a military action. Both sides filled canteens there. Men on both sides would sing, "Oh, I went to Spangler's Spring where the waters so cool," to one another and to the opposing side as well. Soldiers exchanged goods: tobacco, food, newspapers, gossip, and talked army tittle-tatter, flibbertijibutt, scuttlebutt for entertainment at the spring. No shooting allowed, or politics.

Then on 2 July the phenomenon appeared. In the official records of a Massachusetts' regiment it was called "omen" several times. Yankee troops were frightened in the darkness as the tale thickened, was bloated out of proportion before the next day's battle. It scared the beegeebers out of many Northern soldiers. The next morning was disturbing to much of the

Northern army as men woke to tales of devils or ghosts of dead comrades floating through the woods and around the spring house before morning of the next day, the 3rd of July's fatal battle.

Contrariwise, next day on the field of battle it was not Federals who were ruffled, discombobulated, chagrined.

SELAH!

Father Lee could see his daughter's hand begin to quiver above the page. Clearly they had both given their all to the session and earned a well-deserved night's rest.

The following morning he quietly motioned for Mildred to retrieve her writing tools, hope upon hope that she would not abandon their project when it was now so close to completion.

By the mid-day rays, she once again gave written voice to her father's missive:

The uncanny phenomenon disturbed our army only slightly because it was easily explained since many Southern soldiers knew from proximity about the phenomenon. Such knowledge, however, didn't help us the next day on the field of battle. We lost terribly 3 July '63.

In actual fact, Friday night, 2 July 1863, was a full moon. During the early evening there had been a light rain, and a mist had developed in swampy areas around the spring house. Those conditions caused a moonbow.

A moonbow?

When there are corresponding conditions in daytime the bright sun causes a rainbow of colors opposite the source, the sun. Night-time the moonbow, from far less intense moonlight also causes a faintly colored bow refracting light that sometimes is a spooky white in the otherwise clear upper sky. Sometimes a nebulous orb-like reflection seems to hang in the misty atmosphere shimmering in opposite direction from the full moon. To the uninitiated it eerily hangs among the trees and shimmers in a breeze. If a person doesn't know what to expect and is trying to get to sleep at full moon in a misty atmosphere with a dreadful attitude at night and possible death on a battlefield next day the situation could be utterly terrorizing.

Northerners basically had never seen nor heard of such a phenomenon.

Some of our troops from the upper South knew of it because there is a recurring moonbow at Cumberland Falls, in southeastern Kentucky near Corbin, the second largest waterfall in the Eastern United States. Those knowledgeable men spread the word about the moonbow, so hardly any consternation obsessed Southern troops.

Many Northern troops were frightened that July night and felt the moonbow was a disaster-about-to-happen, a harbinger of something horrible to happen next day on 3 July. Most Southerners retired as per usual before a battle; even if they thought of a moonbow. Harmless as it was, our men slept.

That's the trouble with omens; they're human creations; like human beings they can be interpreted either as good or evil—maybe as nothing at all if one is of scientific bent.

The next day was Pickett's Charge. Six-sevenths of the actual division were killed, wounded, or captured. Accompanying units suffered nearly as cruelly.

The omen's effect must have changed from North to South when the moon went down: The results of the battle were a disaster for us.

After the war various Northern vacationers visited Cumberland Falls for good belly laughs about moonbow omens.

Before that infamous charge I had met with division commanders in the morning on the edge of Spangler's woods where we sat on a log. We reviewed plans for the attack on the center of the Federal line. When we finished they rose and returned to their units. I remained seated through the conflagration. I needed firm support under me and something unmovable to hold onto.

I was not on my steed Traveller on high ground observing the action. Then I mounted up when our defeated troops staggered back needing moral support.

The charge was a do-or-die event. The Northern Campaign died 3 July 1863.

It was a ghastly day. My men kept pressing onward up a small rise in the ground, over rail fences, out in the open moving onward and upward as broad swaths of our open ranks constantly widened while explosions terminated squads... even companies at a time... in mere minutes. And then from two sides, furious firing by Union troops hidden in the tall grasses as well as those ahead from behind their low stonewall atop the rise at the copse of trees. Our bewildered men kept marching upwards to the trees but Federals kept appearing out of the tall grass on the left then the right shooting them point blank like sitting ducks. A few reached the low stonewall, fewer crossed it. The slaughter was a butcher house—"and there's no dis-charge in the war," as the Bible says.

"It was my fault. It was I who lost this fight," I said. "You must help me out of it in the best way you can."

And then I made an inane remark: "Though the army did not win a victory, it conquered a success."

What did it mean? I've never been able to understand it myself! War produces as much vacuous expression as it does stout-hearted insights.

I continued the absurd wordage saying, "We must now prepare for heavier blows and harder work. But my trust is in Him who favors the weak and relieves the oppressed, and my hourly prayer is that He will 'fight for us again' I uttered in mystifying double-talk."

Why would God help an army trying to preserve human slavery?

"God will do the heavy work the next time!" I declared. Vacuous? The answer was clear before Appomattox.

If George Washington had made such a statement after a defeat he would have been relieved of command and General Horatio Gates would have become Revolutionary War commander-in-chief as the Conway Cabal sought in 1777-78.

After 4 July I decided we must leave the field of battle. From the presence of countless blue coats on the battlefield it looked as if we had at least drawn a tie. The Army of Northern VA could return to its home base in Virginia. We left with a wagon train 17 miles long, and it rained. Then more. Storm after storm. It flooded the Potomac River so torrentially it could have carried Noah's Ark out to the Chesapeake Bay onto the Atlantic Ocean!

When I finally did realize that we had been roundly defeated I tried to resign from the Confederate Army, as I had the Federal. I wrote a month later but President Davis would not accept my resignation since there was not a younger officer prepared for the task, which was, for me, a deplorable reason to stay on the job. "How is a defeated general better than an untried younger officer?"

So, friend James, Gettysburg does not a saga make. Not a legend. But it's not a fable, by any means. Certainly the Northern Campaign wasn't King Arthur's roundtable of dedicated knights where we would uphold virtue, win glory forever with peace throughout the continent.

Assuredly the Northern Campaign was nothing like a Valhalla of heroes in which one is killed in battle and believed to feast with the god Odin for eternity. It was a plain failure, not a literary story.

Not quite an epic, Tour Guide James. I am a loser, defeated in battle but not life. I'm not quite anything but a small town American resident undefeated in start-over-again America!

No more than president of a small college in a tiny corner of the United States of America, whose students and parents trust Washington College will perform good things together with their sons to influence both sons and parents positively in years ahead.

Finally, sick and dying yet loved by wife, by family, by friends... it's now a beginning! I have distances to go and duties to do... duties to God; duties to others; and duties to myself for I realize 'I am not my own but belong to my precious savior, Jesus Christ'.

Yr obt sert
R. E. Lee

CHAPTER 38

Denouement
(The end that never ends: rains, words, human life)

During the last weeks R. E. Lee lived, the terrors of life increased, more for loved ones than for him, as is often the case when dying is evident and death a close-by breath-taking experience. His self-identity was clouded over but neither compromised nor destroyed.

In the act of dying the old president had to remake himself, so to speak, realizing he had but days, and eventually, mere hours left. As many who are dying he had to gauge his strength and how much reserve he had.

His thoughts returned time and again to words that old unknown philosopher had written. *He must have been old,* Lee thought, *maybe even dying, himself.*

Ah, yes, "The end of living is not simply a stop, an edge a human being simply drops off. To be exact, it makes way for another human tenure, a new lease on life. Or better yet, a lease on a new life, some other human being to take the human place." Lee relished that idea.

One day, struggling to remember, he returned to his desk where the pages containing those words lay. *I'll move them to my bedside,* he thought, as he read a passage he had previously overlooked: "Dying embraces maturing, a ripening of what occurs in all natural phenomena: it is auspicious, promising, and providential for the future of the species.

"As a result, the process of human dying is not *per se* negative; it is reasonable and may become a spiritual grace to

285

participate in the future. As such, every person is capable of being more than solely what has met our five senses and the brain in three score and ten years. One ought not, even dare not, purposely set out to end life... for such an act does not obey Nature's law of fecundity."

At that moment pain surged through his left arm. He instinctively grabbed that arm with his right hand and began rubbing it as he sank into his desk chair. *I'll just sit here, quietly, a while, save more reading until later,* he reasoned.

When Lee's angina pectoris seemingly developed rapidly the family couldn't help but realize the truth. He had arteriosclerosis and heart disease. His health had not been compromised by rheumatism as medical people for years had diagnosed. Most people close to him wanted to believe that error, though, because rheumatism is not *per se* life threatening.

Some of the general public amateurishly thought his diminishing health was because of calcification of the heart because the term sounded scientific, therefore true. It took years for the family to learn his dire condition.

Obvious physical findings to support formal diagnoses did not exist in 1870, especially in back woods, mountainous western Virginia. Lee's physicians made guesses... some educated... while others were hazarded out-of-the-blue by family and friends; still others were conjectured based on his complaints. Treatments in house included the proverbial "everything but the kitchen sink." Home remedies included hot mustard plasters, doses of ammonia, even turpentine, and enemas, always enemas. Such efforts were standard home medical treatments in mid-19th century America.

In the months before Lee's death, without an accurate medical history to guide them, physicians diagnosed stroke, or rheumatism, or pneumonia. Some of those diagnoses may have been exact, some not.

No one but R. E. Lee knew how close to his heart he held the dictum Henry David Thoreau had pronounced in *Walden: Or Life in The Woods* seven years before the Rebellion. Thoreau's dictum was "live deliberately." To live life deliberately is to live powerfully, fully and unashamedly, to live it as a balance of differing forces, as tasting the delectable and trying the new or unusual, both "this and that," beholding things in equity and parity to derive the best of everything.

There is a corollary to "live deliberately." The corollary is to "die deliberately." Lee knew it. It means to participate in one's dying, to live through the act of dying. It means to be as fully cognizant as possible to our experience as we diminish, slow down. It means to alter our selves to detect the slow movement of living into the even slower movement of giving back to life what has intrigued us and sustained us during our deliberate, thoughtful, steady lives. In dying we also experience something new, something for the first time.

His first intimation that such is so had happened when on his Northern Campaign in the Chambersburg, Pennsylvania area in June 1863. He'd made a practice of attending various churches at each of his military posts, developing into "The Compleat Churchman," somewhat like Izaak Walton's earlier creation, *The Compleat Angler*. Lee would write home to Mary about each church service he attended almost as if it were a sport... information about the clergy, the sermon, the music, and the congregants, a happy errand shared with his bride of yesteryear.

One Sunday in June 1863 he'd attended a worship service in a German Reformed Church in Chambersburg, Pennsylvania. The pastor noted the new hymn the congregation was about to sing had been composed by one Henry Harbaugh, professor at the nearby Mercersburg Seminary. The hymn explored both life and death of a Christian believer. Lee was impressed to the point of contentment, so copied the words to send home to his wife and children:

Jesus, I live to thee, the loveliest and best;
My life in thee, thy life in me, in thy blest love I rest.

Jesus, I die to thee, whenever death shall come;
To die in thee is life to me in my eternal home.

Whether to live or die I know not which is best,
To live in thee is bliss to me, to die is endless rest.

Living or dying, Lord, I ask but to be thine;
My life in thee, thy life in me, makes heaven forever mine.

Lee's spirit resonated with the message of there being "newness" in dying. With the anticipation of a "best" in dying as there is in living. Thereafter, he felt deep in his bones a sameness of living deliberately and dying deliberately.

Reciting the words to Harbaugh's hymn and reading Thoreau's *Walden* became a nearly daily habit as he endeavored to die deliberately.

He informed his family how meaningful that pattern was for him. He decided he wanted them to know, as well, the meaning he'd realized from the old philosopher's writings he'd stumbled upon in his library.

"Mildred," he implored one day, "after I die I trust you will not discard the books in my library willy-nilly. There is much of value in many of the 'tomes,' as you call them, to help you and the rest of the family live deliberately as you age. In particular, I advise you to read first the books by my bedside and on my desktop. They are my special 'friends'."

He chuckled, "Even that old unknown philosopher, the rascal. He's teaching me more about living as I'm dying than I ever expected to learn. I like his style—brusque, direct. I just wish I could remember how I came upon his papers."

"Of course, Father," Mildred promised. "And I will tell the rest of the family what you just told me."

That September in 1870 in western Virginia it rained the proverbial cats and dogs, and more, in Lexington. Constant rain caused minor flooding that threatened extra of the same. Lee really didn't want to venture into the damp, falling darkness on the busyness that churches sometimes "cook up" for themselves. As Chief Warden of the official governing Vestry body of Grace Episcopal Church, Lexington, however, it was his duty to attend and preside at the 28 September 1870 meeting beginning at 4:00 P.M. Supper in the President's House had to be set late for the whole family when he was to return home near six o'clock.

Leaving the brightly kerosene-lit house with air warmed by four lamps in the living room he started into the dark gray afternoon. Then stopped. He turned to a daughter and kissed her saying, "I wish I did not have to go and listen to all that pow wow." He stood still, probably thinking it over, then made a short move onto the porch. A second time he paused longer before descending the porch steps.

"I am duty bound," he said, "and it is the Lord's work." Daughter Mildred heard his commitment and loved him for it.

He had flung his old military cape over his shoulders and walked down the porch steps into the rain without a cap or any head covering. Much like an irritated boy, shivering for a minute or two as he tried to hurry, he slipped several times on wet leaves on the concrete pavement he had designed, as he walked to the end of the college property. *Serves me right. I must be careful.* He carried no umbrella to shield his bare head.

The "pow wow" went past 7:00 P.M. Official church boards take longer than God to create meaning. They keep minutes but waste hours, as the saying goes.

The Vestry made several decisions about financing an addition to the church building and went on to the topic of the pastor's salary. The treasury was short $55 to meet the sum agreed upon to compensate their rector. After what seemed an Ice-Age, Lee made a financial pledge in addition to the amount he had stated previously in order to get home for a late family supper. He had not eaten a bite prior to leaving home to go to the meeting. "I will give that sum," he said. The meeting adjourned.

Those words were the last public words R. E. Lee would say in this world. "I will give." It was his life story from boyhood on, from youth through young adulthood to maturity and into old age.

Out in the rain again after the meeting he shivered almost constantly with his head still bare, his stomach growling, and his leg muscles tightening, especially while walking up the steps of the porch of the President's House. He barely could open the door, and was grateful when son Custis pulled it wide open.

Post haste the son stripped his father of dripping cape. Someone else threw a warm blanket over the old man's head and shoulders. Custis grabbed his father in a bear hug and started to rub him with the warm blanket, face then scalp, then neck then shoulders. Another warm blanket appeared and two of his children walked their father to the foot of the dinner table where he stood as if to say grace, to return thanks. He could not speak; he sat down.

Wife Mary said, "You kept us waiting a long time. Let me pour you a cup of tea; you look so tired." Lee tried to say a bare two words, uttering only throaty, raspy sounds. He sat, positioned upright, not bent over, while one of the women took off the second blanket and put another warmed one around him. Tears filled his cheeks among the hairs of his beard. No further sounds came from R. E. Lee at the table. He did not eat a thing, only picking at the food on his plate. No one could follow exactly what he was doing with his spoon.

Exerting that long drawn-out effort to arrive at the dinner table caused his falling tears to be the blessing of the food. His uneaten meal strangely enhanced the family; their spirited conversation moved him to tears again. Like death itself, tears unsettle and un-map any action.

Wife Mary, daughter Agnes, and son Custis decided that his two physicians should be notified. Mildred offered to perform the chore and enter the cold, wet night. She dressed against the lousy weather, left the house warm and with an umbrella to visit the local physicians to ask their immediate help.

While waiting for the medicine men, family members helped their sire navigate to his familiar easy chair. Again he started to communicate, again the sounds were without any ado to the family and were considered meaningless, only gibberish. No one gave evidence of trying to talk with him as he looked pleadingly at family members for someone to address him and converse with him.

The great soul then became passive, likely abandoning most of his hope of getting through to loved ones who only knew communication with unambiguously clear-headed others. The time was unpleasant; both sides experienced deadly silence.

He did smile an extended time but received no such greeting in return because family did not know what the smile meant. Grave facial expression as response to a smile is like a hammer to a nail: harsh, ruthless. Painful. Crucifixus.

The two physicians arrived with their black leather satchels. One doctor examined him, then turned away slowly and was mute. It was his signal there was not a possibility, or even hope, hope of resuscitation. Lee had suffered a stroke. The medicine men noted his action/inaction but knew the fact about the suffering patient.

Lee's bout with the deep chill, the damp, the stroke, the silence of his loved ones, resulted in a noxious cold the next day. Then over the next almost week, pneumonia, followed by even less human interplay, nil communication from the family again.

During his final month Lee sounded avowals of more than mere sounds only three times. Possible they were discomforts, conceivably dissatisfactions, maybe rantings, even explanatory comments on his physical, intellectual, spiritual condition.

The first one, two days after his shocked condition returning from the Vestry meeting, he said, "I do not occupy myself with things too great and too marvelous for me. I have calmed and quieted my soul." He had quoted from King David's *Psalms*. Family members in the room were surprised, utterly.

Two days beyond that first avowal he observed, "There are three things too wonderful for me, even four: The way of an eagle in the air; the way of a serpent on a rock; the way of a ship on the high seas; and the way of a young man with a maid."

Quoting that biblical passage caused several family members to believe he was recovering health. However, the words could have been spoken from rote memory way back in his boyhood catechism training. Reportedly he had the ability to quote without difficulty the Protestant Episcopal Catechism *in toto* from early youthhood on. The avowal, as well, might have come from the Bible he had studied nightly after he became a Christian in 1853.

The family was electrified thinking he was on the way to recovery, but those two bits of good news, although having a beginning and an ending, held little else of substance. The family's views were wrong, as were the physicians', as Lee continued making sounds, not sentences, both times after he had spoken clearly.

Often he uttered what seemed to be sounds without substance. One personal physician noted he spoke "a word a day."

That phrase still puzzles. It could mean a single sound or could mean an incisive pronouncement of sorts. Be that as it may, seldom does the term mean a logical string of words developing argumentations. The phrase was a curious notation.

The third time there was a strange clarity. No one could make heads nor tails of it. He talked of "Uncle Bin" and "Uncle Ben" and waited for a reply. No reply came from any of the family present, his wife, two sons, and two daughters. Family members recalled no relatives of those names, nor were the names ones of slaves his father-in-law had willed to him decades before. After much of that night and near half the next day the family was about to give up in dismay when daughters Agnes and Mildred hit upon a basis for his naming expressions.

Lo and behold, years previous, someone in the family had given those names to two Mason jars that contained condiments and flavors brought to the breakfast table from time to time.

The dying man possibly supposed at least one family member would remember and speak to him about those breakfast episodes. The conjecture may be a wild possibility. However, the ingredients were memorable and, literally, spiced up a meal and conversation. They possibly could do the same for a dying man.

"Uncle Bin," in fact, was hard apple cider with crystallized ginger and pepper. "Uncle Ben" also was hard apple cider, but flavored with dried sassafras roots and cilantro, sometimes called Chinese parsley, and black pepper.

Both ciders were stored in Mason jars, a recent invention used to preserve vegetables, fruit, jellies, dressings, and sauces. They had zinc screw-on lids lined with milk-colored glass and rubber gaskets to seal them when boiled in water to preserve contents.

Possibly Lee, dying, spoke the names Bin and Ben to trigger some family verbal engagement. He didn't succeed; the topic became passé, immediately. Lee was left in silence, as is the fate of most dying people.

The end was nearer, conceivably as near as night-time, and R. E. Lee had something to say. Wanting to converse but not conversing with others he still was learning: No one was prepared to talk with him—a dying person—no member of the illustrious family he had sired. That phrase he'd repeated at different times during the war and afterward kept ringing true: "The education of a man is never completed until he dies."

The few times he was coherent startled bystanders, took them aback, shocked them into more unbelief and then disbelief... for the dying to the living seemingly have nothing of worth to say. R. E. Lee was a dying human being. The completion of his education was happening in silence... plus his own thoughts.

No one, closely loved ones included, engaged him in conversation. Human talk with another human being, a badge characteristic of the human species for its survival and welfare, unmistakably was absent, leaving the dying man as if he were dead already, uncommunicative. But the dying are not yet dead; they are still alive, needing communication, that badge characteristic of the human species, to help them cross over.

We living human beings abandon our dying. At the crucial moment. We think the dying merely make a sound, "a word a day," whereas they make an opportunity for us to communicate caring and meaning, plus abundant loving acts such as grooming, talking, caressing, talking, singing, talking, always talking with them as they pass over. Non-communication by the living damns the dying terribly. To death in fact.

On the sly, as it were, R. E. Lee had stated the maxim about education being completed only at death to the most brilliant of his children, eldest son, Custis, known as Boo, hoping for a comeback. Custis did not come through—he didn't know what to do with his father's insight about death. He didn't know because the hardest part of living the human experience is making believe we don't know how the tale ends.

Human beings mystify death even more than it is by not talking about it in some ordinary conversations, then terribly... frightfully and unbelievably... when a human being is dying and needs to hear the care, the warmth of life to combat the cold of the unknown we turn tail. We retreat.

If we were to acknowledge from the beginning of life that we are but a moment's sunlight the dying would not die abandoned. Not accepting that we are only a brief moment in the time and timelessness of the Universe we pass away, alone. Sadly alone. The living, in retreat, cause the dying to lose their most essential human characteristic, the use of language.

Generally Lee was able to utter clearly that "word a day." One morning he whispered loudly, "God," but it was not a prayer. Several hours later a daughter heard him, softly above a whisper say, "Rules." Distance between spoken words indicates continuing analysis for truth to flow forth, if only someone listening would recognize it.

He was nearly silent the last week but understood the family knew he was homeward bound joyously in his silence for he smiled often and looked around the first-floor room of the President's House the family had made up for him. It was warm; it was friendly. And his smile seemed to fill it often, remarkably for the family who became snug with pleasant visiting,

He knew they knew it was well with his soul. If only they had asked his acknowledgment days before he would have been able to leave this plane of existence sooner.

That last week was heavy: so taxing. The rains doubled, the North River flooded the low areas of hilly Lexington. His pain evidently doubled for he remained speechless and could barely handle the serio-comic nature of the event, serious and humorous at the same time, an event that often brightened his day weeks before his stroke.

Several weeks before his stroked condition a friendly devotee from Scotland, unaware of his situation, had sent him a homemade afghan to keep him warm and a teapot cozy to keep the brew warm. When Lee had opened the gifts he threw the afghan about his shoulders, put the cozy on his head, and did a brief jig in the parlor of the President's House as daughter Mildred played a sprightly tune on the piano.

Most of the several visitors there delighted in his playfulness to the additional delight of most every visitor that day. One sourpuss thought it was "childish." And so it was. Delightfully childish. Lee did not mind the remark for he had jigged the first time in years, and was distressed only slightly by pain in his knees.

But that playing and jigging were then. This dying was now. However, the dying play, too, usually verbal games but they are still humorous. They fulfill St. Thomas Aquinas' position that human beings cannot be human without being risible, that is getting a rise of laughter, of joy out of life given by God. A sense of humor is a sense indeed, as necessary as the five physical senses we tend to think are the only ones we have.

At the same time as his condition worsened he heard family members talk of the serious flood washing away three caskets the local mortician had recently ordered and were on the dock at the North River. It became laughable when he heard about, then thought about, empty coffins floating down the river. He murmured, "Song... should... be... a..." but no more.

In fact, two teenage boys had rescued one of the coffins snagged in brush along the river away from the town. R. E. Lee knew at least he'd have a box when he needed one, and laughed about it. His wife and one daughter heard his chuckling not knowing the reason. Nor did they ask.

R. E. Lee died in faith and good humor, with wonderful companions plus love from family members and various others, including his physicians. After dying talk and communication no longer were concerns.

When finally he was placed in the newly recovered and dried-out casket, the box was found to be too short in length for his body. The discovery added an element of surprise to the oppressive time. He was buried in the crypt of the Library at

Washington College in that only casket available. Without his shoes.

Surely his burial would have been perfectly acceptable to R. E. Lee because of the humor of the situation. He had realized from his mother-in-law Mary Custis that the Eternal Father has so many facets, so much substance, and is so thoroughly complete that a sense of humor would happily be integral to His divine nature, as valuable as His godly sense of justice. A shoeless pilgrim would have seemed familiar to R. E. Lee, for a sense of humor is a human sense indeed, needed often as much as one or all of the five physical senses.

Had R. E. Lee been able to read his obituary in *The New York Times* on Thursday, 13 October 1870, the day after his demise, there is little doubt he would have accepted it graciously from a former enemy: "The most famous of the Southern officers... during the late terrible Rebellion... by official clemency, which is without parallel in the history of the world, was formally pardoned for the active and effective part he had taken in the mad effort... to break up the Union and destroy the Government... since 2 October 1865 [has kept] so far as possible aloof from public notice and by his unobtrusive modesty and purity of life, has won the respect even of those who most bitterly deplore and reprobate his course in the Rebellion."

That same sentiment was expressed by many other people from the North before he died. Had he been talked to by family and friends there is no doubting he would have been invigorated by such a message from the North.

Lee realized there is: "A time to weep and a time to laugh; a time to mourn and a time to dance." One could say R. E. Lee, shoeless... danced into eternity.

Tears and laughter. Mourning and dancing.

The book of life is never closed. The dualities are two sides of one reality. How we balance them, even blend them, is our human task.

R. E. Lee, at last, was on his way to his Father's home. Repentant. R. E. Lee, the iconic American general, college president, provisional pacifist, reconciliationist, sick and dying human being... a "gorgeous Tragedy sweeping by... where *more* is meant than meets the ear."

People still call him "Lee." Or "Robert E. Lee." Some say "Robert Edward Lee."

Or name him how he named himself: "R. E. Lee."

In document after document, in letter after letter, in love letters to his wife, in caring letters to his children, he was "R. E. Lee." On official documents as well.

He signed unassumingly, nearly bashfully: "R. E. Lee."

His signature was modest, always unpretentious: a duty to himself.

His leaving life mounted up from Lexington to Virginia to America, from American human to God believer, from warrior to Christ-like pacifist, from Earth to Eternity...

R. E. Lee's sequel began straightaway. *Duty to God.*

POST MORTEMS

POST MORTEM: ELEANOR AGNES LEE

Eleanor Agnes Lee adored her father, as did her three sisters, in varying degrees of fondness. The youngest, Annie, had died early in life in 1862 during the Rebellion. The eldest, Mary, was away from home in 1870 gallivanting around Europe on a lengthy world tour thanks to the substantial inheritance two aunts had bequeathed. She fared famously in the upper strata of the European social/political scene as "the famous General R. E. Lee's daughter." Mildred was at home, then away; then home, then away. R. E. Lee died 12 October 1870. Agnes stayed home, and suffered.

As a poet, she suffered for her sisters. Compellingly sensitive to life with its more downturns than glories, she was not desperate to sanction the stark choice of suicide. Her sensitivity to life and love helped her choose something more wholesome... most of the time. She summed it up, writing:

> *Soon where the shrapnel fell*
> *Petals shall wake and stir.*
> *Look—she is here, she lives!*
> *Beauty has died for her.*

Eleanor Agnes had dated William Orton Williams, a young Confederate officer as handsome as her father was when young. Intriguingly, he was a cousin of Mary Anna Randolph Custis Lee, her own mother. Williams had grown up in "Tudor Place," a mansion within sight of Arlington, her own mother's home. His sister was Markie Williams, who regularly corresponded with R. E. Lee throughout the war. Agnes' parents were not particularly fond of W. O. Williams, thinking he drank too much alcohol; their vision of their daughter with Williams turned out to be a sight—not to their delight.

Agnes' love—if that was the depth of her feeling—for Orton Williams had ended during a long evening of private conversation in the Lee home. No reason was given for their ending the relationship but the family knew well Father Robert's disfavor, usually voiced against precipitous decision making and abrupt actions. During the war William's fate resulted in appearance with a comrade behind Northern lines in Union uniforms; both men were captured and executed summarily as spies. Agnes suffered in silence. Times, many times it seems, silence is not golden. Oft times it is gilded with guilt.

Agnes' feeble emotional well-being and physical health never completely recovered from the fractured relationship. The "recover-health-trip" for her father after the war she imagined would help her, too; it never exactly materialized. Imagination which adds much beauty to human lives can also easily trap them into frightful disorders if people do not apply a particle of good sense or a dash of rationality to decision making.

Three barren years after her father died, and in which her uncertain and wavering health worsened, Agnes died on 15 October 1873. Still grieving for her father. She had stated her thoughts mournfully about death to her mother, a father's death especially. Never recovered from the grief she experienced, she remained latched onto life unknowing of a reason. The winds of fortune blew dust and debris her way and everything in those three years was a mere footnote to living... not even a side note placed where the human eye could see it, read it, or receive nourishment from it.

Hesitantly Agnes would speak of her own demise but in the scantiest of terms. Next to nothing in self-discernment. No one in her family or among her few friends had followed Solomonic wisdom to "rescue those who are being taken away to death" by talking with her in the language of dying, the language of loving, the language communicating humanness even to the end. Otherwise Death was but a cloud, an uncharted hovering or wandering; everything about it obscure and unsung. Or else bewildering and trivial. Eleanor Agnes existed on a clouded over, darkened, bleak orb.

Her mother, Mary Anna Randolph Custis Lee, soon after died—three weeks later, 5 November 1873. Overwhelmed by Agnes' death, Mother Lee also was not "rescued" by human communication, human communion one with another while dying. Tears fell but no words; ruptured feelings but not solid fare, no sturdy sustenance of human communion though words, the language of human species. Not only was the cloudiness of death hanging over her but it permeated everything Mother Lee. The end of her generation; so very little to live with, to live for. The dreadful day ended: it was a Wednesday. One good turn of Earth for a dismal leave-taking.

Sire and Mother gone; children gone; life which had sprung from their love decades before seemingly broken, depleted, spent, vanished.

Therefore, Christian, die!

Why die?

Yet why?

Yet?

Yes, yet! That death die! That Life fuller, grander be!

Mother Lee hummed last rich sounds like a nightingale at night with piercéd heart echoing in her as prayer:

Lead, kindly Light, amid the encircling gloom, lead thou me on;
The night is dark, and I am far from home, lead thou me on.
Keep thou my feet; I do not ask to see the distant scene;
One step enough for me.

POST MORTEM: MARY CUSTIS LEE

And then there was one.
The last one.

I'll sing you one, Ho.
Green grow the rushes, Ho.
What is your one, Ho?
One is one and all alone
And evermore shall be so.

In 1918, the oldest daughter at age eighty-three was one alone of the Lee family.

The one who followed in her father's pacifist footsteps.

Her oldest brother Custis had died in 1913. Brother Robert E. Jr. in 1914. Brother Wm. H. F. "Roonie" had died in 1891 earlier than both his brothers.

Her sibling, Anne, was actually first of the immediate family to die, in 1862, during wartime. Sister Agnes died in 1873 just weeks before their mother Mary. Sister Mildred had died in 1905.

Daughter Mary in 1835 was the first daughter but second born after brother Custis. And by happenstance, it was she, daughter Mary, who had introduced Robert Edward Lee to the Trustees of Washington College, in a roundabout way. Mary and another young woman happened to speak one day to a member of the trustees, former colonel Bolivar Christian. She noted, "while Southern people were willing to give her father anything, no actual offer had been made by which he could earn a living." At a subsequent trustee meeting Trustee Christian thought he should at least mention the name R. E. Lee. Immediately another trustee moved that the names of all other nominees be withdrawn; the motion passed unanimously. Thus, Daughter

Mary's casual remark instigated her father's great academic career at Washington College.

While living in Europe she became friends with the German royal family, eating various times at Kaiser Wilhelm's table. As well she was friends with the British royal family though she never dined at the table of King George V. When war broke out in 1914 Mary skedaddled back to the States and opposed the war for four years as a true pacifist, even when America entered the fray in 1917.

Back in 1829 R. E. Lee's mother Anne "put off dying" until a month after her son had graduated from the Military Academy at West Point, her task "*accomplished.*" Daughter Mary reflected a similar condition, when she "put off dying" until after the 11th hour of the 11th day of the 11th month of November 1918. Then the armistice agreement between the Allies and Germany was signed in a railroad car outside Compiégne, France, ending World War I. The same month Mary died, her task accomplished. Or so she thought.

Mary Lee didn't realize the peace treaty would be enforced severely by the European Allies against Germany thereby triggering incitement for another war—a mere twenty-one years later in the 20th century, September 1939, to be exact: World War II a global war across Planet Earth.

BY AN UNKNOWN PHILOSOPHER: THE FLAWED ORIGIN OF RACISM

Hatred for a segment of humanity is deadly in the long run as it easily sneaks into hatred of all humanness by human beings. Second place always labors to become first place. And R. E. Lee was racist, before, during, and after the Rebellion; to what degree is not easy to ascertain except his membership with other die-hards.

A rigid form of such racism can be found in India's ancient system of caste and class. Technically it is called an ancient Sanskrit word, *varna*, meaning color, and comes via Middle English *varnisch* via West German into English. That term *varna* appears in the *Rigveda,* Hindu scriptures from the oldest Iron Age about 1200-1000 B.C. after the Aryan invasions of the sub-continent of India. The four castes varied visibly in skin color from light brown through to dark brown; those people without any Aryan blood were Outcaste, that is darkest brown, even black in color. Racism was readily evident in India.

Popular origins of Western world racism are recorded in the Judeo-Christian scriptures, which many consider factual. The story, though, is a sorry mixture of drunkenness, compassion, sexuality—possibly homosexuality between son and father—of blame, and confusion of human racism with God grading the different races.

Viewed together the biblical story is a correct evaluation for poor human behavior on the part of a father and a different, supposed poor behavior on the part of a son. Both these errors in judgment result in gross misdirection of punishment for what began as an act of respect of a son for a drunken father lying naked in public.

The story is suspect, a baffling part of the canon of Jewish/Christian literature. It is marked by a bedlam of blurred human reactions that can't be seen distinctly because of ambiguity of purposes of the *dramatis personae* in the story. That old story compounds errors of omission through centuries-long wrongful transmission by countless textual scribes from various religious traditions in the Near East. Yet many people consider it to be a factual representation of why some people are considered less than human.

Bafflement results when, as in the story, there is a quadruple mixture of volatile issues: sex and religion, morals, and racism. It becomes a witches' brew far more potent than the "double trouble, boil and bubble" of Shakespeare's witches that occurred in Endor of the Bible, then in *Macbeth*, ending as "dung for the earth." Little or no benefit comes from mixing combustible subjects such as sexuality, religion, morals, and skin color—they mushroom into hatred for a group of human beings.

The biblical story is recorded in *Genesis* 9:18-29 and is a mix-up of gigantic proportions for ordinary readers and scholars alike. The story, in a vernacular summation, goes:

> The three sons of Noah were Shem, Ham, and Japheth. Hundreds of years after Noah's Ark had landed, the great flood having subsided, sailor Noah became a tiller of the soil. He planted a vineyard, harvested the fruit, and made wine. He drank his own product from a great crop, got thoroughly soused, fell over buck-naked to the earth—and was bare as a jay bird on the ground. Son Ham saw his father's nakedness, realized the disgrace this drunken stupor would bring upon his father, so told his two brothers about Noah's fallen condition. Shem and Japheth opened a blanket, held it at shoulder height and stepping carefully backward placed it over their father, covering his nakedness.

When drunkard Noah awakened he noted undeniably his sluggish, listless condition on the ground. He was shocked. Not at his drunken state, however, but by the answer he received when asking who covered his nakedness. Who had seen his blatant nakedness and had done this supposed unforgivable deed of covering him. The two sons informed Noah it was brother Ham who saw his blotto, sloshed nakedness; they informed "dear old dad" to save their own necks. It was the depth of depravity to see one's parent naked. The pits, the worst thing an offspring could do, worse than murder, even patricide. Human beings may not behold their parents' organs of origin; it is the direst sort of error, so to speak, to see where one came from. Seeing one's origins for humans is a secret not to be known; naked parents is getting too close to reality. The secret is of sacred origin. God may see nakedness because nakedness is true of all creatures in Nature, unclothed. God may see it—but not human beings about human nakedness of one's origin.

In the story, immediately Noah was wroth, filled not with ordinary wrath but with cruel wrath—and cursed Ham's son, Canaan. That's right, not Ham, who had discovered his father's fallen estate but Ham's son Canaan! An unexplained error. Noah must still have been drunk for he did not curse the one who saw him naked but the son of the one who saw him naked. Some grandfather. Some story!

"Cursed be Canaan: a slave of slaves shall he be to his brothers," the old drunk said and added, "Blessed be the Lord, God of Shem, and let Canaan be his slave. God enlarge Japheth and let him dwell in the tents of Shem, and let Canaan be his slave."

Thus, discovery of where and how we came to be sexual is unquestioningly the first sin in the Bible, as in Adam and Eve's awareness of their nakedness.

Canaan, obviously, was guiltless but was cursed by Noah totally unfairly. The guzzler still did not think clearly: too much of his own juice and an innocent grandson was cursed.

The story is horribly contrived to justify slavery, subservience.

In the scriptural account Shem is the father of the S[h]emitic peoples, Hebrews in particular; Japheth is the father of other fair-skinned peoples. Ham is the father of dark-skinned peoples from Africa, called Hamites in different languages, particularly from the land of Cush, Ethiopia. Thus, dark-skinned people are cursed to be slaves forever, according to a jumbled, garbled lie.

The story is bowdlerized, the purging of anything deemed offensive to one's aesthetic sense or religious sensibility. Though nakedness is a minor expression of sexuality it is still sex—a no-no of the first order for many primitive minds.

As we know from history, Canaan was the enemy land of Canaanite people the Hebrews fought and finally conquered *over centuries*. Canaan, the area between the River Jordan on the east and the Mediterranean Sea on the west, that Jewish legend contends God gave to the Israelite people—without telling Canaanites he gave it to someone else. They were the largest group of enemies of the Jewish people and one way or another Canaan and Canaanites had to be shown to be cursed by God.

The meaning is heavily nationalistic, complicated by religion and distorted by psychology. Canaan had to be demeaned, not only militarily but also socially, especially religiously—yet the Canaanites were not black! Hamites were black but not Canaanites.

This Noah story is as impactful culturally as the Great Flood story yet is missing elements, such as who actually did what? It has obscure emphases like sexuality, sibling rivalries, and strong hatred for people of differing skin colors. Loaded with insular emotion, it is bare of facts.

Nonetheless, it makes a riveting, salacious, and absorbing tale. The scriptural account is easily acceptable to explain to uncritical minds in Western culture how some people of dark skin color differ from white- and yellow-skinned peoples worldwide, emphasizing such people are "naturally" better human beings than others. And thus, others are less human.

That fact alone, therefore, makes God less than omnipotent if, in fact, he accepted Noah's curse as his own divine curse after Noah blatantly misconstrued who discovered his nakedness—as if nakedness *per se* is such a bad thing. We all come to know what another human being really looks like under clothing, and where s/he came from, and usually know how it occurs, otherwise we would be as unknowing as a god of any religion who superficially accepts the first account of a story without verification. Such a god is not God, but a devil notwithstanding still being denominated a god.

And so in our Western tradition some people accept a lie that makes black people inferior, each of them a patsy, a person being cheated or blamed for something. It was and is stupid to blame slavery on slaves; and erroneous to blame God.

With no help from R. E. Lee, the culprit is God—a play god who listened to an old drunk, Noah—and nothing human beings, especially Southerners, could do about it.

The blue-blooded Lee, soon after he became a Confederate field commander in early 1862, conveniently and ignobly avoided the derring-do of a slave and his compatriots on a Confederate warship.

Robert Smalls, a black man, a year and a month after U.S.A.'s Fort Sumter was bombarded in South Carolina's Charleston Harbor, marking the beginning of the Rebellion, performed an unheard of feat. He commandeered, hijacked, a Southern man-of-war.

With other slaves Robert Smalls, in May 1862, on the *CSS Planter* seized the vessel in Charleston Harbor and sailed it out of Confederate control passing at least five checkpoints fearlessly. As a twenty-three-year-old married man with two young children, he and his fellow slaves rescued his family and some others as they escaped in the purloined ship, when some white sailors had gone ashore and others below deck to sleep.

Smalls was more than brave with other brave men; he was intelligent as well. Dressed in the garb of the former captain of the *Planter*, Smalls particularly waved the captain's hat *a la* the captain's manner as the ship passed various checkpoints, thereby fooling watchmen and guards time after time.

Their efforts were made easy because some of the white crew and captain had left the ship, so to speak, high and dry, letting their prejudice against blacks overreach their naval discipline, thinking nothing adverse would happen to the vessel. They misjudged those black human beings, thinking blacks were neither intelligent nor brave enough to do anything unfavorable. Lee's prejudice was: wherever blacks are, then things go to the dogs. Lee's dogma bit the South... and it lost a sea-going man-o-war.

Smalls' crew navigated skillfully and successfully until they met a Union warship and showed a white sheet in surrender. The *Planter* contained valuable information for the Northern navy including a code book, and information about underwater mines in the Charleston Harbor. Those "lazy slaves" rightly became heroes up North. Southern folks didn't know what to make of the news. Lee fell silent.

Robert Smalls was king-sized up North. He had met President Lincoln and military officials. It is true he may have been used for propaganda purposes but it was helpful in convincing people up North that their cause was right, indeed righteous. Just and merciful as well.

After the war, Smalls was the first black person elected to the Congressional House of Representatives. Sometimes truth, goodness, and beauty come sweeping by, on water as well as land.

In 1861 the hotspurs of South Carolina were the first to rationalize their action, calling it "A Declaration of the Immediate Causes Which Induce and Justify the Secession of South Carolina from the Federal Union." Cataloging its grievances, the document highlighted "an increasing hostility on the part of the non-slaveholding states to the institution of slavery."

The declaration attacked New York State for prohibiting temporary slavery, the action of Palmetto State citizens who, to escape summer heat and humidity, vacationed in the cool Catskill Mountains of southeastern New York State. Some people took their slaves along to serve them, and wanted them to be slaves in a free state.

New York had made it clear in 1860 that it was a free state and any slave brought therein would automatically become free.

Everything political came apart in South Carolina. Officially it countered by contending that in "the supreme law of the land [blacks] are incapable of becoming citizens" because the *Constitution* in Article 1, Section 2, Clause 3 termed blacks as only three-fifths "other persons." South Carolinians cried, literally, that the North had "denounced as sinful the institution of slavery" thereby evoking a religious purpose as basic to Christian Faith.

Copy-cat states marched along in lock-step order to South Carolina's. "A blow at slavery is a blow at commerce and civilization," bellowed Mississippi, as if Mississippi ever were a bastion of learning and culture. Each Southern state had its own bone to pick with the North, and didn't want to sell its cotton north of the Mason-Dixon Line between Maryland and Pennsylvania. Stupidly, Southern cotton farmers cut off their noses to please their white faces.

Southern leaders wrote a new constitution that protected the institution of slavery at their national level. The Confederate constitution maintained a state did *not* have power to interfere with central government's protection of slavery. So much for states' rights *a la* Southern protection of such rights. States' rights has been recurrently a red herring for dullards to follow.

Slavery, obviously, was not the only cause of secession. The South also seceded over *machismo*, white male supremacy. White Southerners quickly came to see the four million blacks in their midst were an absolute social threat. Many predicted catastrophe, an out-an-out, knock-down campaign of primitive sticks and stones, home-made knives, spears, harpoons, lances, hammers, plus iron skillets and kettles free-for-all race war were slavery ever to end legally. That facet of Southern ideology vindicated for them the support poor white Southerners—even those who did not own slaves nor had a possibility of owning any—mobilizing readily to protect white supremacy of males, gratuitously *later* adding women, even children as supreme.

Another strident wing of that movement to "explain" the Rebellion was spearheaded by one of Lee's lower commanders, Jubal Early. He violently disobeyed Lee's General Order 73 during the Northern Campaign, an order informing officers and men they were assiduously to avoid doing damage to Pennsylvania property. Lee wanted peace to have a chance. Real peace.

Nonetheless, Jubal Early purposely violated Lee's order against Thaddeus Stevens, a known anti-Southern businessman and Pennsylvania Congressional Representative. Stevens' Caledonia Iron Works at Caledonia Furnace, on the road between Chambersburg and Gettysburg, was destroyed by Early's order, affecting the livelihood of 200-plus workmen.

R. E. Lee was thrown into a wretched disorder that his edict had been so blatantly disobeyed by one of his generals. He ordered his Chief Commissary Officer to provide rations for the 200 Pennsylvanians involved, shorting his own rations for his troops. Wars, and causes, are lost off battlefields as well as on them.

If that disobedience were not enough, Jubal Early, in his Official Report, stated he had been directly ordered to burn the major bridge over the Susquehanna River between Wrightsville and Columbia, thus isolating York County from Union forces to the east of the river such as those from Philadelphia. Early blatantly *countermanded* Lee's direct order and wrote his own orders *not* to burn the mile-and-a-quarter long bridge. *Sacré bleu!* Napoleon would have had such a disobedient general shot on the spot!

Early's "craziness" continued on the battlefield of Gettysburg to the point that General John Bell Hood wrote:

> *General Early broke up General Lee's line of battle on the 2d of July by detaching part of his division on some uncalled for service, in violation of General Lee's orders, and thus prevented the cooperative attack of Ewell ordered by General Lee.*

It is no wonder—no wonder at all—R. E. Lee later had to cashier, relieve Jubal Early from command. *Good riddance of bad garbage!*

As well, it is no wonder Early sought revenge. He beat a hasty retreat in disguise to Mexico. Returning via Canada, he used a trick to get back in Lee's good graces. The technique he used—is it believable?—to idolize Lee.

He lionized Lee through the pages of the Southern History Society founded 1 May 1869 while Lee was still alive. It published the *Southern Historical Society Papers* with the motto *DEO VINDICE*: "God avenges!" A god who avenges was not the God of R. E. Lee. Shame under wraps, *a la Jubal Early* under cover, drives human beings as much as does fame out in the open. It appears necessary we should put shame on shame if that be possible.

MORE BY AN UNKNOWN PHILOSOPHER

Notes on Dying and Death

We fear death. The living fear death. The dying fear death. No wonder we do not want to talk about it.

We don't know what to do with dying persons so we remain silent, closed, close-mouthed, uncommunicative. Dumbfounded, we send the dying off, abandoning talk with them.

Human communication is far more thorough, far more useful, than solitude and silence. Through the interchange that happens with language it isn't "survival of the fittest" that is paramount but the freedom of personhood manifested in willingness to join in a relationship of conversation... whether with a living or a dying person. The willingness to join other personhoods in "the grand old pageant of man" in relationship is paramount. The willingness to be a person in the miracle of relationship with the Universe and the Universe's relationship with the spiritual ultimate we call God is paramount.

But we abandon talk with the dying, thus, we disregard their personhood, and abandon them. We think it over-reaching to expect dying people to "talk" while dying, especially to talk about dying. We say we don't know what to talk about.

The dying still want to communicate; we do not talk to them. What can they do but become fearful? Not only fearful of the unknown in death but fearful loved ones have abandoned them.

What a terrible way to go beyond this life, all because we say we don't know what to say to them.

Hear this idea: If need be, talk of the weather. Far, far better is to talk of our love for them, our respect for them, our happiness that they have given some meaning, some purpose, some glory to our lives.

But talking about the weather is an option, too. We're conceived within weather, born into weather, and, as well, live and die within it.

"Is anyone listening?" becomes a simple question the dying ask themselves, disquieting their human hearts, for the living do not manifest interest. In cases where people, including family and dear ones, pay minimal attention to what seems without content, the living give minimal time for hearing what is spoken by the dying, discerning it as purposeless. Verbalizations by dying people generally are thought babblings without substance, less than an infant's burble and prattle. Coherent words, if any, go by unregistered and are considered atypical: curious, thin, unusual, meaningless, disconnected from reality. Then forgotten.

We make the dying face death alone because we do not communicate with them during their dying. Then we groan, we cry, when the dying one is dead. Late. So late. Too late.

When people are dying and thought to be mere dotage, declined, worn out, semi-human, almost every dying sound is written off, cast aside, not considered a language because it is slightly different from ordinary communication. Nearly always people turn their backs on what the elderly dying say or how they say it.

Most people do not make an effort to listen to the sounds from long-lived human beings who have had countless experiences, ventures galore, continual ups and downs. Late in life we consider the old to be frayed, fallen to pieces, in the ruins of their lives, incompetent, so the living speak not to the dying.

I doubt it right not to pay them heed. I see it as opportunities missed for last chance souvenirs, interesting insights, and testaments of lives well-lived as human.

The human species has many ways to communicate: linguistic speech, physical motions, pauses, shouts, emotional innuendoes, stagnant pauses, whispers, vibrant hesitations, songs, volume, even silence. There is a language of love, a rhetoric of hatred, an oratory of praise, a faction of "fake news," a catalog of advertising, a pigeonhole of obscenities, parties of political obfuscation, cults of religious mystification, teams of play, and unions of workers, each and all with their own grammar, their own syntax, their own morphology. It is likely—actually, decidedly likely—there is also a discourse of the dying in our species.

Human dying, as with all else that lives, is universal—everyone comes to an end. Something so universal as death must serve some purpose, some good in creation. Therefore it surely seems natural and proper that mutterings and rustlings, murmurings and whisperings, clarity and ambiguity during the dying process are, nonetheless, truly human forms of communication seeking communication with more actively living human beings.

Being human is an intense interiority—while we are living and while we are dying. Yet most living souls seem all too ready to deny the same dynamic of interiority to our dying companions. We do not embrace the inner dynamic of the dying. We put them into the silence of the grave before they have drawn their last breath of earthly air.

The most essential feature of human interiority is actualized more through the use of language than anything else. Humanity needs humanity to survive as human through whatever befalls it, even dying. Humanness is the interiority, the spiritual air we breathe, and, without it we pass away with nothingness into the Beyond, whatever that may be or may not be.

The human dying deserve human hearing.

We do not help people dying to "gird up their loins now like a human being... to deck themselves with majesty and excellency, and array themselves with glory and beauty [as well to] cast abroad the rage of their wrath and behold everyone that is proud and abuse him... and bring him low and tread down the wicked in their place, so their own right hand can save them," as God confessed unto us as true in the book of *Job*. We don't promote the living personhood of dying people because we don't think talking with the dying is natural.

We deny the dying the glory of being majestic, of being excellent, of being glorious, of being beautiful with ability to strike down arrogance and wickedness in evil persons one last time.

When we believe so little about the fullness of being human at the end of life we cause ourselves to fear those dying. Then we are less than worthy of any of the grandeur as human beings that we actually are. For God to proclaim us, living and dying, as self-saving is almost unimaginable to many, and heresy to some others.

When we believe so little about the fullness of being human at the end of life we fear our own dying and death. Consequently, we cover our fear by denying we will die... until we actually are dying.

Our fear and denial of our own dying and death rebuff and veto the others who are dying an earthly victory. We turn on a red light to them, purposely not listening to their dying talk, fearing what they will say.

The dying have not lost their humanity. We who do not listen to the dying lose ours. No wonder the Bard wrote, "What fools these mortals be."

How we speak to the dying is more important than how we speak to the living because the dying have a thinner buffer to deal with negative words and phrases. For example, when dying people admit to feeling poorly when asked how they feel, the admission worsens them; they feel as though they indict themselves of a crime. On the other hand if dying persons say they are "feeling fine," or even "better," then they cause themselves to have to make intelligible why it is they are still linked to a bed or chair.

Rather than ask the condition of dying persons we would do better to greet them with a particular non-confrontive Polynesian greeting shared when meeting someone: "THERE YOU ARE!"

The greeting, so different from "Hello," "Hi," or "How are you?" is a healing poultice beholding the excellency of anyone, including a dying person. Immediately the greeted one has standing. Excitement accompanies the recognition of "THERE YOU ARE!" The phrase is invitation for them to engage in conversation.

THERE YOU ARE is an avowal to dying persons that they still are worthy of being spoken to, thought of, accepted as human though dying, as still viable beings who talk and listen.

THERE YOU ARE is an earthly form of a mystery solved, a problem overcome, an obstacle surmounted, a lost pearl of great price found, a journey soon to be taken and now being prepared for.

Those three words tell addressees they are important, alive, and ready for the future whatever it may be.

Those three words grant status to the addressees. They say, "Talk with me. Tell me."

Maybe the dying want to tell us something about dying. Maybe they want to teach us. Maybe they want to share a new truth. Maybe they want to reassure us that dying is acceptable, natural. Maybe they want to comfort us. Maybe they want to bring us up short in our lack of attention to those dying around us. Maybe they want to help us navigate on all the seas of God. Maybe they want to guide us. They can't and won't do any of those things unless they know we want to listen to them and find them worth listening to.

They also won't share their end-of-living questions with us unless they know from our willingness to listen we are as brave as they are. Know we can bear asking questions without receiving clear answers.

Questions are the bravest way of living the human experience because they open up a whole universe of values for us, far more than declarative words, even the powerful greeting THERE YOU ARE.

Questions are the bravest way of dying, too. Questioning while dying continues humanness.

Human languages that are foreign to us number about 6,500 natural tongues in the world today. Anthropologists predict most are in such flux that about 3,000 will vanish in a few hundred years.

Any language of the dying in Western culture is so alien to us it will join the disappearing tongues one-by-one-by-one by countless thousands every day as people and cultures die.

The language of the dying strikes us as offensive. When we are negative about death sounds we are not receptive to the ones who speak the sounds. We pay no attention to the spoken, hummed, sung, muttered, whispered, undertoned sounds of the dying, even to those sounds of loved ones dying.

By ignoring the sounds of the dying we ignore them as persons. Given our tendency to confuse famous with heroic we do not see the dying sound-makers as heroic. But they are heroic as they try to voice sounds foreign to them until their present condition.

There is a plea of anguish at the time of dying, a sound unformed in our usual linguistic style and formulation. The plea of the heart is as plain as the cry for help, yet not stated with language competence or linguistic styling. The varied human cries of distress surely are human language, too, even if without common syntax or any rules for analysis.

And tears.

Tears of suffering. Tears of joy.

They are human language.

If only the living listened.

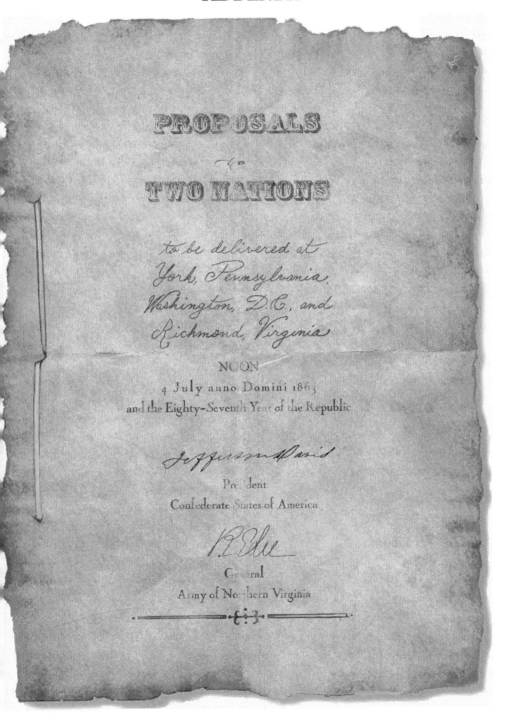

PROPOSALS

to

TWO NATIONS

*to be delivered at
York, Pennsylvania,
Washington, D.C., and
Richmond, Virginia*

NOON
4 July anno Domini 1863
and the Eighty-Seventh Year of the Republic

Jefferson Davis

President
Confederate States of America

R.E. Lee

General
Army of Northern Virginia

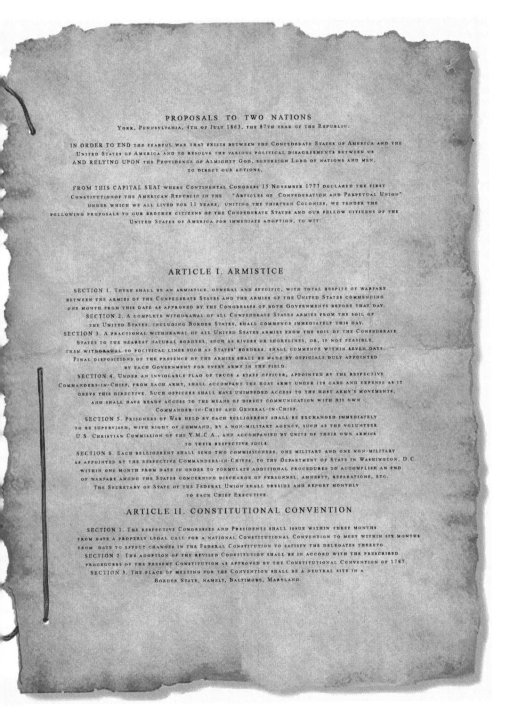

PROPOSALS TO TWO NATIONS
York, Pennsylvania, 4th of July 1863, the 87th year of the Republic.

IN ORDER TO END the fearful war that exists between the Confederate States of America and the United States of America and to resolve the various political disagreements between us AND RELYING UPON the Providence of Almighty God, sovereign Lord of nations and men, to direct our actions,

FROM THIS CAPITAL SEAT where Continental Congress 15 November 1777 declared the first Constitutionof the American Republic in the "Articles of Confederation and Perpetual Union" under which we all lived for 11 years, uniting the thirteen Colonies, we tender the following proposals to our brother citizens of the Confederate States and our fellow citizens of the United States of America for immediate adoption, to wit:

ARTICLE I. ARMISTICE

SECTION 1. There shall be an armistice, general and specific, with total respite of warfare between the armies of the Confederate States and the armies of the United States commencing one month from this date as approved by the Congresses of both Governments before that day.
SECTION 2. A complete withdrawal of all Confederate States armies from the soil of the United States, including Border States, shall commence immediately this day.
SECTION 3. A fractional withdrawal of all United States armies from the soil of the Confederate States to the nearest natural borders, such as rivers or shorelines, or, if not feasible, then withdrawal to political lines such as States' borders, shall commence within seven days. Final dispositions of the presence of the armies shall be made by officials duly appointed by each Government for every army in the field.
SECTION 4. Under an inviolable flag of truce a staff officer, appointed by the respective Commanders-in-Chief, from each army, shall accompany the host army under its care and expense as it obeys this directive. Such officers shall have unimpeded access to the host army's movements, and shall have ready access to the means of direct communication with his own Commander-in-Chief and General-in-Chief.
SECTION 5. Prisoners of War held by each belligerent shall be exchanged immediately to be supervised, with right of command, by a non-military agency, such as the volunteer U.S. Christian Commission of the Y.M.C.A., and accompanied by units of their own armies to their respective soils.
SECTION 6. Each belligerent shall send two commissioners, one military and one non-military as appointed by the respective Commanders-in-Chiefs, to the Department of State in Washington, D.C. within one month from date in order to formulate additional procedures to accomplish an end of warfare among the States concerning discharge of personnel, amnesty, reparations, etc. The Secretary of State of the Federal Union shall preside and report monthly to each Chief Executive.

ARTICLE II. CONSTITUTIONAL CONVENTION

SECTION 1. The respective Congresses and Presidents shall issue within three months from date a properly legal call for a national Constitutional Convention to meet within six months from date to effect changes in the Federal Constitution to satisfy the delegates thereto.
SECTION 2. The adoption of the revised Constitution shall be in accord with the prescribed procedures of the present Constitution as approved by the Constitutional Convention of 1787.
SECTION 3. The place of meeting for the Convention shall be a neutral site in a Border State, namely, Baltimore, Maryland.

EXAMINE THE EVIDENCE

The Essence of Historical Fiction

Inherently historical fiction is a meld, a merging of two literary roles: facts and imagination-based-on-facts. And imagination-based-on-facts is both curiosity and the mind's eye perpetuating truth only so far as it might be able to see rationally. The valuable attribute of fiction-based-on-fact is that it *can be* true yet not factual at the same time.

A clear, even profound, example of imagination-based-on-facts is located on the battlefield at Gettysburg, Pennsylvania. The magnificent statue of R. E. Lee and his steed Traveller on a high pedestal depicts him scrutinizing the lay of the land toward a meager clump of trees on a small rise of land about a mile away. Below the commander is a semi-circle of soldiers' statues pointing at that copse of trees which marked the farthest advance Southern troops made on 3 July 1863: the famous—or infamous—"Pickett's Charge." It was decimated by Northern troops who held their ground as U.S. Army commander Major General George Gordon Meade ordered.

That grand statuary preeminently looms over other sculptures on the battlefield. It has its own paved drive-around, parking places, information devices, and pathways for visitors most any day of a year, numerous from foreign lands. It is spectacular.

Notwithstanding, what the statuary portrays did not happen that way! It is a fiction-based-fact. With stallion Traveller nearby, Lee did view the battle... while he sat on a log or stump of a tree at the edge of Spangler's woods. After the failed attack he did mount up and ride out to meet his routed troops, repeating over and over, "It's all my fault." It was. Then R. E. Lee,

327

magnificent in defeat, nurtured his troops, agonized with them, and acknowledged honorably his plan *had been* faulty.

Nor, as that statuary might sadly suggest, was he a conquering hero, like a victorious Caesar returning to Rome. Lee was a penitent loser: a masterful human leader.

ACKNOWLEDGMENTS

The people who made the writing of this narrative worthwhile deserve plaudits from more than a quarter of a century ago plus a decade of its writing unto this publication date.

My younger brother Glenn Winston Winter, gifted radio/television engineer and brave paratrooper, who seven decades ago inspired me about R. E. Lee.

My wife of 36+ years, Dr. Elva Joan Shertzer Winter... psychotherapist, professor, potter, poet, author... persistent gadfly like Socrates of old, keeping me to the decades-long task about American icon R. E. Lee.

Dr. Demi Stevens, editor without equal, matchless yet pleasant throughout the process... even when on my writing-back.

Debbie Hummel, teacher and another editor, delightful and bouncy who loves the English language; a supporter even when correcting errors.

Greg Neuhauser, lawyer with a keen eye and keener sense of truth, goodness, and beauty; as well my "man-Friday."

Leif Ellsworth Winter, my eldest son, with huge full beard and full huge heart attuned to other human hearts.

Kristin Kest, both artist and musician, whose *joie de vivre* infuses her conversation, days, and efforts with beauty.

Kenneth Anthony (surname either Smith or Dupre, as suits his fancy!) with whom I sailed marvelously in Florida on his wooden sloop. Brother of my heart without stint.

Kristen Woolley, social agency founder and photographer, dear friend through my wife, whose generosity makes friendship a holy gift.

Donald Miller, pen-name Donald Motier, former student, unfaltering author to find truth, who gifts me with books concerning R. E. Lee.

Dr. Paul E. Stambach, a pastor primarius, college professor, and fellow traveler to graduate studies; strong brother in the Faith Incarnate.

Jean Ruth Hoffman Winter, teacher, my first wife so long in death and longer in memory; mother of our Leif Ellsworth, Arn Ellsworth, Jeannine Alicia, Val Ellsworth, and Alicia Jeannine. Jean Ruth knew I was good for something; after decades our children have come to similar conclusions.

ABOUT THE AUTHOR

JOHN ELLSWORTH WINTER, Ph.D., 92 years old, is Professor Emeritus of Philosophy at Pennsylvania's oldest state-owned university, which in 1863 sent students to Gettysburg "to put down the fierce rebellion." Additionally, he had been Guest Professor of Philosophy at the University of Vienna, Austria. He has taught at three colleges, lectured at thirteen others, and delivered papers on human rights at the World Congress of Philosophy and the Inter-American Congress of Philosophy.

Dr. Winter has toured the battlefield at Gettysburg over a hundred times. He attended the 75th anniversary of the battle in 1938 (as a Boy Scout) when President Franklin Roosevelt dedicated The Eternal Light Peace Memorial, and the 100th anniversary in 1963 with two of his sons. He presented a paper at the 150th Anniversary in July 2013.

He is married thirty-six years with the author, poet, professor, and psychotherapist Dr. Elva Joan Winter. They share a blended family of nine children, fifteen grandchildren, and four great-grandchildren.

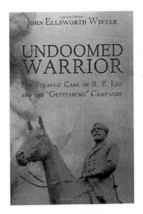

Undoomed Warrior: The Strange Case of Robert E. Lee and the Gettysburg Campaign

R. E. Lee realized in September 1862 the South could not win the war. He recommended that President Jefferson Davis send a peace proposal to the North. Davis refused. In May 1863 Lee again proposed to proclaim peace, taking his army into the North for the 4th of July at the place Continental Congress had forged the first American constitution in 1777. The accidental battle at Gettysburg interfered with Lee's "wisest, grandest, most imposing" plan. The South went down to defeat.

Made in the USA
Columbia, SC
07 November 2018